BASIC HANDLOADING

AN OUTDOOR LIFE BOOK

BASIC HANDLOADING

George C. Nonte, Jr.

OUTDOOR LIFE BOOKS
New York

STACKPOLE BOOKS
Harrisburg, Pennsylvania

Published by

Outdoor Life Books
Times Mirror Magazines, Inc.
380 Madison Avenue
New York, NY 10017

Distributed to the trade by

Stackpole Books
Box 1831
Cameron & Kelker Streets
Harrisburg, PA 17105

Library of Congress Catalog Card Number: 77-26482
ISBN: 0-943822-11-4

Sixth Printing, 1982

Manufactured in the United States of America

Contents

1

Handloading: What and Why

WHAT AND WHY? Unless you thoroughly understand what and why, you'll not be able to determine whether you really want to get into the fascinating, productive, and profitable game of handloading. First of all, that word "handloading." Some of the old-time aficionados differentiate between "handloading" and "reloading." Actually, the two words describe almost exactly the same mechanical operations, which are performed for the same purpose—to produce safe, reliable, and accurate ammunition for rifles, handguns, and shotguns. Based upon past usage, "handloading" means assembling *new* components into complete cartridges. You start with a *new* cartridge case, add a primer and powder charge, then seat a bullet, and the job is done. "Reloading," on the other hand, means reloading or reassembling a *fired* cartridge. But since the bullet has gone downrange after firing, the powder has been consumed, and the primer is destroyed and must be replaced, the only difference is that in handloading you use a factory-new case, and in reloading you use a reclaimed or salvaged case which has already been fired at least once. However, the two words are used interchangeably by present-day gun buffs, and we'll do so in this book.

You need four components to assemble a loaded metallic cartridge, one of which you already have—the fired case. You simply add a fresh bullet, powder, and primer.

In original manufacture, the ammunition manufacturer makes the cartridge case, primer, and bullet from raw materials. Since the propellant powder is a highly specialized item, it is manufactured by another independent company and is then purchased by the ammunition manufacturer as it is needed. These are the four basic components of a metallic cartridge. About half the materials cost of the factory load is attributable to the bullet, powder, and primer—though in light loads primer cost may be higher than powder cost—and when the cartridge is eventually fired, all these components are destroyed. But the cartridge case, which accounts for approximately the other half of the cost, is not destroyed. The case is slightly larger after firing than before firing, but is generally still quite serviceable.

Since that fired case represents roughly half the materials cost of a factory-loaded cartridge you might buy to replace it, casually tossing cases aside is a ridiculous waste not only of your own money, but of the natural resources and energy employed to make them. In this respect, handloading can be a very valuable conservation measure. For example, if you fire 1,000 rounds of .30-06 ammunition this year, and discard the cases, that represents approximately 28 pounds of brass that is simply lost. If, on the other hand, you fire the same 1,000 shots by buying 100 rounds of ammunition and reloading the fired cases nine times, you will have *utilized* (as opposed to *wasted*) less than 3 pounds of brass, and may still be able to get even more use from it. You'll have saved over 25 pounds of copper and zinc, as well as all the energy consumed in mining, smelting, processing, and forming those other 900 cases. In these days, such a saving, 90 percent, is no mean accomplishment in and of itself, regardless of all the other benefits you'll discover in handloading.

However, only centerfire cases may be reloaded. The various rimfire cartridges, of which the .22s are by far the most common, with roughly 4 *billion* fired each year, do not have a removable, separate primer; therefore the fired case cannot be reprimed except with sophisticated and costly tools and equipment. Even then, the operations and the materials employed are quite dangerous, and are performed in ammunition factories only under rigid safety precautions. You can save the brass and perhaps sell it, so that it isn't wasted, but you can't reload it.

To better understand reloading, you need to understand what happens inside the gun when a cartridge is fired. The trigger is pulled, the firing pin strikes the primer, and the tip of the firing pin indents the primer cup, crushing the pellet of priming compound against the anvil. This ignites the priming compound, which burns very rapidly with a fierce flame that rushes through the flash hole and ignites the propellant powder. The propellant also burns rapidly, though less rapidly than the priming com-

Sorry, but the smooth-headed rimfire case at left can't be handloaded; for reloading to be practical, the case must contain a separate, removable primer like the case shown at right.

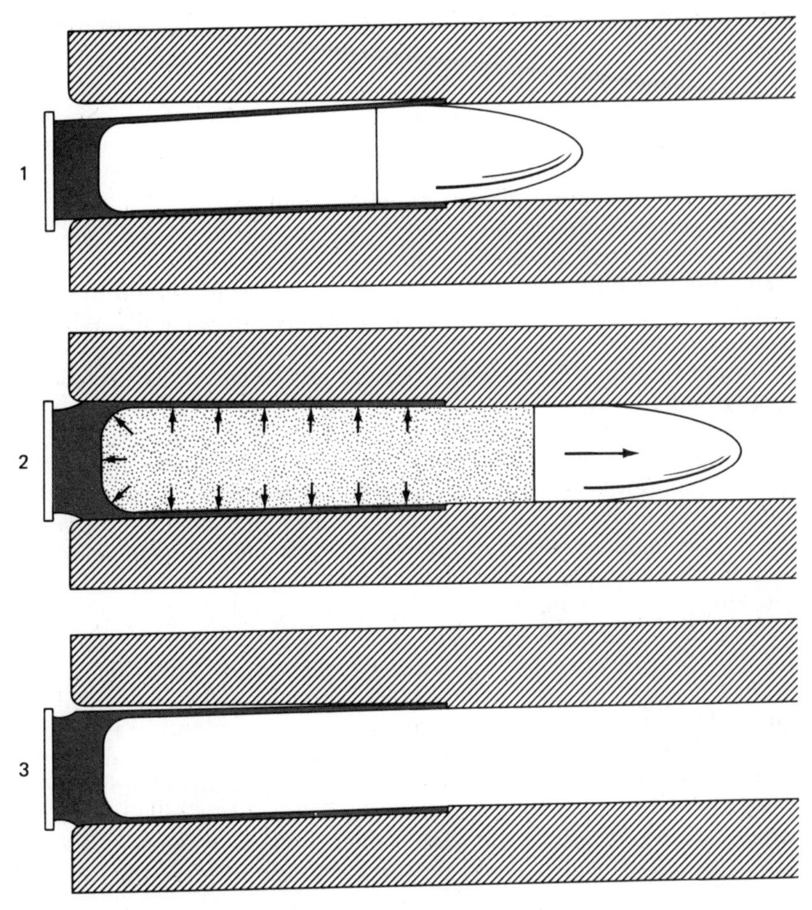

A somewhat simplified sketch showing the three conditions of the cartridge case, beginning with it in the chamber before firing, with substantial clearance between the case and the chamber walls. Then, the case is expanded at the instant of firing to tight contact with the chamber walls. Finally, after firing, the case has sprung back toward its original dimensions, but not quite all the way back.

pound—*it does not explode.* It burns at a controlled and predetermined rate, generating many times its own volume in high-temperature (up to 3,500°) and high-pressure gas. Generally, as gas pressure increases, the rate at which the powder burns increases. In modern, high-performance rifle cartridges such as the .270 Winchester, .30-06, or 7mm Remington Magnum, gas pressures inside the case and chamber may well approach or exceed 50,000 CUP (copper unit of pressure, roughly comparable to pounds per square inch). This gas pressure forces the bullet out of the case, into the rifling, and on out the barrel; as the bullet exits the muzzle, gas pressure has dropped considerably and dissipates very rapidly into the atmosphere.

The brass of the cartridge case is a very ductile metal (meaning that it will stretch or deform easily), and so as soon as gas pressure begins to build up, the case expands until it meets the walls of the chamber. It is held tightly in contact with those chamber walls until the bullet clears the muzzle and the gas pressure drops. The walls of the case are forced into contact with the chamber walls *before* the bullet has left the case, and thus the case acts as a very efficient "plug" for the rear of the barrel and prevents any gas from leaking out the chamber to the rear, where it could cause damage. This sealing action by the case is known as "obturation."

In a chamber of standard dimensions and at normal working gas pressures, the solid portion of the case head does not deform during firing. However, the thin walls do, and the case diameter is increased by several thousandths of an inch as it is forced against the chamber walls. When the gas pressure drops, the brass "springs back," reducing its diameter so that it is no longer tight in the chamber. This leaves the case relatively loose so that it may be extracted and ejected easily. Unfortunately, the brass does not spring back quite as much as it was originally expanded, with the result that the case diameter remains greater after firing than it was before. The amount by which it is greater depends upon many factors—the physical characteristics of the brass, the gas pressures involved, and the dimensional relationship between the chamber and the case. The result of all this is simply that the fired case is larger in diameter through all of its length after firing, except for the solid head.

If the case is to be reloaded, this increase in diameter becomes quite important. First, it prevents the case from gripping a new bullet tightly; second, it may prevent the case from seating properly in another chamber of the same caliber, simply because chambers cannot be identical in all guns.

Thus, the first mechanical operation in reloading a given fired case is to reduce its diameter enough so that it will enter freely any chamber of the same caliber, and that it will grip a bullet tightly. This is called "resizing," and while it may not reduce the case diameter all the way back to what it was when it left the factory, it will reduce it enough to serve the purposes.

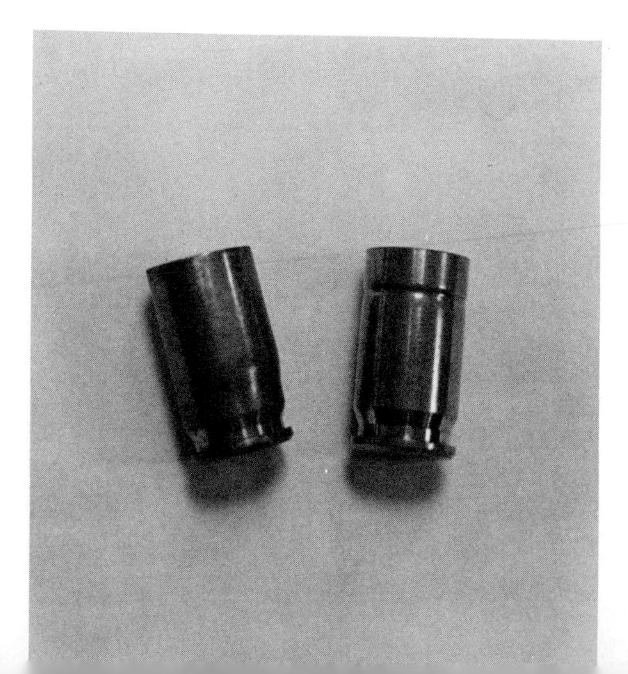

The obvious bulge on the case at left shows it has been fired, and in a rather loose chamber at that. Compare it to the neat, straight new one alongside, and you see why fired cases must be squeezed back into shape before loading.

The sparkplug of the cartridge—the boxer-type, centerfire and removable primer. Side, top, and underside views.

In addition to resizing, preparing the case for reloading requires that the fired primer be punched out of its pocket in the case head, so that a new, factory-made primer can be seated. Once the fired case is prepared, handloading consists of performing exactly the same operations that the factory does in seating a primer, placing a propellant charge in the case, and finally seating and crimping a bullet in the case mouth.

Basically these are the standard procedures in loading any metallic-case, bulleted cartridge. However, when loading paper or plastic shotshells, you also must place the proper wads over the powder and put in an appropriate number of spherical lead pellets rather than a bullet. The final operation in loading shotshells consists of crimping the mouth of the case to hold the shot in place, either with or without a thin disc of cardboard beneath the crimp, depending upon the type of case and type of crimp involved. As we progress through this volume, we will cover all of these operations in more than sufficient detail to enable you to apply them properly for almost any kind of load.

Naturally, handloading is not performed with the contents of the typical home toolbox. Special tools are required, and they are available from a variety of manufacturers in considerable profusion. While tool designs differ in detail, they are all intended to turn out loaded cartridges that will function correctly in any properly made gun in good mechanical condition. Ex-

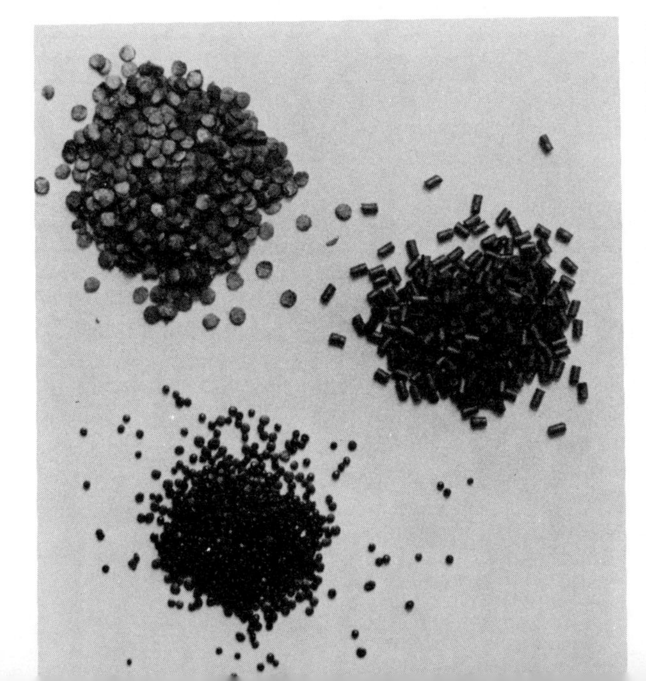

Three different forms of smokeless powder you'll undoubtedly encounter. Reading clockwise from upper left, we have Hercules Unique (pistol and shotshell), consisting of thin, solid discs from long strings of extruded propellant; perforated DuPont IMR 4064 (big-bore rifle), which is also extruded in long, thin strings containing a hole through the center, then chopped into relatively short lengths; and last, what we have come to call "ball powder," this being W-W 680 (also big-bore rifle), though many of them have been flattened between rollers to achieve the desired thickness.

cept for certain "progressive-type" tools designed to produce ammunition at a high rate of speed, tool operating procedures are generally quite standardized. If you become familiar with one tool, you will generally be able to operate another make or model of the same general type without difficulty.

You must always keep in mind that handloading consists of a very simple series of easily performed mechanical operations. Neither the operations nor the tools are complex, and pre-teen-age children often learn the rudiments and turn out perfectly safe and functionally good ammunition after only an hour or so of instruction. Unless you are totally incompetent in things mechanically so simple as tightening a door hinge or installing storm windows, you will be able to learn handloading without difficulty. I know people who can't replace a light switch or change an oil filter, but have become quite competent handloaders.

There are many reasons for handloading, and we have mentioned conservation and economy briefly above. Economy is the reason most often given, and it is certainly reason enough standing alone. Even when you buy all the components (primer, powder, bullet) at retail prices, handloaded cartridges of the .30-06 class can be assembled for a materials cost that is only one-third to one-quarter the price of factory-loaded ammunition. That is for full-charge loads duplicating factory ballistics; if lighter loads, especially with lead bullets, will serve your purpose, then the cost becomes much, much less. Full-charge handloads suitable for 95 percent of all ordinary shooting in .45 Automatic caliber need cost no more than 2 to 3 cents each, compared to the factory-load cost of 25 cents or more. Less savings

The basic tool setup needed for handloading any caliber—the loading press, the die set in its plastic box, and a powder scale. How far you go beyond this basic setup depends upon the ease and convenience you want, the amount of money you want to spend, and how far you might want to deviate from basic handloading.

are possible when reloading shotshells, but it is still quite possible to cut the per-shot cost well below half that of factory ammunition.

Of course, we have talked here only of materials cost; you also have an initial investment in tools. But when cared for properly, handloading tools will generally last the lifetime of the owner unless he assembles an enormous amount of ammunition. If you amortize a typical tool investment of about $200 over twenty years at $10 per year, the per-shot cost becomes so small as to be imperceptible. So, even with a sophisticated handloading setup costing several hundred dollars intelligent handloading can still produce per-shot savings of at least 50 percent, ranging upward to 90 percent, depending upon the type of load.

But economy is by no means the only reason for handloading. As an example, the ultra-powerful .44 Magnum revolver cartridge was available in *only* a single, full-charge loading for twenty-two years. This load is more than most shooters can handle, and, in fact, far too powerful for 95 percent of their shooting needs. Anyone wishing a less powerful load was actually forced to handload to obtain it, thus producing a load suited to his needs which was not available by any other means. The fact that such loads could and can be produced for only 2 to 3 cents each, compared to 32 cents for factory cartridges, was simply a welcome economic bonus. As that example shows, handloading enables you to produce all manner of loads and performance levels not commercailly available to suit your particular shooting needs. Until just recently, it was patently impossible to purchase factory-loaded handgun ammunition in most calibers which would be especially effective for defensive use against antagonistic humans; consequently, such ammunition could be obtained only by handloading. Other examples are legion.

While accuracy is important to all firearms users, it is especially important to riflemen who shoot competitively or hunt big game or varmints at abnormally long ranges. Inasmuch as factory-loaded ammunition is made to safely produce *acceptable* performance in *all* guns, more often than not it is not capable of delivering maximum accuracy from a *particular* rifle. The handloader can overcome this situation simply by careful experimentation with various powders, bullets, and weights of powder (along with other lesser factors affecting accuracy), and often he can produce ammunition that is much more accurate in his particular rifle. Thus, again, handloading offers one the opportunity of obtaining ballistic performance of a degree that cannot be had from factory-loaded ammunition.

So, when all factors are considered, handloading can be so useful and productive for all types of shooters that it actually can become more a necessity than a convenience or economy measure. On top of all this, don't overlook the simple fact that ammunition you load yourself will give you a special feeling of satifaction and accomplishment. *Anyone* can buy factory ammunition and make it go bang; but only the handloader can have that intimate feeling of kinship with his equipment, and that feeling of accomplishment that comes from having *done it all yourself*.

2

Choosing Tools and Equipment

LOADING PRESS

With the exception of the so-called "pocket" loading tool, the basic handloading tool is a loading press, which provides the framework and the leverage for processing fired cases into complete cartridges by means of various dies and accessories. Presses are generally categorized by the geometry of their frames, and thus are known as C-type, H-type, O-type, and assorted variations thereof. The photographs show the differences far better than words. The C- and O-types may be made of either steel or aluminum, while every H-type I've encountered has been of steel. Of the lot, assuming good design and workmanship, the O-type is the strongest, and the H-type next. Though the C-type is least strong, it is the easiest and cheapest to make, and for 99 percent of all handloaders, it is quite adequate to the task. The C-type is also the most convenient to operate, there being no upright posts (H-type) or surrounding arm (O-type) to interfere with quick and easy handling of cartridge cases.

Modern presses of all three types contain a "ram" which moves more or less vertically to force the cartridge case into a die screwed into the top of the press, then to draw the case out of the die. It is aided by a separate, removable "shell holder" seated in a T-slot in the top of the ram, and contains a T-slot in its own upper end to accept the rim of the cartridge case. This type of shell holder originated with RCBS and has since become the standard of the industry.

The ram is raised and lowered by a handle and a "linkage" which converts rotary to linear motion, and offers a substantial mechanical advantage to permit processing of cases without excessive effort. Some O-type presses, particularly the RCBS "Rock Chucker," employ a compound linkage originated by RCBS and since employed by other makers. Where great force is required—as in reforming cases or swaging bullets—a press of the O-type with compound linkage is to be preferred.

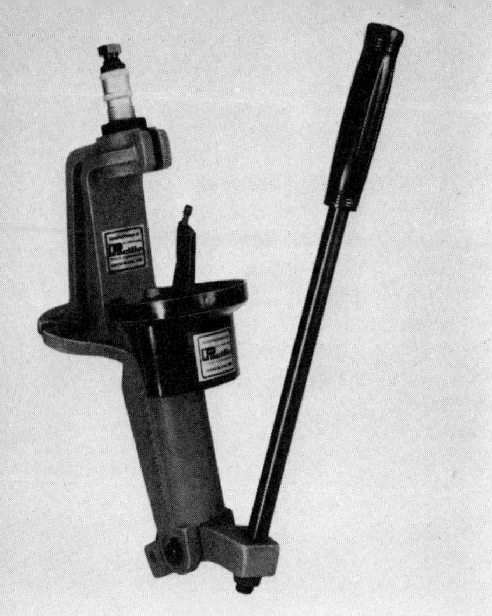

◀ This is the basic C-type press, which is usually the most economical and is suitable for all but the most arduous handloading operations. This particular tool by Pacific happens to be fitted with a plastic catcher for fired primers. Saves mess on the floor.

The basic O-type press as manufactured by RCBS. This is the "RCBS Jr." model, complete with primer arm and primer catcher installed. Note that this is essentially a C-type press with the open end of the C closed by an integral arm of the frame. ▶

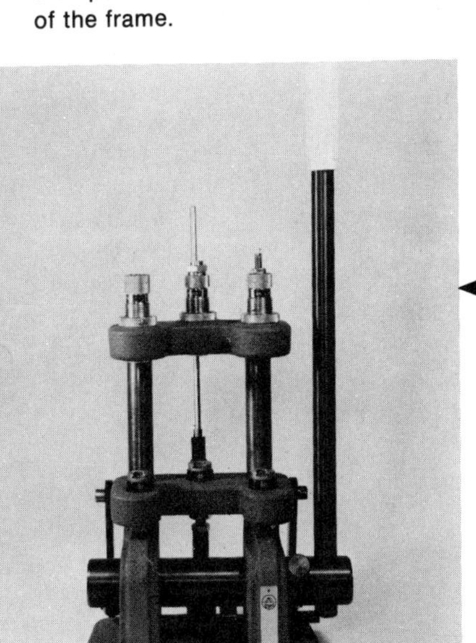

◀ An example of the H-type press. This particular model by Bear is of three-station configuration, allowing all dies of a three-die set to be installed simultaneously so that cases may be individually processed through the complete loading procedure.

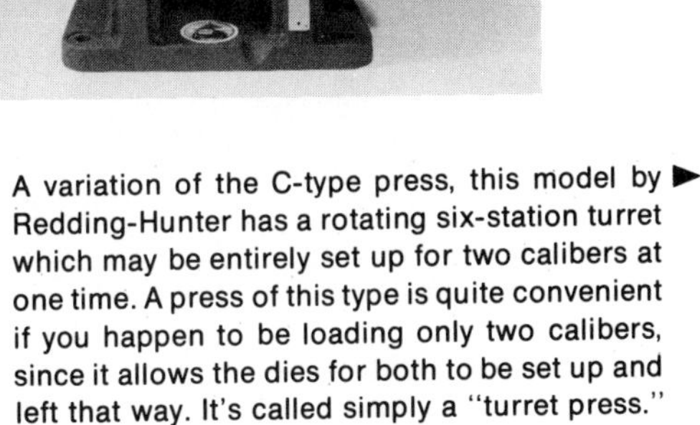

A variation of the C-type press, this model by Redding-Hunter has a rotating six-station turret which may be entirely set up for two calibers at one time. A press of this type is quite convenient if you happen to be loading only two calibers, since it allows the dies for both to be set up and left that way. It's called simply a "turret press." ▶

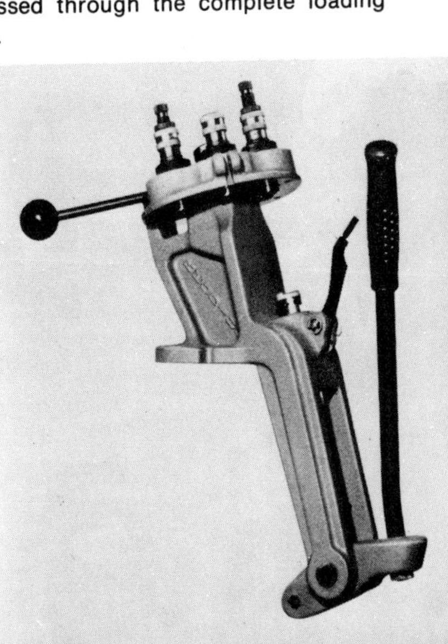

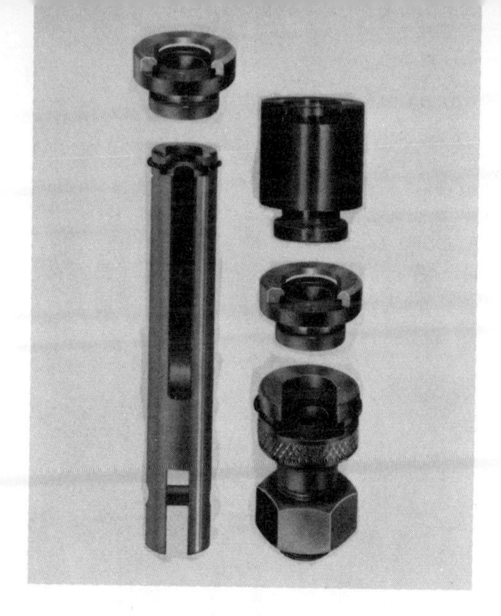

At left, a conventional ram and removable shell holder head. At the upper right, a shell-holder extension used for some case-forming operations with very short cases. Beneath it is the standard removable head, and at the bottom is a typical shell-holder ram for an H-type press. Note the latter uses the same head as the more common long ram.

Virtually all presses made today incorporate a "primer-seating punch." In O- and C-type presses, it is normally installed at the top of a pivoted, spring-loaded lever shaped like an inverted L. The punch proper, at the top of the arm, may be changed to suit the size primer being used. A slot in the ram allows the priming arm to be rotated inward, positioning a primer so that as the case is drawn from the die, it is forced down over the primer. The arm then swings clear, and the case may be extracted.

The average neophyte handloader may be confused by the large number of presses on the market at widely varying prices. For normal use, not including the swaging of jacketed bullets, the basic C-type press of steel construction is the most practical selection. A number of companies supply this type, and the Pacific "Power C" is typical. If you do anticipate swaging bullets and other heavy work, then an O-type press with compound linkage is a better choice. Probably the best and most practical of this type is the well-engineered RCBS "Rock Chucker." It will cost about two-thirds more than the average C-press, but for heavy-duty work and ease of operation, the extra money is well spent.

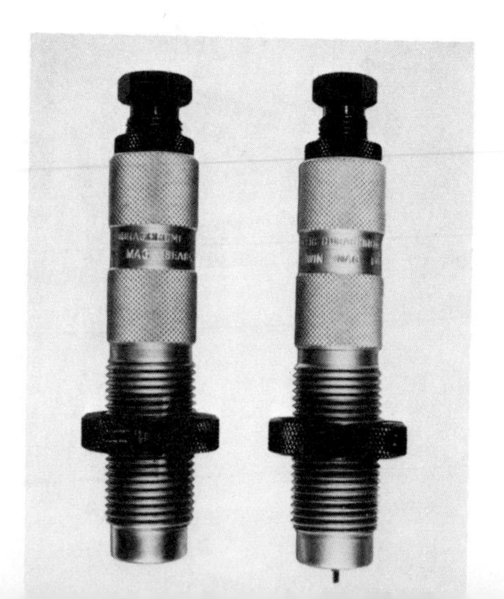

A typical two-die set for loading bottleneck cases; this example from Pacific.

RELOADING DIES

Next in importance comes the reloading die set. Dies are threaded into the top of the press, and over the past three decades, the threading has been standardized at $\frac{7}{8} \times 14$, so that dies by one manufacturer may be used in a press by another. Theoretically, because of different tolerances used by different manufacturers, one should obtain dies and shell holders from the same maker as the press. Dies for bottleneck cases normally come in sets of two—one for resizing, decapping, and neck expansion, and the second only for bullet seating and, where necessary, crimping the case mouth on the bullet. Dies for straight or straight-tapered cases come in sets of three—one for resizing, one for decapping and expanding the mouth, and a third for seating and crimping the bullet. In straight handgun calibers, a four-die set is also available from RCBS; its third die seats the bullet, while the fourth forms the crimp separately. A better and more uniform crimp—and thus theoretically better accuracy—*may* be obtained with the four-die set.

Reloading dies are not as complex as they might appear. The resizing die consists of a bar of steel containing a cavity shaped exactly like the cartridge case, and dimensioned so that when the case is forced into it, the case will be reduced in diameter to standard dimensions, allowing for springback. The interior of this cavity is made very hard and is polished quite smooth. The internal dimensions, hardness, and finish are very important to the quality of your ammunition and to the ease of operation. Likewise, the dimensions of the neck and bullet portion of a seating die are important to accuracy because they control the alignment of the bullet in the case. Bargain-basement dies are not consistently good enough in these areas to produce first-class ammunition. It is false economy to buy cheap, roughly finished dies. RCBS has a top name in dies, as do Pacific, C-H, and others. Good dies will produce good ammunition in almost any press; poor dies will produce poor ammunition in almost any press. If you will not be buying dies and press of the same make, then buy a shell holder matching the dies; this way the critical headspace dimension for bottleneck cases is more likely to be correct.

A typical three-die set for loading handgun or other straight cases—the resizing die at left, followed by the neck-expanding and decapping die, and the bullet-seating die. Some manufacturers place the decapping setup in the resizing die.

A number of the older references and publications recommend "neck-sizing" only, and while dies may still be purchased to accomplish this, I recommend that *only* full-length-resizing dies be used. The pure accuracy buff can justify sizing only the necks, but for practical, everyday use, ammunition should be loaded in cases which have been resized full length.

POWDER SCALE

For general-purpose handloading, you'll need a powder scale. This is typically a simple beam balance, and one design or another is offered by almost all makers of handloading equipment. Designs vary a good deal, and this, too, is an area in which I feel it is false economy to purchase on price alone. Since it is seldom ever possible to check the accuracy of an individual scale after you have obtained it, you should buy the best you can afford and care for it tenderly. Scales using only a simple sliding weight on the beam may be the most convenient to use, but it is also quite easy to make mistakes with them. Over the years, I have come to prefer the micrometer-adjustment type developed by Ohaus Company several years ago and now offered exclusively by RCBS. It also contains an "approach to weight" feature which makes operation more rapid and convenient. There are quite a few cheaper scales, but properly cared for, this one will serve a lifetime. When

Sectioned view of a typical bottleneck-caliber loading-die set.

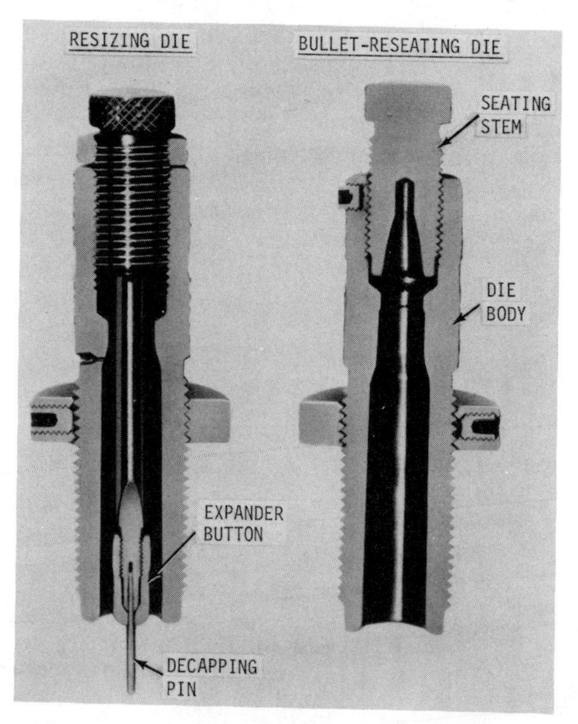

purchasing a scale, also obtain a cover or container for it; airborne dust, dirt, and grit will collect on a scale and affect both sensitivity and accuracy. It should be kept covered except when in use.

POWDER MEASURE

While it is possible to handload with only a scale for determining the proper powder charge, a powder measure is far more convenient and will allow ten or twenty charges to be thrown in the time it ordinarily takes to weigh only one on a scale. However, for ordinary loading, a measure may not be substituted for a scale, simply because the scale is necessary to set an adjustable-charge measure to throw a particular amount of powder. In short, while you can get along with only a scale, to use a measure, you must have a scale as well. As a result, many beginners buy only a scale, and then add a measure later. There are fixed-charge measures, commonly called "pistol-type" measures, but they are useful only within narrow ranges, and are not suitable for general handloading.

A micrometer-type adjustable measure is the best all-round choice, and for maximum versatility, it should possess both rifle-size and pistol-size "metering chambers." Powder charges for rifle calibers seldom go below 25 grains, and usually fall in the 40-50-grain range. Further, the small kernels of pistol powders are measured much more accurately in a small-diameter chamber, which is not at all suitable for the larger-kernel rifle powders. A variety of measures are available, and most follow the same basic design—a housing and a cylindrical, rotating drum containing a cylindrical cavity that functions as a metering chamber, combined with a movable plug which is used through a micrometer device to vary the volume of the metering chamber and thus the amount of powder it will contain. With the handle in the "fill" position, the metering chamber connects to the powder reservoir and is filled with powder by gravity; and when the handle is moved to the "dump" position, the powder is dumped out of the metering chamber, through a "drop tube," and into the cartridge case. In many of these designs, the entire drum or metering chamber is replaced to adapt the measure to either rifle or pistol use.

The measure I have found most convenient—and quite accurate as well—for combined rifle and pistol use is the Ohaus "Du-O-Measure," which contains both size metering chambers and adjustment devices in the same drum. The change between rifle and pistol metering chambers is

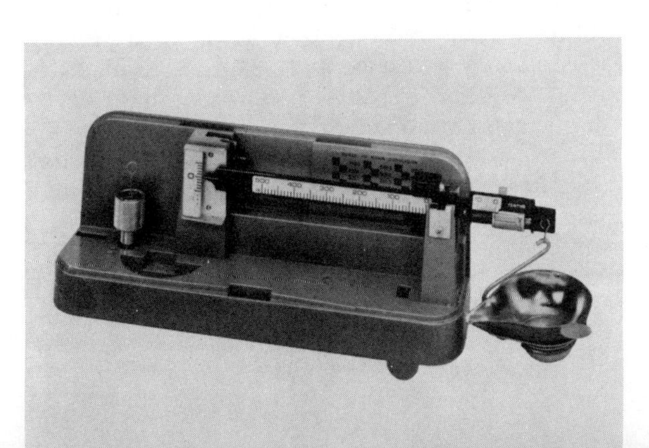

One of the better powder scales, the Ohaus design with micrometer adjustment, now distributed exclusively under the RCBS name. Basically this is a simple beam balance.

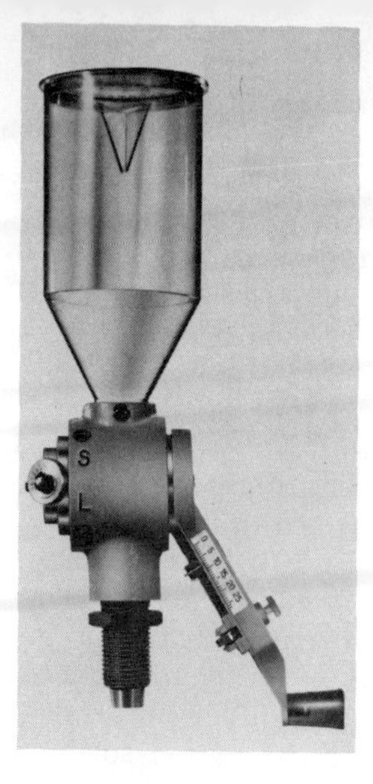

This Ohaus "Du-O-Measure" is a conventional micrometer-adjustable volumetric type, except that it incorporates a pistol-size metering chamber on the left side of the drum in addition to the rifle chamber on the right.

made simply by removing a stop, rotating the drum about 180 degrees, and repositioning the stop. Thus there is no need for the lengthy process of changing drums, nor are there any spare parts to be mislaid or lost. Better yet, the changeover can be accomplished in less than ten seconds. As with other tools, there are satisfactory measures which cost less, but I prefer the Ohaus "Du-O-Measure" for its pleasing combination of convenience, speed, and accuracy.

Those are the basic tools you'll need, and you can actually get by for quite a while without the measure if money is tight.

ACCESSORIES

There are quite a few smaller and fortunately inexpensive accessory items, some of which are almost essential and some of which are simply convenient.

You'll almost have to have a powder funnel if you're using a scale, and most manufacturers offer one. They are simple plastic affairs with a tapered spout which fits over the outside of the case mouth. The typical funnel will fit calibers from .22 up to .40 or .45 without difficulty. For smaller calibers such as the .17, a special funnel is needed. Almost all of these funnels are round, and so they roll off the bench when you lay them down. The single exception is the RCBS funnel, which has a squared flange around its upper end so that it can't run away from you. It's good.

You'll also need some means of deburring the inside of case mouths. New or once-fired cases will have a squared edge and a slight burr on the inside of the mouth, which interferes with proper seating of bullets. It should be removed by paring away the edge to form a very slight bevel. While you can do this with a sharp knife blade, the Lee deburring tool is cheap and remarkably efficient, consisting simply of a knurled split steel ring with a male conical edge for doing the inside of the case mouth, and a female conical end for doing the outer edge.

If you'll be reloading any military cases, you will need some means of removing the primer crimp; if it is not removed after decapping, it will either prevent new primers from being seated, or will deform them and thus

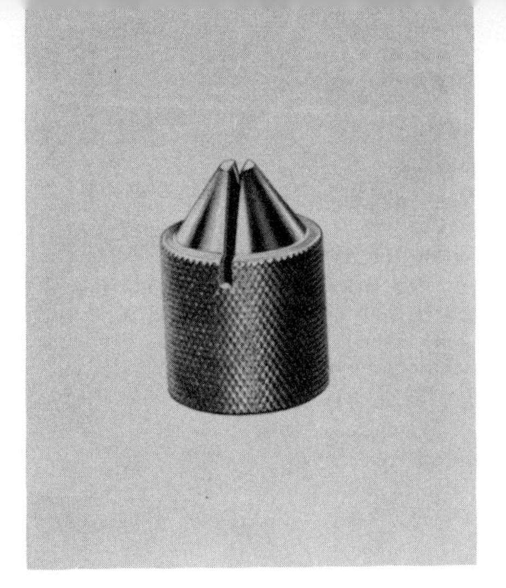

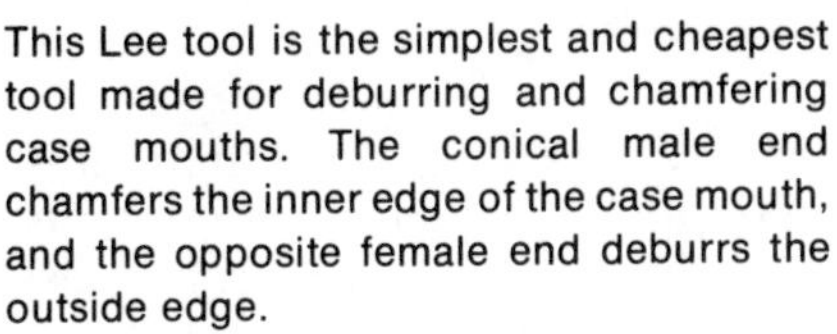

This Lee tool is the simplest and cheapest tool made for deburring and chamfering case mouths. The conical male end chamfers the inner edge of the case mouth, and the opposite female end deburrs the outside edge.

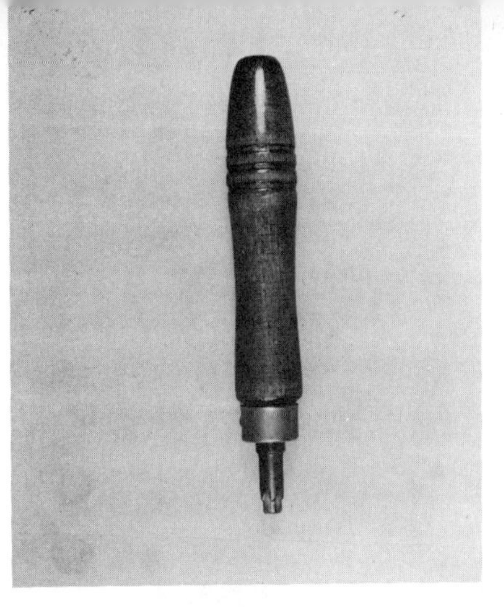

A very handy tool for removing the primer crimp from military cases after decapping. This Lyman primer-pocket reamer is inserted in the pocket after decapping and given a couple twists to cut away the intruding crimp.

spoil their performance. This, too, can be handled with a knife blade, but the low-cost primer-pocket reamer made by Lyman is quite effective and convenient. Just remember that primer pockets come in two sizes, so you might need this tool for both large and small primer sizes.

You can handload without a loading block, but it's damned inconvenient. Several firms offer cheap and simple molded-plastic blocks which will hold your cases upright for charging with powder. However, if you prefer, just drill holes in a section of ½-inch board, glue something over the bottom to keep the cases in place, and you'll have a perfectly good loading block at no cost.

If you'll be weighing out all or most of your powder charges on a scale, you'll find that a "powder trickler" will make the job much more rapid and convenient. This is a funnel-like gadget which contains a small amount of powder that comes in contact with a horizontal tube passing through its base; rotating the tube causes powder to run out through the tube and trickle out its open end and right onto the pan of your powder scale. Several companies make tricklers, of both plastic and metal, but for a long time I've obtained excellent results from the one supplied at low cost by Redding-Hunter.

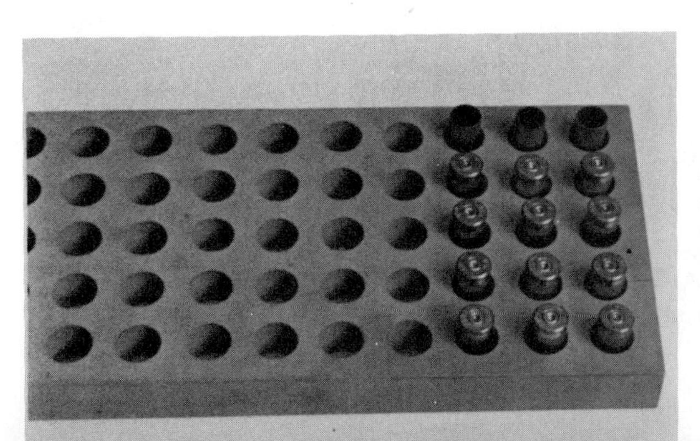

A loading block is a great convenience, and if you make your own by drilling holes in a piece of board like this, it will cost you next to nothing.

A very simple little gadget, the powder trickler allows very small quantities of powder to be transferred to the scale pan and thus simplifies weighing precise powder charges.

You'll also need some means of applying a very, very small amount of lubricant to cases prior to resizing. If you doubt the need for lubricant, just go ahead and run a dry case into a dry resizing die, and watch it jam fast. By the time you have fought it clear, you'll be convinced. A *cloth,* not rubber, ordinary stamp pad treated lightly with the resizing lubricant supplied by most tool makers will do very nicely. Several toolmakers offer this as a standard item, and it is not costly. Actually, you can get by without this quite easily, just moisten your thumb and finger with lubricant and twist the cases through them before resizing.

While you probably will never encounter any problem with stretching of handgun cases or straight rifle cases, bottleneck rifle cases tend to stretch or elongate with repeated use, the degree of stretching dependent somewhat upon the loads employed. While you can keep an unfired case in a particular caliber and compare fired cases with it to learn if they've stretched overmuch, the job is much simpler if you obtain one of the plastic vernier calipers supplied by Ohaus and some other handloading-tool manufacturers.

Once stretching has reared its head, the excess length must be removed, or it will interfere with accuracy and increase chamber pressures, possibly to the danger point. This is accomplished with a "case trimmer," which in its basic form is nothing more than a simple hand-operated lathe. Almost every manufacturer has a case trimmer, and for general use, I see little to

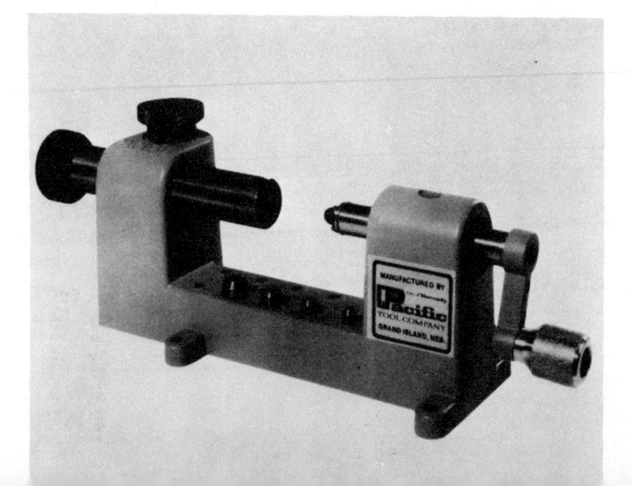

A conventional case trimmer, this particular model by Pacific utilizes the shell-holder head from the loading press to hold the case while the cutter, attached to the crank at right, is rotated to trim away excess brass.

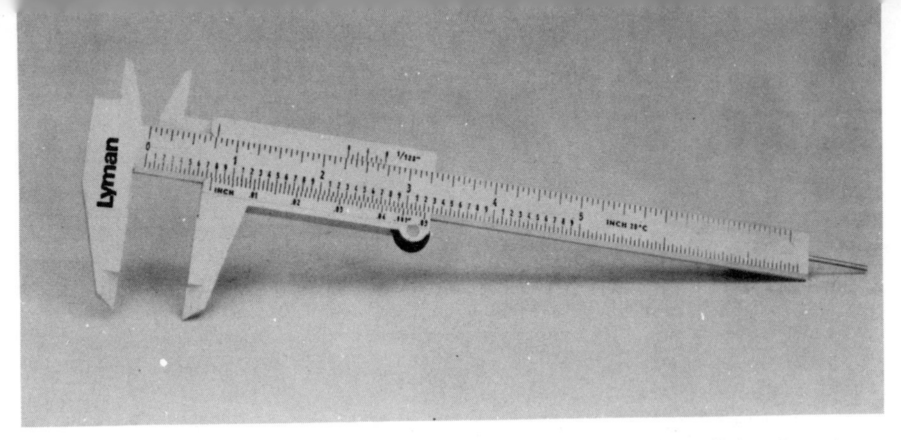

A low-priced vernier caliper such as this Lyman plastic model is entirely adequate for checking length of fired cases, and lets you avoid the purchase or fabrication of more complex and sophisticated gauges.

choose from between those of low and high cost. Some are more convenient to use than others, but trimming is a boring and tiring operation any way you look at it. The most convenient to use are those which utilize a stepped collet to grip the case head and which open and close that collet by a knurled ring or simple handle. For many years now, I've been quite satisfied with the trimmer made by Forster-Apelt. It is reasonably priced, has the added virtues of accessories allowing it to be used for neck reaming, and can be converted for use under power in a drill press. I don't think you can go wrong with the Forster case trimmer.

LOADING BENCH

You will need some form of loading bench. Because of the force required for resizing and some other operations, the press must be mounted solidly; a card table or typical kitchen table won't do, even if you're allowed to drill mounting holes in them. A sturdy workbench is what you want, and if you don't have one, you'll need to build something. Plans for a most excellent handloading bench are available for a small fee from the National Reloading Manufacturers Association. The plans are quite complete, and almost anyone can follow them and make an excellent bench with hand tools.

If you're too cramped for space to put up an ordinary workbench, make up a simple "pedestal mount" for your press, then use some sort of folding table next to it to accommodate the other items. The simplest pedestal consists of a 30-inch length of 1-inch pipe, both ends threaded; two pipe flanges to match, screwed on both ends of the pipe; a 12-inch square of *doubled* $^3/_4$-inch plywood screwed to the top flange; and an 18× 24-inch piece of $^3/_4$-inch plywood screwed to the bottom flange. The larger piece of plywood forms the base of the pedestal, and your loading press is bolted or C-clamped to the thicker top. A powder measure may also be mounted on the top, and the scale, components, loading blocks, etc. can be placed on a card table erected alongside. This type of pedestal works quite well, and if you are forced to do your loading in the kitchen or living room, the entire outfit can be whisked out of sight in only minutes.

The bench shown in the drawing lies between the pedestal and the

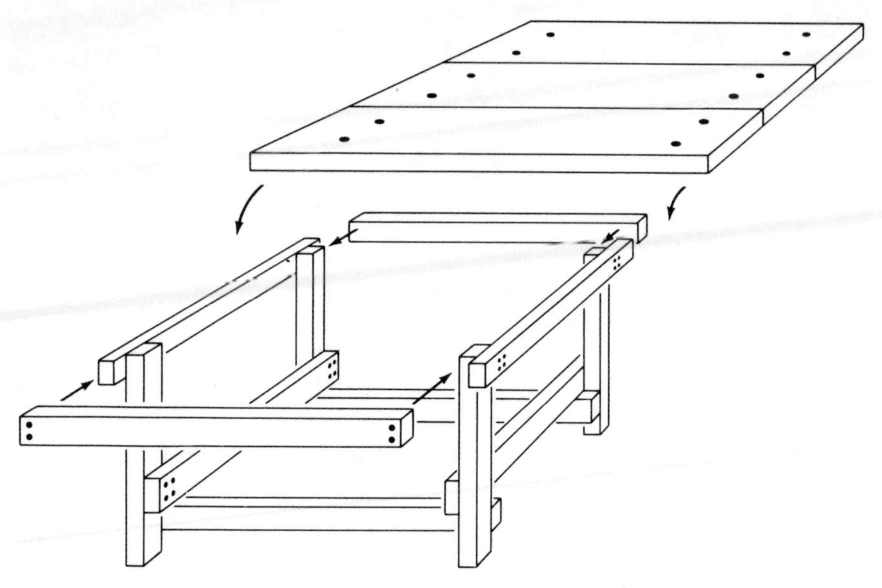

This drawing shows how to put together a very simple but sturdy bench that will serve for almost any handloading job you might wish to do.

NRMA bench. It's as simple as you can make it, utilizing stock-size lumber which may be bought cheaply in most areas if you just watch for sales. The top of the loading bench need not be large, at least for ordinary use; I consider 6 square feet of area about right. Typically that would be a top 2 × 3 feet, and that is plenty provided you have some other place to store the items not in use. Most of all, though, make the bench *solid,* so that it doesn't wobble around when you're putting plenty of beef on the press handle.

That's about it as far as selection of tools, equipment, and accessories is concerned. Other items will crop up as you dig more deeply into handloading and as you gain experience. As we move along in this book, we'll describe those items as we come to the particular operations for which they are needed.

3

Cartridge Components

As I mentioned in the first chapter, the typical centerfire metallic cartridge is composed of a brass cartridge case, a primer seated in a recess in the head of that case, a smokeless propellant powder charge inside the case, and a bullet of either lead or jacketed design held tightly in the mouth of the case. The case serves as a container or "envelope" for the entire assembly and ties it into a rugged, waterproof, oilproof package which must stand all manner of abuse, including heavy stresses and impacts placed upon it in feeding, chambering, extraction, and ejection. Few handloaders realize just how heavily the cartridge is stressed during feeding through autoloading actions. Factory loads have the strength necessary to resist these stresses, but handloads often fail in this area.

CARTRIDGE CASES

The case is the mechanical heart of the cartridge, and it is the obturating metallic case which made modern firearms practical. In addition to all of its other functions, it must seal the high-pressure powder gases inside the chamber and bore, preventing even the slightest escape to the rear. The brass from which cases are made is not ordinary brass; it is known in the trade as cartridge brass and is especially formulated and manufactured for the job. It is of a very high degree of purity, and the long coils of it supplied to cartridge plants must be exceedingly free of mechanical defects. Any defect in the strip brass may show up as a defect in the cartridge case, causing at best a malfunction of the gun, and at worst destruction of the gun and injury to the shooter.

A brief description of case manufacture will help to explain all this. Cases begin as a strip of sheet brass which is fed into an automatic press that simultaneously punches out discs and forms them into short, thick-walled cups. These are known in the trade simply as "cups" and are carefully designed and dimensioned to suit the particular case which will be made from them. An alternative method of forming the cup is called "impact extrusion," wherein a short, cylindrical slug of brass is contained within a die

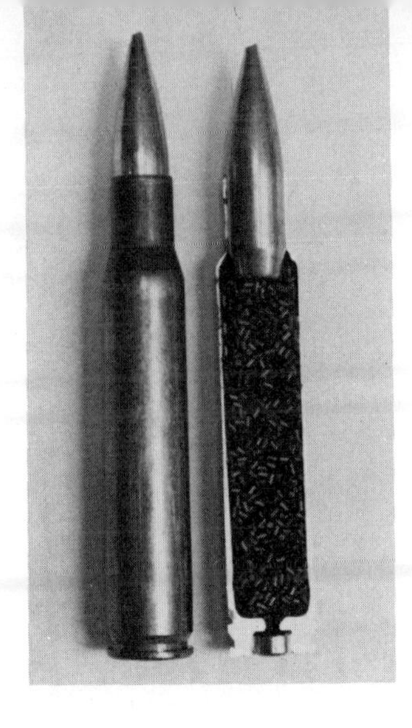

A typical rimless bottleneck centerfire cartridge on the left (actually .30-06), and on the right, the same thing with the case sectioned to show the manner in which all four components are assembled.

while a punch of smaller diameter is forced into it; as the slug is pierced by the punch, brass flows up around the punch, forming a cup which may be as much as half the length of the finished cartridge case. The cups resulting from the two different processes are in themselves different, and require somewhat different processes to form them into cases. However, for now, we'll stick with the first method described.

The cups are lubricated and drawn out, forced by punches through ring dies which reduce them in overall diameter, lengthen them, and reduce the thickness of the walls. The head or web remains thick. With annealing, washing, and lubrication after each drawing operation, the case proceeds through several draws (as many as five) until the proper length, diameter, and wall thickness are achieved. At this point, the case is cylindrical, and the head is not formed. The primer pocket and headstamp are then formed by a punch which slams into the bottom of the cup while it is held tightly in a die. At this point, the rough case will appear to have a rim, formed by excess brass flowing outward, even if it is intended to be a rimless or belted case. This is followed by a head-turning operation which brings the rim or extraction groove to proper dimensions and profile. The mouth of the case is trimmed to eliminate any cracks or raggedness which might interfere with subsequent operations; tapered by being forced into a die; given proper neck and shoulder dimensions and profile by another die; and finally trimmed to proper length. The last operation consists of annealing the neck and shoulder to give the brass there the proper degree of hardness. In some factories, the case is still without a flash hole at this point, it being formed by a punch as part of the priming operation; however, cases intended for sale to handloaders or to other loading plants will have the flash hole formed earlier.

Once the case has been completed, it represents about half the total materials cost of the cartridge. In order to withstand its first use, it has been given the strength and other physical properties that will enable it to withstand many firings under good conditions. Under the closely controlled conditions employed by a bench-rest shooter, a rifle case may very well be suitable for a hundred or more loadings. Under the more stringent conditions of ordinary handloading with full-charge loads, it may serve for only seven to twenty loadings, but with light loads and careful attention, it may last for twenty-five or thirty or even more.

PRIMERS

The primer begins as a strip of thin sheet brass. The brass is fed into an automatic press, which punches out small discs and simultaneously shapes them into the cup which forms the shell of the primer. After inspection and gauging, these cups are placed in holes in steel plates, awaiting insertion of the priming mix. This mix is highly explosive and quite dangerous. When it is used wet (to reduce the danger), a small lump of it is placed upon a plate containing holes which matches those in the cup plate, and the mix is squeegeed across the plate to fill all the holes uniformly. Then the plate containing the mix is aligned over the plate containing the primer cups, the two are placed in a press, and a plate with matching punches forces the pellets of wet priming mix firmly into the bottom of the primer cups. Still in the plate, the cups pass under a "foiling press," which punches out small discs of waterproof paper or foil and presses them on top of the priming mix. This may be followed by application of a small drop of waterproofing lacquer on top of each priming pellet. Those typical three-legged cone-shaped "anvils" have also been punched out of thin brass sheet in the same manner as the cups. They are now placed in a perforated steel plate which is aligned over the plate of charged cups, and a multiple punch forces them into the cups, seating them friction-tight, with the proper amount of pressure against the moist priming mix. Following this, the plates of primers go into a drying room or oven where the moist mix is brought down to the desired moisture content.

This is the traditional method of primer manufacture, but changes are taking place. Because of the hazardous nature of primer manufacture, it is being automated and done by remote control as new equipment is developed. I visited a primer factory in Scandinavia several years ago where the entire operation was done by remote control behind heavy reinforced-concrete barricades, using a *dry* priming mix. I suspect that eventually all primer manufacture will be done by remote control behind barricades.

All primers are made in this fashion, whether they be small or large, rifle or pistol, some special size, or "standard" or "magnum." Magnum primers differ from the standard variety only in that the pellet of priming compound is designed to produce a larger jet of flame for a slightly longer period of time. The resulting increase in heat and the length of time over which it is produced is needed to ignite some powders more efficiently.

The primer pocket in the case and the primer cup are very carefully matched in dimensions so that the primer becomes a tight, waterproof fit, yet is not distorted by the pressure required to seat it in the case. Any distortion or deformation is likely to fracture or crumble the priming-mix pellet, thus altering its performance when ignited.

Manufacture of "battery-cup" shotshell primers is quite similar, except that the cup containing the priming mix is pressed into the steel battery cup, which has already been fitted with its separate anvil.

The primer pocket in a metallic case, in this instance the .45 ACP, which uses the Large Pistol size. This is a fired case; note the hard, blackish ash adhering to the bottom of the pocket. The pocket is made slightly smaller than the primer to provide a tight interference fit which will be gas-tight, and the mouth is smoothly radiused to permit the primer to enter easily. The bottom of the pocket is flat to permit the primer anvil to seat solidly.

Primer manufacture is one of the most closely controlled and heavily inspected processes in the manufacture of ammunition. It is not only a very dangerous operation, but performance of the entire cartridge depends upon the efficiency, reliability, and uniformity of the primer.

POWDER

Powder manufacture is beyond the scope of this book. It is sufficient to say that it is a complex, costly, and dangerous process performed in special plants where everything and everyone is controlled by safety considerations. All operations are barricaded and conducted by remote control wherever possible. Not only is the manufacture of powder dangerous, but the materials themselves, especially nitric acid and (for double-base powders) nitroglycerin, are very hazardous. The propellant powder you purchase for your handloading is remarkably stable and quite safe as long as some care is used in handling it; however, up to the point that it is completed, tested, and packaged, it is mighty hazardous.

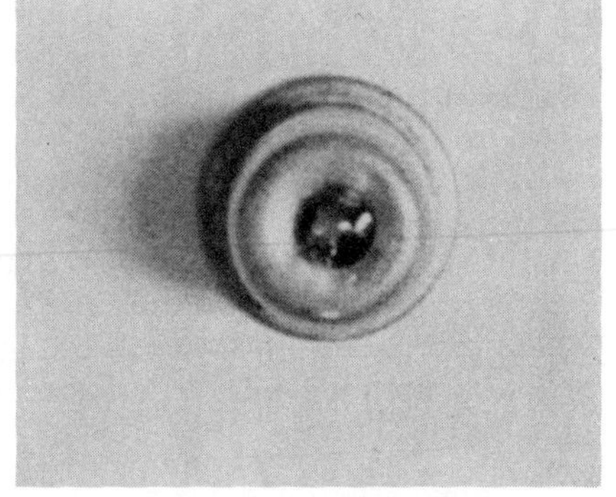

Side and end views of the typical shotshell battery-cup primer, so named because the flanged steel cup into which the primer and anvil are pressed was originally referred to as a battery cup. In the end view, note the hole in the bottom of the cup which permits the flash to reach the powder charge.

LEAD BULLETS

Ammunition factories no longer cast lead bullets. They haven't done so since well before the beginning of this century. Instead, bullets are formed in automatic presses fed by a coil of lead wire of the proper hardness and diameter, which is sheared off into "slugs" of the proper size and weight. The slug is then forced into a die by a punch, upsetting it to fill the die and giving the bullet its proper shape and weight and dimensions. Excess lead—and the slugs are cut a wee bit heavy—bleeds off through a hole in the die. The bullet is then ejected from the die, and is in its final form except for the lubricating grooves. The bullet is then transferred to a canneluring or grooving machine, where it is spun by finely serrated wheels which roll grooves into the bearing surface.

The bullet is then fully formed, and lacks only lubrication. This may be applied by dipping in molten lubricant, by tumbling in dry lubricant, or by automatic machinery. Once all this has been accomplished, and the lubricant has dried if it was applied wet, bullets are ready for loading.

Virtually any shape or size lead bullet may be formed this way. The process is known as *swaging,* and the lead slug is simply compressed in a die between two punches shaped to form the nose and the base. Traditionally, the factories use relatively soft lead, because it is easier to swage into shape and places less strain on the machines. Harder alloys can be used, but production rate is lowered and machine and tool wear is increased. Considering, then, that factory bullets are usually quite soft and that they are far more expensive than the home-cast variety, we find that relatively few handloaders use them. However, in the past few years, the independent bullet makers have begun to offer excellent swaged lead bullets, and usage by handloaders has increased substantially.

Both of these are factory-swaged lead bullets. The one on the left is used by Winchester-Western in .38 Special match cartridges. It features the traditional rolled-in lubricating grooves. The other, a new handloader's bullet by Hornady, substitutes knurling of the entire bearing surface for those grooves.

JACKETED BULLETS

The making of "jacketed" bullets is another matter entirely, and much more complex. The process begins just as in case manufacture, with cups being punched out of thin sheets of copper-alloy jacket metal. Depending upon the bullet, the cup may be drawn to greater length as a separate operation. Wall thickness and concentricity of bullet jackets are critical to accuracy, substantially more so than in case manufacture. Ideally, jackets should be absolutely concentric, with wall thickness perfectly uniform throughout. Manufacturers strive toward this goal, but they never quite reach it at a cost that shooters can afford to pay. During forming, the jacket is given any special, internal contours intended (such as a pentagonal or octagonal section to promote uniform expansion) and is then trimmed to length. Following this, the jacket goes to a bullet assembly press, where in a number of operations in sequence, a slug of lead wire is cut to length, formed roughly to shape, then placed in the jacket, and the two are assembled tightly in a die. Following that, a cannelure will be rolled into the surface of the bullet if one is specified, and it will then be washed and inspected.

These manufacturing processes apply whether the bullet has a thick, tough jacket extending clear to the tip, a thinner jacket extending only about three-quarters of the way to the tip, or the so-called "half jacket" of some handgun bullets. The number of individual operations varies from one design to another, not only in final bullet assembly, but in the forming of the core and the jacket.

What we've just described is the basic process for producing an elementary, jacketed, soft- or hollow-point bullet. Many variations are made—some utilizing two-part cores, one of hard lead and one of soft; others using specially contoured or unusually heavy jackets to control expansion; and full-metal-jacketed bullets in which the process is essentially the same but the jacket is inverted with the core inserted from the base. Regardless of the type or the process, expansion in game depends upon design and construction appropriate to the impact velocity, and accuracy depends upon uniformity of dimensions and weight, combined with concentricity and squareness of the base.

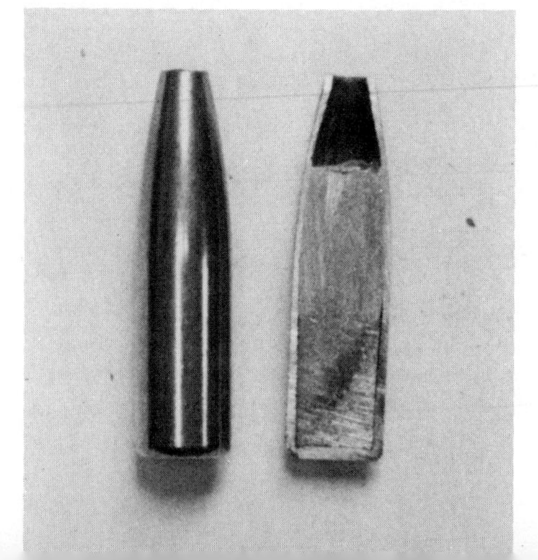

A typical jacketed hollow-point bullet shown whole and sectioned.

SHOTSHELL COMPONENTS

Shotshell components, with the exception of the primer and propellant powder, are an entirely different matter. The bulk of today's shotshells use either one-piece or built-up plastic cases, so we'll look at the case first. The so-called "compression-formed" case, first introduced by Winchester as the AA, is formed under considerable heat and pressure from a specially compounded tough plastic in female and male dies. Consequently, this single operation produces a completed case, with flash hole and primer pocket formed, requiring only the addition of a thin steel or brass "head overlay" which reinforces the rim for better extraction and gives the case the traditional look which shooters expect. The overlay is formed from thin sheet metal into a cup, much as a cartridge case begins but from thinner metal. The overlay is then placed over the plastic case head and formed down tightly against the case and into final shape. The overlay metal over the primer pocket is pierced and turned down into the pocket. The overlay is also usually lightly knurled at several points ahead of the rim to secure it more tightly to the case. The less costly "standard" plastic case is of built-up construction, made essentially from a length of very tough extruded-plastic tube of the correct wall thickness and diameter. One end of this tube is closed with a snug-fitting plastic or fiber (normally) "base wad," and then a steel or brass cup is swaged tightly over the head, forming the rim and primer pocket. This metal head, too, is knurled forward of the rim to make the entire assembly tighter.

Paper cases, not often used these days, are made essentially the same way, except that the body is made up of many layers of thin, tough paper rolled into a tube and impregnated with wax, and the base wad is also a paper pulp or composition material. While paper cases are cheaper, the advantages of the plastic case are so great and so numerous that plastic is almost universally preferred in this country. Aside from everything else, the plastic case is vastly superior for reloading, giving far greater case life. Some plastic cases will last for more than twenty-five reloadings, while even the best of the old paper cases did well to hold up for four or five loadings.

Modern shotshells generally use a one-piece plastic "wad column" which serves not only to seal the powder gases behind it but to cushion the shot

A typical built-up plastic case cut apart to show how the single-unit plastic wad column/shot cup is used.

A typical shotshell manufactured as a display dummy to show the different components and their locations inside. This is a compression-formed plastic case utilizing a cupped cardboard over-powder wad as well as conventional fiber filler wads.

against the initial shock of acceleration and to protect the shot from the steel bore. These complex-shaped wads are injection-molded in very sophisticated dies from polyethylene or similar plastic.

However, some loads are still assembled with the old-style "conventional" wad column. The "over-powder" wad is formed in a die from stiff, tough waxed cardboard (or plastic) and is shaped into a very shallow cup. This cup is seated over the powder, mouth down, so that the powder gases expand the edges tightly against the bore and thus seal themselves in. Above the over-powder wad we have the so-called "filler" wads, which may be any resilient material which will cushion the shot against the initial shock of acceleration by the powder gases. Many materials have been used for these wads, but the most common greatly resembles fiber insulating board such as Celotex. These wads are simply cut from sheets of the material of the proper thickness. An automatic press does this with sharp-edged, hollow punches operating at a very high speed.

Lead shot is simply small, spherical balls of lead, normally hardened by about 3 percent antimony. Traditionally it is made by pouring molten lead alloy through an oversize iron frying pan containing multiple holes in its bottom. Hole size, lead temperature and composition, flux, and

A bottom view of the cupped cardboard over-powder wad used for many years in almost all factory-loaded shotshells, and still used in some loadings.

other factors control the size of the droplets that come through the perforations. Then the droplets fall over 100 feet through the air, during which time surface tension pulls them into spheres, and they become partially hard. At the end of the drop, they fall into water and are quenched and cooled. Since this method doesn't produce absolute uniformity of size or shape, the shot is then taken from the water, dried, and sorted automatically for size and roudness by rolling over angled steel plates and screens. The shot is then finished by tumbling it with a small amount of very fine powdered graphite.

A much more modern method of making lead shot is used by the Murdock Lead Company. A stream of molten lead is allowed to fall against the surface of a rotating plate; this breaks up the stream into individual droplets, which are hurled through the air and eventually fall into a water tank. Many factors determine the size and roundness of shot produced this way, and they must be watched constantly. Assuming both methods are under proper control, there is no apparent difference in the quality of shot they produce; the second method has the advantage of not requiring a tall and tremendously expensive "shot tower."

As this book goes to press, steel shot—sometimes called soft-iron shot—is in the news. Federal waterfowl regulations have been changed to require the use of steel shot to reduce deaths of waterfowl due to lead poisoning. Birds feeding off the bottom of ponds and potholes ingest lead shot pellets which are ground up in the crop and absorbed into the system, with death resulting. Steel shot eliminates this problem since it is not toxic when ingested. Federally mandated use of steel shot is a highly controversial and involved subject, and I won't get into that aspect of it here. The fact remains that steel shot is required by law.

Steel-shot waterfowling loads are available from the major ammunition manufacturers, but only in 12 gauge. Because of insufficient development time and ballistic problems not yet overcome, steel-shot loads are not yet available in smaller gauges and have not been developed in ten gauge. As of September 1977 waterfowlers using 12-gauge guns had to use steel-shot ammunition. And lead shot will probably be banned for all other gauges before long.

If you are accustomed to assembling your own waterfowling loads, you may think you can load your own steel shot as you loaded lead. Unfortunately, you can't. First of all, the steel shot used by the ammunition manufacturers is highly specialized and very costly, and it's not yet available to handloaders. Even though it is as soft as existing technology can make it, it will still eventually deform modern shotgun barrels, and it will actually gouge and groove older guns with barrels of softer steel. In the best of modern barrels, this damage usually occurs as a slight bulging of the barrel behind the choke, and as some enlargement of the choke. In older barrels, it may also show up as longitudinal grooves in the bore surface, and as extensive bulging and choke enlargement. If you attempt to use other steel balls as shot (BB-shot, bearings, etc.), the damage will far greater, even for the strongest barrels.

In addition to the effect of steel shot on the barrel, there are other problems. First of all, barrel damage is minimized in factory ammunition

Lead shot pellets, unusually uniform, in company with "Grex" granulated polyethylene filler introduced in some Winchester-Western magnum shotshell loads during 1977. Both shot and filler came from a 20-gauge 3-inch magnum.

by the use of extra-thick plastic shot cups which are not yet available to handloaders. Along with this, shotshell powders developed for use with lead shot cannot deliver proper ballistic performance with steel shot because of their greatly different densities. Special powders have been developed for steel shot in twelve-gauge (which are not necessarily suitable for other gauges), and even the powders in use have not been the best ones for steel shot. These powders, too, are not available to handloaders, and the use of conventional shotshell powders with steel shot is fraught with many problems. Lastly, because of the special powders required with steel shot, existing conventional shotshell primers do not provide efficient ignition. So new primers have been developed. These primers are not yet available to handloaders.

There are other problems, but the ones I've just mentioned are the most significant. It all boils down to the simple fact that no matter what you might think or want, you simply cannot yet assemble steel-shot loads that are either safe or efficient. As if that weren't enough, any steel shot loads you might try to brew up would be almost certain to cause irreparable damage to your gun.

I'm not trying condemn the handloading of steel shot forever. Eventually proper components for steel-shot handloads will be produced in quantity and made available through normal channels to individuals. However, it may be 1980 before that will happen. As it stands right now, the case is the only shotshell component available to you that is suitable for steel-shot loads. So don't load steel shot until proper handloading components become available.

The only component of the shotshell remaining for discussion is the "over-shot" wad, which is seldom used. It will, however, be found on buckshot loads and some others. It is simply a disc of relatively thin, brittle cardboard fitting snugly inside the case mouth and held in place by the mouth of the case being turned over through 180 degrees to press down tightly against it. This is known as a "roll crimp" as opposed to the much more popular "star crimp" which is found on most loads. The over-shot wad is intended to hold the shot charge securely in the case, but yet break up as the charge emerges from the muzzle. If it does not break up, it may mask a portion of the shot charge and cause what is called a "blown pat-

At left is the traditional "rolled" crimp with the mouth of the case turned inward 180 degrees to secure a circular cardboard over-shot wad. At right is the more modern folded or star crimp; the entire mouth of the case is folded in upon itself to meet in the center and in factory loads is often heat-sealed as can be seen here. The old-style rolled crimp requires special equipment for the handloader, while the star crimp is formed very easily.

tern." This means simply that there will be a hole somewhere near the center of the shot pattern.

Shot sizes are described in Chapter 12.

MAKING YOUR OWN COMPONENTS

In metallic cartridges, the only component you can actually make from scratch yourself is the bullet. You may cast simple lead bullets, or you may swage the most complex double-jacketed, compound-cored, controlled-expansion, jacketed bullets. In shotshells, it isn't practical to make ordinary shot, but you can cast the larger buckshot sizes in a round-ball mold, and you may also cast bore-size balls or hollow-base slugs for specialized loads. The only other shotshell component you may make yourself is the wad column of the old-style, conventional type. A wadcutter punch may be made or purchased in the proper size, and over-powder wads may be cut from cardboard, or the filler wads may be cut from composition board such as Celotex.

Aside from those items above, you must depend upon commercially manufacturerd components for both metallic cartridges and shotshells. Maximum economy is achieved, of course, when the fired case is combined with as many home made components as possible.

With the foregoing background on manufacture and function of the various components, you'll be able to understand better the procedures in selecting and assembling loads to suit a particular functional purpose, or to achieve maximum economy.

4

Loading Metallic Cartridges

PROPER RELOADING BEGINS with fired cases, and if safe and efficient ammunition is to result, those cases must be carefully inspected and selected. The average neophyte will usually have a hodgepodge of fired cases scrounged from ranges and donated by friends. The history of such cases is unknown, and some of them may have been fired and loaded many times. One really should start with cases in the best possible condition and *known* to have been fired only once. Ideally they should also be of the same make.

WASHING

Assuming you do have a mixture, the first step in preparing cases for loading is to wash and sort them. Dump them into a kettle of water and de-

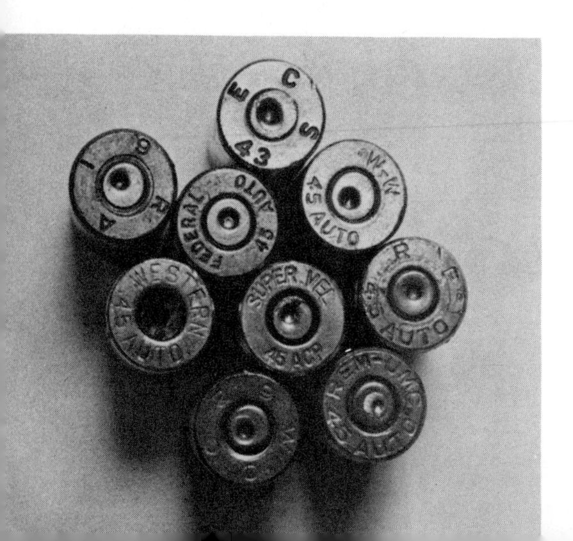

Nine different headstamps, both commercial and military. A good many more will be encountered, and while all are good if not damaged, cases should be sorted by headstamp and kept separate. Cases of one headstamp will most likely perform just as well as those of another, but differences in hardness and internal capacity will cause them to shoot to slightly different points of impact. Mixing them up will enlarge groups. Note the "E C S 43" at the top; though nickel-plated and apparently the same as the others, it is actually a relatively hard, steel case which does not lend itself at all well to reloading.

These are defects that may be encountered in fired cases. In addition to the splits in the neck and shoulder area, note that the case on the right is substantially expanded ahead of the extractor groove, indicating an undersized case and/or oversized chamber. Note also that there is possibly serious thinning of the wall just ahead of the solid web.

tergent on the range, and bring the water to a boil, agitating vigorously when the water starts to bubble. The detergent will clean off all the loose dirt and grease, and the agitation should loosen any foreign material that's accumulated inside the cases. If the water becomes very dirty, dump it out and repeat the process. Then rinse the cases under the hottest water your tap will supply. When all the detergent and dirty water are flushed away, drain the cases, using an old colander or french-fry basket, agitating them all the while so that water inside will have a chance to run out. Spread them out on an old towel or piece of carpeting to air-dry. Drying can be speeded up by setting an electric fan to blow across them, or a small portable electric heater containing a fan will do the job even better. Don't use direct heat to dry them, because until you've obtained some experience, it's possible to apply too much heat and spoil the hardness of the cases, setting up a serious accident.

SORTING

Once the cases are dry, sort them by headstamp. Inspect them for condition, setting aside any that show more than very minor dents, flattened mouths, large amounts of expansion ahead of the rim, primer leaks (a black smudge or corrosion around the primer), blown primers (indicated by a hole rather than a dent in the primer), primers that appear excessively flattened, surface pitting or heavy corrosion, lots of parallel longitudinal scratches which indicate previous reloading, bent rims, and anything else that seems significantly abnormal. Many of those rejects may be salvaged later when you've obtained more experience, but in the beginning, you should work with near-perfect cases. You'll learn better and faster, and will encounter far fewer troubles.

Range pick-up cases such as this batch of .32 ACP can be salvaged mechanically, since their dents and bending will be smoothed out by resizing and mouth expansion, but sand and grit are so deeply imbedded in the brass that no normal cleaning would remove it; the resizing dies would be ruined.

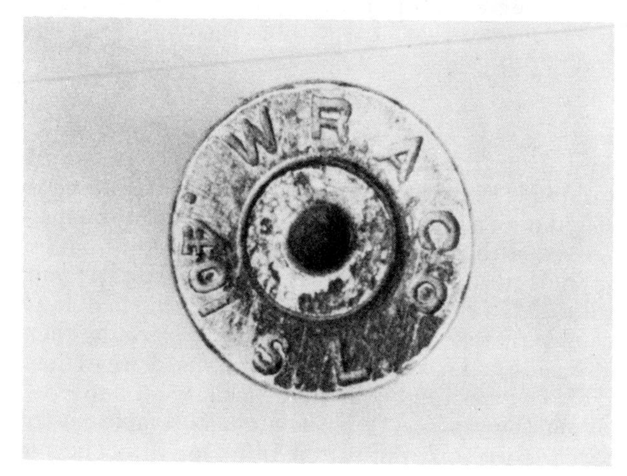

The head of this .401 Winchester case shows not only a heavily flattened and perforated primer, but a primer leak, evidenced by the dark stains on the head. All this indicates excessive pressures, which have most likely damaged the case internally.

RESIZING

Resizing is the next step. In most rifle and some handgun calibers (those with bottleneck cases), decapping (punching out the expended primer) is performed simultaneously with resizing. First of all, you should think only in terms of resizing *full length.* Resizing the necks only is suitable for some special purposes, but not for general-use ammunition. Cases that are not resized full length will usually not chamber in all guns of the same caliber, and may not chamber smoothly and easily even in the gun in which they were originally fired. Take the shell-holder head of the proper caliber and place it in the ram of your press. Screw the full-length-resizing die into the top of the press, and with the press ram at the top of its stroke, turn the die into the press until it bumps solidly into the holder. Retract the ram a bit, turn the die in ⅛ turn, then run the ram all the way back up. The holder should bump the die, and you should feel the press linkage pop "over center." This should not require any great amount of effort, just a slight

With die properly adjusted, it will protrude about this far through the press head and will be contacted quite solidly by the shell holder; note the approximate correct amount of decapping-pin protrusion. So the case must be pushed fully into the shell holder and must remain there as it starts into the die.

increase as the linkage pops over. This places the press frame in tension, and pretty well eliminates the possibility of its stretching under the load of resizing and thus keeping the case from going all the way into the die. At this point, screw down the lock ring on the die body snug against the press so that the die won't work loose from vibration during use. Lock the ring on the die with its screw. Loosen the lock nuts at the top of the die and adjust the decapping stem until the decapping pin protrudes about $\frac{1}{4}$ inch from the die mouth. Lock the stem in place and make certain that it is solid in the die and that the decapping pin is centered in the die mouth.

Before doing all that, it's an excellent idea to remove the decapping stem entirely and wipe out the die cavity with solvent and a lint-free cloth. The dies are shipped coated with a preservative, and may well have picked up a bit of grit and dirt since you first opened the box; if not removed, this material will scratch both cases and dies. Minute scratches won't really cause any serious harm, but they'll make your cases look sloppy, and die wear will be somewhat accelerated.

Once the die has been properly adjusted, the locking ring must be screwed down snugly and then clamped securely in place with its own lock screw.

The full-length-resizing die adjustment described is standard with all makes of dies, and is the one you should use in the beginning. Other factors enter into die adjustment for special purposes, but this is covered in considerable detail in another chapter. Those things can come later after you know the basics.

Fired cases *must* be lubricated before resizing, with the single exception covered in detail in Chapter 7, which applies only to handgun calibers. Most tool manufacturers offer a resizing lubricant, but plain anhydrous lanolin from your pharmacist works equally well and is much cheaper. Also, STP oil additive works beautifully, and a single can contains enough to last you for years. Do *not*—repeat, do *not*—attempt to use ordinary oils and greases. Generally, they lack the high film strength necessary to withstand the high pressures involved and may cause a stuck case. Only the slightest trace of lubricant is necessary; if there is any excess, it will be trapped between the die and case (most often in the shoulder area) and will form a big dent (called an "oil dent"), or in extreme instances will actually split the case.

If lubricant is not applied to the case, excessive effort is required to force it into the die and to extract it; *usually* it will not extract, with the rim being torn off instead. That leaves you with a case stuck immovably in the die, and the job of removing it is lengthy and frustrating. That problem, too, will be covered in a later chapter. Cases can be quite adequately lubricated by merely moistening the thumb and finger of one hand with lubricant and rolling the shoulder area of the case between them as you insert it in the shell holder. The first two or three cases into the die will spread the lube throughout the die cavity, and this is your insurance if you skip one or two. Even if you absent-mindedly quit lubricating, several more cases can be processed safely, but you'll feel the progressively greater effort required. That's your warning.

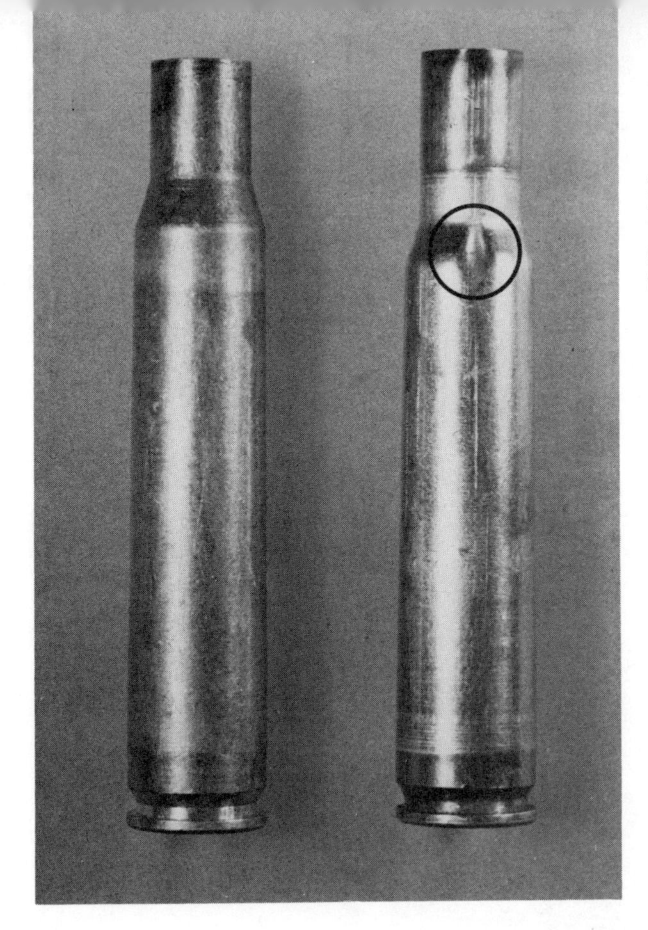

Application of too much lubricant will produce "oil dents" along the shoulder area, shown in the circle.

Lubricant must be kept off the head of the case to avoid contaminating the new primers when they are seated. A contaminated primer may not ignite, or it may not fire well enough to ignite the powder charge, and that is even worse because it will force the bullet and part of the powder charge a short distance into the bore. This is a dangerous condition which must be avoided.

With the case lubricated, slide its rim into the T-slot of the shell holder, making certain it seats all the way and that there is no dirt, powder, or other foreign material packed in the slot to prevent the rim from seating properly. Run the press handle down, and the case *should* enter the die mouth smoothly, passing over the decapping stem and the expander plug in the process. However, it's a good idea to guide the case with your thumb and finger to be certain that it passes over the expander plug and decapping pin. In the smaller calibers, particularly if the loading press is not vertical on the bench (and many are designed with a built-in slant), the case might lean enough to snag on the end of the decapping rod, damaging the mouth, probably spoiling the entire case. With just a little practice, you'll be able to guide the case instinctively as it passes between thumb and finger without losing a bit of time. Run the case all the way into the die in one single smooth stroke until you feel the linkage barely pop over center. If you don't feel it pop over, look closely and make certain there is no gap

With the case rim seated fully in the shell holder, guide the case initially with the fingers until it moves up over the decapping pin. Then run the case fully into the die with a single smooth stroke of the press handle. If the stroke is interrupted, a great deal of additional effort will be needed to start the case moving again.

between the shell holder and the die mouth. If any light can be seen between the two, you'll have to screw the die a tiny bit deeper into the press. Some presses have more spring to them than others, and some calibers and cases require more sizing effort than others—with the result that some presses require deeper die adjustment.

Note as the case seats home in the die whether the fired primer is completely expelled and falls through the slot in the ram. If it does not, you'll have to adjust the decapping stem just a bit lower.

Now, extract the case from the die with a single, smooth stroke, take the case out of the shell holder, and look at it closely. There shouldn't be any heavy scratches, feathers of scraped-up brass, wrinkles or dents, or bending or deformation of the rim. Dents result from excess lubricant as already described. A deformed rim is most likely due to lack of lubricant, which causes excessive extraction force. The other problems result from the die

The swinging primer arm on this RCBS press is a typical on-press type.

or from dirt and grit on the case. Look in the primer pocket and you'll see a hard black crystalline residue produced by the burning priming compound. Unless there is an excessive amount of this material, I see no particular need to remove it. However, many handloaders prefer to do so for the sake of uniformity. A cheap screwdriver filed into a scraper which enters the primer pocket easily can be twisted to remove the residue.

At some point during the extraction stroke, you'll feel—and perhaps hear—the expander ball or plug as the case neck is pulled over it. In fired condition, the inside diameter of the neck is sufficient to pass over the expander; then the die reduces the neck substantially, which is then *expanded up* to the proper diameter to hold the bullet by being pulled over the expander plug on the extraction stroke. It must be done this way because of the variations encountered in case-neck wall thickness and in dies. Accept that for the time being, and don't attempt to get by without this automatic expanding operation.

Priming During Resizing

You have an option before extracting a case from the resizing die. The case may be primed quite adequately during the extraction stroke, using the swinging-arm priming device supplied with the press. To do so, before beginning the extraction stroke, pick up a fresh primer and seat it in the sleeve, anvil up, of the priming arm; then press the arm forward until it comes to a positive stop inside the priming slot in the ram. Then begin the

I much prefer to seat primers separately, using this RCBS bench-type priming tool. Priming begins by placing a primer anvil-up in the bushing in the center of the shell holder, with the handle lifted.

extraction stroke slowly and easily, *feeling* for the added resistance as the case is pulled down over the primer. With practice, you'll be able to feel the primer seat against the bottom of its pocket, and no further pressure should be applied. Any crushing or deformation will alter the primer's flame characteristics, resulting in reduced accuracy. Then ease the ram up about $\frac{1}{4}$ inch, and the priming arm will be moved back to its rest position by a spring. Then you can complete the extraction stroke. Take care when running the ram up to free the priming arm, or the decapping stem will punch that fresh primer right back out.

Priming as a Separate Step

This priming method is satisfactory for "ordinary" ammunition, but substantially more uniform primer seating can be obtained from a bench priming tool such as the RCBS. The problem is simply that the average press linkage develops a high mechanical advantage which reduces one's feel for primer seating, and the amount of friction involved in the entire press reduces it even further. A bench priming tool offers very sensitive feel, and allows much more uniform seating of primers.

There's one other factor which has an effect upon when and how you reprime the cases. Military cases—calibers .30-06, 7.62mm/.308 (NATO), .223/5.56mm, .38 Special, 9mm Parabellum, and .45 ACP—will normally have a ring crimp around the mouth of the primer pocket, applied after the original primer was seated. The purpose of this crimp is to make certain that primers do not back out when fired in automatic weapons with loose headspace. Once the fired primer has been expelled, the crimp must be removed before a fresh primer can be seated safely or correctly. The simplest way of doing this is with the small primer-pocket reamer made by Lyman and sold for only a few dollars, though a creditable job can be done with the point of a thin, sharp knife blade. Either way, remove no more metal than is necessary to clean out the crimp so that a fresh primer can enter freely. Do not hog out so much metal that a significant bevel is

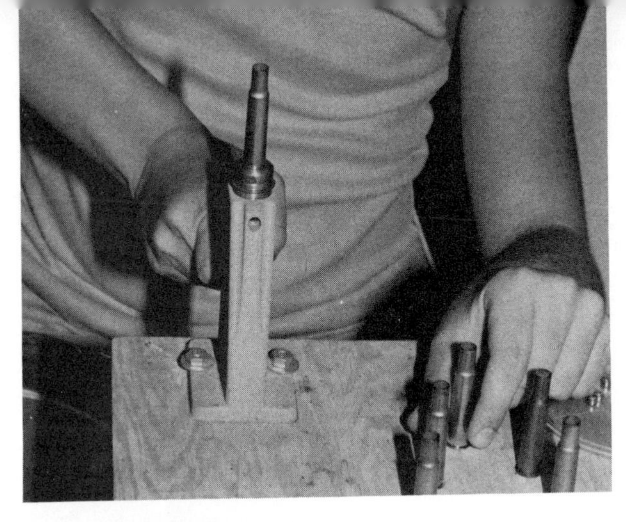

The case is slipped into the shell holder, taking care that it is fully seated, and the primer is then seated by pressing the tool handle downward, *feeling* carefully for the point where the anvil contacts the bottom of the pocket. Don't use too much pressure.

Be particularly careful that primers are fully seated and don't protrude beyond the case head like this.

produced on the mouth of the primer pocket. This serves no purpose other than to reduce the amount of support the pocket walls give the primer and thus encourage primer leaks. A better method is to use a primer pocket swage, which simply forces the crimp back without removing any metal.

Lubricating the Inside of the Case

The expander ball often drags rather heavily on the case neck. If the upper end of the plug is smoothly beveled and highly polished over its entire bearing surface, and the inside of the case neck is clean, there usually won't be any trouble. However, many of the older expander plugs have a sharp edge that scrapes brass off the inside of the case neck and the finish isn't necessarily as smooth as it might be. Expander plugs like this should be smoothly polished and the sharp upper edge gently radiused. Depending upon the relationship between die diameter, plug diameter, and neck wall thickness, it may take quite a bit of force to pull the plug through the neck. This can get tough enough to deform the case shoulder, so unless the case pulls over the plug easily, some lubrication should be used. It's easiest to use a fluid lubricant, essentially the same stuff you use on cases, but this

Military primer crimp will prevent proper seating of a new primer and must be removed as shown at left.

leaves the inside of the case neck moist, causing powder granules to cling there later, and if done to excess, might even contaminate the powder charge. Finely powdered graphite does better, and eliminates the contamination problem. A bore-cleaning brush dipped occasionally in graphite and passed through the neck provides adequate lubrication. Bonanza makes a very handy little "Case-Neck Graphiter." It consists of a plastic base with space for a supply of graphite, and several bore brushes of different sizes mounted vertically in it. With this gadget clamped or screwed to the bench top, you simply plunge the case mouth over the appropriate-size brush before resizing, and there'll be no more problems.

CLEANING AND DEBURRING

Once cases have been resized, the lubricant should be completely removed. Even though only a trace is present, it will reduce friction between case and chamber on firing, and thus increase backthrust on the bolt of the rifle. If an excessive amount is present, it can cause pressures to skyrocket. If you're priming on the press, then it's not practical to remove the lubricant until after priming; but if you're priming on a separate tool, the lubricant should be removed first to prevent primer contamination. If there are only a few cases, a cloth moistened in lighter fluid may be used to wipe the cases clean. However, if there are many, moisten a large, thick towel *lightly* with lighter fluid or other solvent, dump the cases on it, roll them in the towel, grasp either end, and shuffle them back and forth between your hands for a few minutes. The solvent-moistened nap of the towel will remove all traces of the lubricant, leaving the cases clean, dry, and grease-free.

Assuming the cases are only once-fired and have never been processed before, only one more thing remains to be done and they'll be ready to load. The mouth has a sharp inner and outer edge; the inner edge, even though it's relatively soft brass, can gouge into the bullet as it is seated, or scrape up jacket metal, flawing the jacket and perhaps interfering with accuracy. The sharp outer edge doesn't cause any trouble, but it's common practice to break the sharp edge with a deburring tool. The inner edge must be deburred and lightly chamfered, and this is generally done with the same tool, which incorporates a male cone with at least one cutting edge at one end for the inside, and a female cone at the other for the outer edge.

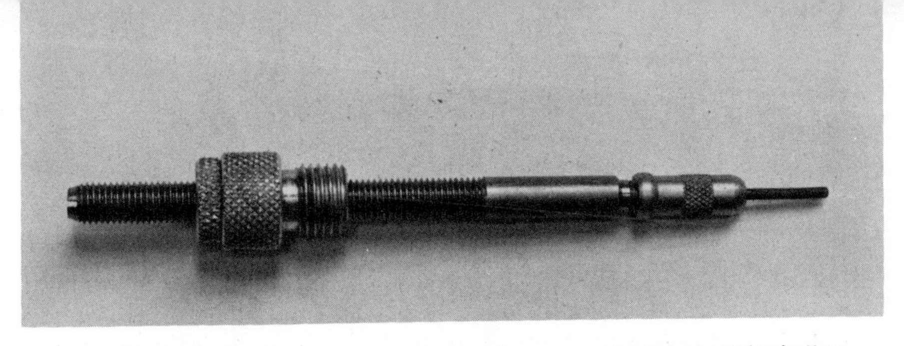

Decapping stem for conventional bottlenecked cases carries the expander button, whose work is done by the raised ring to the left of the narrow, knurled portion on the button holding the decapping pin. This area must be polished smooth and neatly radiused or beveled at both ends to prevent case damage.

Simply inserting the cone into the case mouth and giving it a twist or two with light pressure will peel off the burrs and leave a slight chamfer. Don't overdo this, because it will simply weaken the case mouth. Slip the female end over the outside of the case mouth and give it a twist or two, and the outer edge is deburred. Lacking a deburring tool, the inner edge can be easily done with a sharp knife blade, and the outer edge with a file. In either case, go lightly, and remove no more brass than is absolutely necessary.

CHARGING

Charging the case with powder comes next, and for both safety and accuracy, this is probably the most critical of all the operations.

Set up your scale, making certain it is level, using the leveling screws and following the manufacturer's instructions. Set it up where it will *not* be in any strong drafts from fans, air conditioners, open windows, etc. Even an almost unnoticeable draft can affect the scale and make its use difficult. Make certain also that the scale is zeroed, that movement of the beam is free, and that the pan is clean and is dry. Set out the powder you'll be using, then double-check the label against the loading data sheet, making *abso-*

Before adding powder and bullet, new or once-fired cases require that the inside of the mouth be chamfered. This simple and economical Lee tool does the job well.

lutely certain that the powder you have is the one specified in the data. It's easy to make mistakes in reading labels, especially when they are as similar as 4320 and 4350; use of the former in a load intended for the latter will certainly produce excessive pressures, and possibly wreck the gun. *Never, never* use unlabeled powder simply because it *looks* like the right one. Powders *cannot* be positively identified by appearance.

Pour powder out into a cup or small bowl, set the scale for the charge weight you want, and with a spoon, dribble powder onto the scale pan until the beam starts to move. Do this gently and slowly at first, or you'll dump too much powder on the pan and simply have to remove part of it and start over. When the pan starts to move, watch the pointer at the end of the beam very closely, and continue to dribble only a very few kernels of powder at a time until the pointer comes to rest at or very near zero. In an *undamped* scale, it will take the pointer quite a while to come to rest. However, most modern scales are magnetically damped, so the pointer will stop very quickly. In a damped scale, you can just keep dribbling a couple of kernels at a time until the pointer reaches zero and stops there. In an undamped scale, dribble powder until the pointer is swinging an equal distance on either side of the zero mark. So long as the pointer is doing this, you need not wait for it to come to a complete rest. With the pointer either resting on zero or swinging an equal distance on either side, the weight of powder in the pan is equal in grains avoirdupois to the setting you placed on the scale. Recheck it to make sure it hasn't been accidentally moved, and the powder charge is correct.

In Chapter 2 I mentioned a powder trickler. It will simplify weighing charges. To use it, fill its reservoir with powder, then rotate the knob until powder starts to trickle out the end of its tube. Now, spoon an amount of

After the bulk of the charge has been placed in the scale pan, a powder trickler is used to feed in the rest and bring the pointer to zero. Rotating the tube passing through the trickler feeds individual kernels of powder to the pan. The setting on this scale is 53 grains, 50 of which are accounted for by the poise indicated by the left arrow, and three grains accounted for by the micrometer adjustment at the right.

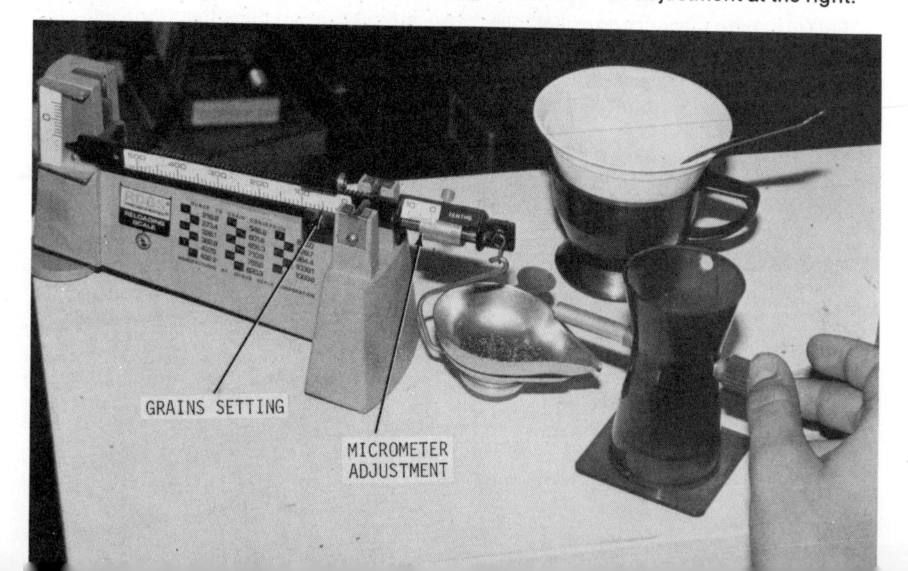

powder on the pan that you know is just a bit less than the charge you want; then move the trickler over so its spout is over the pan, and rotate the knob slowly, feeding a steady but sparse stream of powder granules into the pan. Continue this until the scale pointer reaches zero.

With the powder charge weighed out, simply place your primed and prepared case in a loading block to hold it upright, set a powder funnel over its mouth, and pour the powder charge directly into the funnel. With some powders, you'll encounter "bridging," which means that the granules pack together in the throat of the funnel and won't flow down into the case. Tapping the side of the funnel or case with a piece of rod or a cartridge case will cause the powder to flow on through. As a beginner, you shouldn't be using a powder charge so large that it fills the case completely full; but if it appears to do so, tap the side of the case gently to settle the charge. If the case still looks overfull, pour the charge back in the scale pan and reweigh it and recheck the amount with your loading data. The one thing you don't want is an overcharge. If you determine that the charge is correct and that it still overfills the case, you'll simply have to select a new load that uses less powder.

Using a Powder Measure

Use of an adjustable powder measure will greatly speed the operation, but still requires very careful use of the scale to verify proper charge weight. Clamp or bolt the measure down solidly; it is almost impossible to throw consistent charges from a wobbly measure. Fill the reservoir with the *proper* powder, and simply by guess, set the metering chamber adjustment at about its middle point. Set the powder scale for the charge you intend to use, then operate the measure handle to drop a charge into the scale pan. Note whether it is over or under the weight desired, and reset the adjustment. Continue this process until you have approached closely the charge weight desired; then, operating the measure handle as smoothly and consistently as possible, throw five consecutive charges into the pan, weigh

After the charge is weighed, powder is poured into the case through a typical plastic powder funnel.

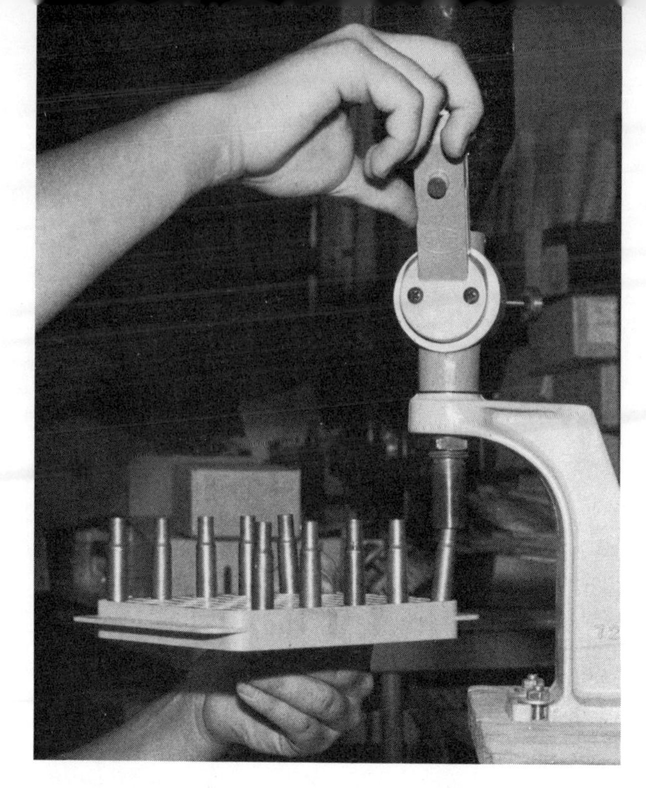

While you can get by quite well with only a powder scale, charging cases can be greatly speeded by use of an adjustable volumetric measure such as this Ohaus Du-O-Measure. Consistency of operation is most important to ensure charge uniformity.

them together, then divide the weight by five to obtain the *average* weight. Make minor adjustments and repeat this until the average of at least five consecutive charges is the weight of charge called for. Until you have become quite experienced in the operation of a powder measure, setting it by a five-charge average, rather than an individual charge, will produce more accurate and consistent results. In fact, it's a good idea to always set the measure by the average charge weight.

It is not so much the exact weight of charge as it is its uniformity or consistency that affects accuracy. A volumetric powder measure is mechanically capable of throwing very consistent charges (the smaller the powder granulation, the more consistent), but to do so it must be mounted very solidly and the handle must be operated as uniformly as possible from charge to charge. It must be moved smoothly through each arc of its travel with uniform speed and force. It must come to rest at both ends of each stroke with equal impact. If it hangs up—as it will sometimes with coarse-kernel powders—in the middle of a stroke, dump that charge back into the reservoir and not into the case, for it may be lighter or heavier than its companions. The amount of powder in the reservoir will affect the charge weight—the less powder there, the lighter the charge—so add powder frequently to keep a fairly uniform "head" of powder. And, of course, check the adjustment frequently to make certain it has not changed or loosened from vibration. Most measures have a micrometer scale on the adjustment mechanism so that a quick glance will tell you whether anything has shifted. Feel the adjustment knob, too, to make sure it remains tight. Even if everything appears to remain the same, periodically weigh a single charge to verify that nothing has changed. It's a good idea to weigh a

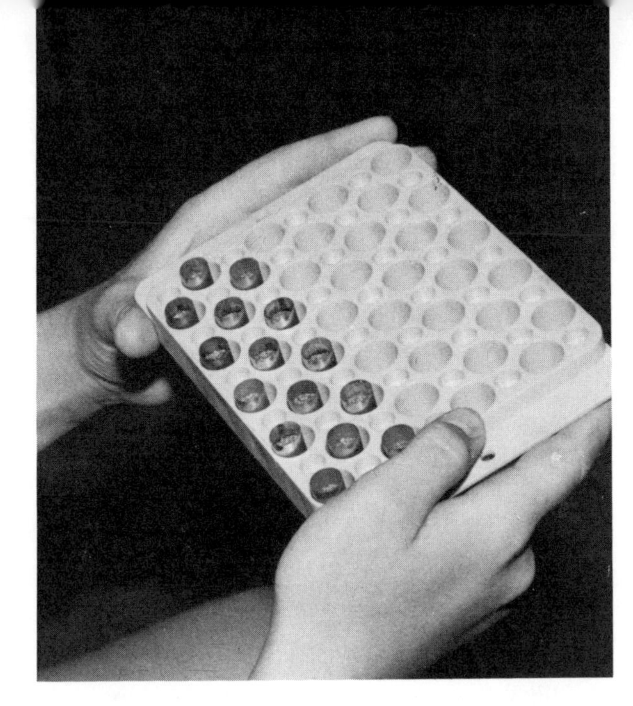

Regardless of the caliber and whether charges are heavy or light, *every* charge should be visually examined like this to ascertain that every case contains powder and that charges bulk up approximately the same.

charge after you've filled all the cases in each loading block, before seating bullets. That way, if there has been an error, you'll know it before the cartridges are completed. If you discover an error after forty or fifty rounds have been completed, there may be no way to identify the cartridges that contain the error. Another check that should always be made is a simple visual inspection of the powder level in each case before a bullet is seated. This is best done with charged cases in a loading block, held under a good light, looking into the mouth of each case and noting whether any particular charge seems to bulk higher or lower in the case than its neighbors. If it does, dump it back in the measure and do it over. If a charge seems to bulk much higher than the others, look inside the case after you've dumped it to make certain there isn't some foreign material stuck in there. Usually, a charge that bulks abnormally high or low will do so at the expense of the charge thrown immediately before or after it. A light charge in the case might mean that some powder remained in the drop tube, and so was probably added to the next charge thrown; an overcharge probably indicates that powder hung up in the drop tube from the previous charge, making it less than it should be.

If it seems that I'm dwelling overmuch on powder charging, remember that this is the most critical of all the handloading operations to safety. You'll get no joy or profit from handloading if a mistake or an oversight causes a gun to be wrecked or a shooter to be hurt. Handloading is essentially a very safe practice, *provided* one adheres to the basic safety requirements and concentrates on the job at hand.

SEATING BULLETS

Once a loading block full of cases has been properly charged with powder, bullets should be seated immediately. Don't quit for the night at this point and plan to finish the job tomorrow or next weekend. Left exposed, the charges might become contaminated or absorb moisture, or they might get knocked around and spilled.

Seating bullets is the last of the mechanical operations. Since case mouths are not normally crimped on the bullets in rifle calibers (except those intended for use in tubular-magazine rifles), we'll not get into that at this time. So, take the bullet-seating die and screw it partway into the press. Place a sized but *uncharged* empty case in the shell holder and run the ram to the top of its stroke. Screw the seating die in farther, until you feel it contact the case solidly; then back the die out about ⅛ turn and lock it in that position. Now, back out the bullet-seating screw most of the way. Place a bullet in the mouth of the empty case and run it fully into the die. Depending on how far you backed out the seating stem, it may not contact the bullet at all; if not, screw it in until it does. Now, alternately running the case into the die and screwing the seating stem in farther, keep seating the bullet deeper into the case until the proper overall cartridge length is achieved. Lacking a table of specifications for this purpose, simply seat the bullet so that cartridge length is the same as that of a factory-loaded cartridge utilizing the same bullet type and weight. Once this has been achieved, lock the seating stem in place.

Now, you have created a dummy cartridge which handloaders commonly call a "seating dummy" and it should be saved for future use in adjusting the seating die. Mark it in some way with the bullet weight and make, and to make certain it will never get mixed up with loaded ammunition, drill a ⅛-inch hole completely through the case from side to side, or simply file large notches in the sides. The best place to keep this seating dummy is with the dies of that caliber. Then, in the future, to adjust the seating dies, simply run the ram up with the dummy in place, screw the die into the press against its lock ring, then adjust the seating stem to contact the bullet firmly. It's a lot quicker that way.

After the die has been set up and a bullet seated in an *unprimed and uncharged* case, a hole should be drilled through the case, and the entire unit preserved as a "seating dummy" to permit quick and easy seating-die adjustment in the future.

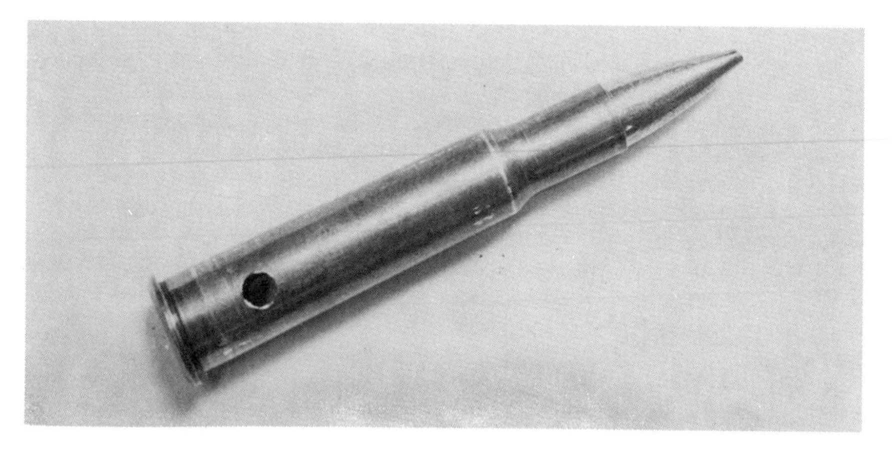

Once the die is properly adjusted, seating bullets may be performed quickly and easily. Place the case carefully in the shell holder, making certain that you don't spill any powder. Place the bullet on top of the case mouth with the thumb and finger, pressing it into the case mouth if it will go, then run the case into the die, allowing it to pass through thumb and finger to keep the bullet in alignment until it has entered the die. Then continue the press-handle stroke smoothly until the end of the stroke is reached. You'll feel added resistance as the bullet comes up against the seating stem and the case neck is forced over it. If excessive force is required at this point, you'll know something is wrong; perhaps the bullet has tipped, or the case mouth has dug into it. When unusual resistance is met, don't try to force the bullet the rest of the way. Instead, extract the round and determine the trouble. This will be most commonly encountered with bullets having a very sharp-edged, square base, where the base digs into one side of the neck and crumples the case, or causes the case to dig into the bullet. When this happens, both case and bullet are usually ruined. *Don't* attempt to salvage such a cartridge by ramming the bullet on in, regardless of the mess it makes. Such a defective cartridge may chamber and fire, but it certainly won't be accurate, and it might produce excessive pressures.

INSPECTION AND PACKAGING

Once bullets are seated, you still aren't quite finished. Each individual cartridge should be inspected closely for any visible defect. Pay particular attention to primer seating depth and condition; the primer should be seated slightly below the surface of the case head, and it should not be smashed or

Bullet seating requires that the bullet be finger-started in the case, and it should be aligned as closely as possible with the case, not excessively canted as shown here. This bullet is leaning so far to one side that it might very well strike the mouth of the die and ruin the case.

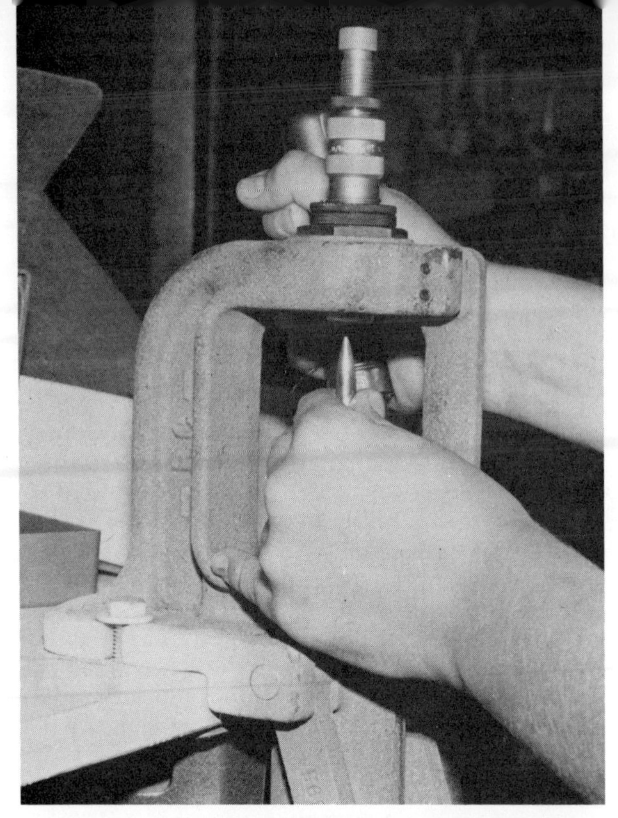

The bullet and case mouth should be grasped between thumb and finger, and given guidance to ensure that they enter the die smoothly as the press handle is operated. As the bullet enters the die, it and the case neck can be allowed to slide smoothly between thumb and finger, thus maintaining proper alignment.

The bullet is completely seated, and the finished round is shown extracted from the die.

deformed in any way. Look for dents, wrinkling or bulging of the case neck over the bullet, and anything else that doesn't look perfect. Surface blemishes and defects won't present a safety hazard, and they probably won't affect accuracy much unless on the bullet, but they do look sloppy. A badly deformed or crushed primer, though, is certain to produce an erratic shot, and it might leak, letting hot gases back into the action and possibly into your face. A primer that protrudes above the case head could cause what is known as a "slam fire," which is the cartridge firing as the action of the rifle is closed. This is far more likely to occur in an autoloading or pump action, and it *is* dangerous because the firing can occur before the breech is fully locked. This can result in wrecking the gun and injuring the shooter.

After inspection, loaded cartridges should be packaged and labeled. This should be done immediately, so that the load's identity is not lost. Modern jacketed bullets are so alike that you can't really depend upon appearance for identification, and anyway, you might very well be using the same bullet with different powder charges and this would make visual separation impossible. Cartridge boxes are best, with a pasted-on label filled out with bullet make, type, and weight, as well as type and weight of powder. Other information is useful, but that is essential. Lacking anything better, simply place the cartridges in plastic bags along with a strip of paper having the identification data written on it. The method doesn't really matter, but the ammunition needs to be packaged to protect it from dirt, moisture, and grit; and it *must* be properly identified.

CLEANUP

When you're finished loading, the dies should be wiped clean, inside and out, and placed in a tightly closed container along with the shell holder and the seating dummy. Most dies today come packaged in a plastic box which also contains a bit of VPI (vapor phase inhibitor) corrosion-preventing paper or cardboard. This will prevent rust for several months, but once the VPI material becomes aged, you'll have to take other steps. A die that rusts inside its cavity will never be quite right again, even though the rust is thoroughly removed. I don't like storing dies in sealed plastic bags; moisture may condense inside and cause rust. It's also an excellent idea to cover the press with a cloth or plastic bag to keep out airborne dirt and grit. This is especially true if your loading bench is set up in a garage, attic, or basement. Cared for properly, good equipment will last a lifetime.

Protect your loads by boxing them snugly, and retain their identity by filling out and affixing a label such as this one, which is supplied free with Speer bullets.

5

Selecting the Best Load

HANDLOADERS, particularly those of limited experience, seem to have an unexplained proclivity for diving head-first into a loading-data manual and then choosing a load which is either ballisticly inefficient, poorly suited to their use, or overly expensive—or, sometimes, all three. Often such less-than-perfect selections are made purely on the basis of muzzle velocity or because of a desire to use a particular propellant powder or powder/bullet combination because it is either readily available or cheap, recommended by some writer or authority (?), or locally popular. A good deal of this trouble arises, in this scribe's opinion, because the publishers of loading manuals compete with one another to offer the greatest quantity of loading data. The attitude appears to be that if some loading data is good, more is better, and best of all is to claim a greater number of loads than a competing manual. After all, loading-data manuals are published and sold to generate profit; they are not distributed at cost just to promote products. Free data is published by the major propellant manufacturers as part of their promotion program. However, it is generally in the form of folders or leaflets, and is not in the class of a Lyman, Sierra, Hornady, Nosler, etc. loading *manual.* The effort to present a great mass of loading data results in many highly inefficient propellant/projectile combinations, as well as some that are poorly suited for any practical use.

You'll be served best by a load that is efficient and low in cost.

A load that achieves maximum *energy efficiency* consists of the specific propellant that produces standard velocity or the desired velocity with the lowest peak chamber pressures. A measure of this efficiency is sometimes known as the pressure/velocity ratio,—that is, velocity divided by pressure—and might be expressed as the number of feet per second per 1,000 CUP. Unfortunately, most loading data does not contain chamber pressures, so there is no way that the efficiency of a given load can be determined accurately. You can generally assume that the top loads shown for any given propellant/projectile combination produce normal working pressures for that caliber, so we can determine a rough measure of efficiency. It's not very accurate, but it's better than nothing. Thus, you can assume that a top .30-06 load produces approximately 50,000 CUP; and from that you divide the velocity by 50, and come up with a value that may be used to compare the energy efficiency of that load with others.

A load is most *cost-efficient* when it produces the standard or desired velocity at standard or safe pressures with the least propellant *cost.* It is surprising how seldom this factor is given any consideration in choosing a load. Particularly in magnum handgun calibers, it is often possible to produce a load giving the desired performance with one propellant, when only half that amount of another propellant will safely produce the same results. As an example, the 240-grain JHP bullet may be given 1,200 fps in the .44 Magnum by 19.8 grains of Hercules 2400 or 23 grains of DuPont 4227; yet only 11.2 grains of Hercules Unique produces the same velocity. That may be an extreme example, but illustrates the point. The differences are generally less in high-intensity rifle cartridges such as the .270 Winchester, but even there differences of up to 20 percent or more in charge weight may be discovered. If you shoot a lot, 20 percent of the powder bill can add up to a substantial amount.

In most loading manuals, you'll find from five to a dozen or more powders listed with each bullet weight and type. Also, you'll usually find that powders at either end of the scale are not particularly efficient in that case/bullet combination. Those who make up the manuals often list the powders more or less in order of burning rate. Those powders which show the smallest charge as a top load are normally the fastest-burning, while those for which the largest charge is shown are the slowest. Loads for the fastest powder usually don't produce velocity quite as high as those in the middle range, and the slowest-burning powders usually indicate the

The vast number of loads given for some calibers in the various handloading manuals can be confusing. Not only that, they generally contain recommendations for powders which are at best inefficient for the caliber and bullet concerned. Rather than selecting a load mainly on the basis of velocity it produces, you should choose a load that is both energy-efficient and cost-efficient.

highest velocities of the lot. However, the spread is not very wide, and in choosing the highest-velocity load, you are usually selecting an inefficient powder. Generally, in a page of loading data for a given bullet weight and case, the two, three, or four powders listed in the middle of the table are the best suited to that particular combination. The slower-burning powders at one end will usually produce a bit more velocity, but only at the expense of a great deal more powder. The faster-burning powders at the other end often won't produce full standard velocity without exceeding safe pressures. So, in selecting a load from data contained in a loading-data manual, I strongly recommend ignoring those powders at the top and bottom of the table and making your choice from those that appear in the middle.

As a practical matter, it's a good idea to survey your shooting requirements, and then narrow down the different bullets needed in a given caliber to meet those requirements. In rifles, it's often possible to select a given weight and type bullet that will handle all of your needs. For example, a .30-06 which won't be used on varmints will perform quite well on most North American big game and on the target range with a 165-grain or 168-grain (depending on manufacture) bullet. Both game and target bullets in this weight perform extremely well with IMR4350 powder, and may efficiently be given velocities of 2,500 to 2,900 fps by it. Thus, you can standardize on one bullet weight, two bullet types, and one powder for all of your .30-06 shooting. This way, you will avoid tying up money in additional powders and bullets, reduce storage-space requirements, and eliminate confusion around your loading bench. If that same .30-06 rifle is to be used on varmints as well, you'd need to add a 110-grain or 130-grain (some makers offer other weights in between) bullet and a powder suitable for it. IMR3031 is especially efficient and usually quite accurate with bullets in that weight range, and will drive 130-grain bullets up to 3,300 fps, and the lighter ones perhaps 100 fps faster.

Much the same condition exists in both handgun and shotshell loads. A loading manual will list many powders for each load level, when in reality virtually all your requirements can be met with one powder, or at most two. In handguns, for example, except for seldom-loaded calibers like the .25 and .32 ACP, every need except full-charge magnum loads can be met with Hercules Unique. The .41 and .44 Magnums will require H110 or WW296 (either one, not both), so unless you are an inveterate experimenter, two powders will handle 99 percent of handgun-caliber loading you might ever want to do.There are at least a dozen other powders you could use for many loads, but you'd just be tying up money, cluttering up space, and gaining virtually nothing.

The biggest mistake handloaders make is selecting loads on the basis of velocity. An extra 100 fps in a rifle cartridge will make not the slightest bit of difference in game kills. Yet, you may be burning up to 20 percent more powder to achieve that added velocity, working at higher pressures, and achieving a lower degree of accuracy. The additional powder and higher pressures will increase barrel erosion and be generally harder on the gun. The only reason for going all-out on velocity is to be able to tell your buddies how fast it shoots. And I don't believe that ever helped kill game or win matches.

In centerfire rifles, there's no need for full-charge loads and expensive jacketed bullets for fun shooting, plinking, and general shooting under 200 yards. Home-swaged or cast bullets at velocities down around 2,000 fps, or even a bit less, are far more appropriate to such shooting games, cost a lot less, increase the accuracy life of the barrel, and save much wear and tear on the gun. If you do a fair amount of this type of shooting, then select a load that suits it, rather than the full-charge blasters. The same applies to handgun loads. Except for hunting and defense use, and developing proficiency with those particular loads, there is no need for expensive jacketed expanding bullets. Even for training, the velocity, power, and recoil impulse of full-charge loads in virtually everything but the big Auto Mag pistol can be duplicated (or very nearly, so close it makes no difference) with hard-alloy cast bullets. Sure, it's fun to shoot those pretty, shiny, nickel-each jacketed slugs, but as a practical matter, loads employing them are of no other value for the majority of one's handgun shooting. So there's no point in selecting a load from a manual that produces 1,600 fps in .357 Magnum with an expensive, jacketed bullet unless you're going to use it on people or game. The same velocity can be achieved with a properly chosen hard-alloy cast bullet, and the effect will be the same except on live targets. As a practical matter, except for the sheer fun of shooting them, there's no need of full-charge loads in the magnum calibers. As we mentioned earlier in this chapter, you can get very nearly full-charge performance with half as much of another powder and a good cast bullet. In the long run, both you and your handgun will be better served by a cheaper load chosen for its *suitability* to your everyday shooting than one chosen for the noise or speed it develops.

There is less of a problem in shotshell loads. Over the years, handloads have been well standardized along the same lines as factory loads, with there being roughly three load levels in most gauges, and four in 12-bore. In each gauge, we have skeet or target loads, high-velocity field loads, and, with the exception of 16- and 28-gauge, magnum loads. In 12-gauge, we have another bastard load which is generally termed "short magnum," which is heavier than a high-velocity field load, but still is a bit below the performance of the 3-inch magnum. And, of course, there is no skeet or target load in 10-gauge.

The number of entries in a shotshell loading-data booklet would at first seem to belie that statement. Well, it does and it doesn't. Shotshells differ in construction from metallic cartridges; in the former, components are interchangeable in the same caliber between makes. Not so in shotshells. Because of differing designs, tolerances, and manufacturing methods, and the fact that a shotshell contains an additional component, the wad, components are not nearly so interchangeable. For example, Winchester makes its AA case and a wad matched especially to it. The AA wad doesn't work properly in a Federal C-F case, nor in a Remington-Peters case, and neither will wads of those makes work in the AA case. In addition, we have general- and special-purpose wads from the independent manufacturers, and they are made in different sizes or variations to fit the widest variety of cases—yet, when switching those wads from one case to another, powder charges necessary to produce standard-load performance may change. Add to that the fact that there are dozens of shotshell powders which may be used in everybody's cases, and you can see the reason for the profusion of data in a shotshell manual. What we have there is simply as many as fifty different component combinations, all of which produce the same standard level of ballistic performance, whether it be for skeet or trap or a short magnum load.

Selection of a shotshell load consists, then, simply of choosing the component combinations that might be forced upon you by the particular empty cases that are available. The choice is made on components dictated by the case or desired by the shooter, and *not* based on ballistic performance.

There are, of course, minor variations in velocity and shot-charge weight, but the variations are much, much smaller than encountered in metallic load data. The entire velocity spread from light skeet loads up through long magnums is little more than a couple hundred fps. Aside from that small amount of velocity gain, the principal advantage of the heaviest shotshell loads over the lightest is in the amount of shot—both in weight and number of pellets—utilized.

Shotshell powders are far less versatile than others, because of the narrow limits in which they must operate. Even if you load only one gauge, at least two powders, perhaps three, will be required to cover the range from light to heavy loads. And adding another gauge may very well require another two or three powders. Nevertheless, by careful examination of loading-data tables, you can keep the number of powders, and thus your investment, to a minimum.

So, load selection in any of the three categories boils down to plain, common sense rather than flying off on a tangent in search of maximum velocity, or exercising some personal or public prejudice or preference not necessarily based on need or fact. The *best* load selection will invariably be that load which accomplishes your specific shooting purpose at lowest cost and with least stress and strain on the gun—a load that is energy-efficient and cost-efficient.

We can't leave load selection without making at least some reference to "load development." This is a much-overworked and much-overrated process. It *is* possible to improve individual rifle accuracy by varying powder charge and bullet. However, before load development can serve any useful purpose, one must first actually *know* the degrees of mechanical accuracy that a load will give in a particular rifle. It is unfortunate but true—and I do not wish to put anyone down—that the *average* shooter/handloader is not a sufficiently skilled marksman to benefit more than casually or accidentally from expensive load development. More often than not the degree of accuracy change (better or worse) produced by varying components will be less than the aiming error of the shooter. If the shooter can consistently produce only 5-inch groups at 100 yards, then even a 1-inch change in mechanical accuracy brought about by varying components simply won't be visible. Unless an individual is capable of *consistently* shooting groups under 2 inches at 100 yards, it is extremely doubtful that he'll be able to evaluate, or even see, the results of various component changes.

Nevertheless, development of a load for maximum accuracy (and this is only in a *particular* rifle or handgun, remember) normally begins with carefully selecting a standard, recommended load. Several groups are shot with it to determine its accuracy, and then changes of approximately 1/2 grain are made in the powder charge to determine whether they produce any visible effect on target. If the basic load is a moderate one, then it will be possible to vary the powder charge both above and below the original amount; but if it is one of the so-called maximum loads, then certainly no further increases in charge should be made. Actually, a maximum load will seldom give top accuracy anyway, particularly in large-capacity cases. It may be necessary to vary the powder charge as much as four or five grains (in $^1/_2$ -grain increments) in order to determine whether accuracy may be improved. In any event, at each level of powder charge at least a couple of five-shot groups will be required to determine whether any changes in accuracy have occurred. If no improvement is noted, then the two powders lying on either side of the original load in the data table are the next logical step, beginning with a load that produces approximately the same velocity as the one first chosen. The entire process is then repeated with each powder, noting any accuracy changes. If sufficient accuracy increase isn't obtained, then changing makes of bullet is the next step up. A bullet of comparable weight and type should be chosen, and the entire process repeated. As can be seen at this point, the search for ultimate accuracy may well be quite lengthy and more than a little bit expensive.

The average handloader usually doesn't carry load development this far. He either quits when he gets tired of loading and testing, or when he's obtained *any* improvement in accuracy.

In summary, let's just say that load selection should be based on actual needs, and should never be based mainly on velocity. Less-than-maximum loads are cheaper, usually more accurate, easier on the gun, and suitable for any real purpose. Usually the time and money for load development will be better spent on improving one's marksmanship, because that is where accuracy problems lie most often.

6

Loading Shotshells

First of all, we must differentiate between the tools for shotshell and metallic reloading. Today's shotshell tools are quite different. Generally the basic tool is a lightweight, multiple-station, single-purpose tool in which a fired case is run through all of the loading operations before another case is started. Dies are more or less permanently installed at each of the stations, and there is no changing of dies except when converting a loader from one gauge or case length to another. Even the powder and shot measure is an integral part of the tool, so there are ordinarily no accessories to be used separately.

The operations that must be performed do not differ all that much from metallic cartridges. The case must first be inspected and cleaned, though there is less emphasis on cleaning than with metallics. Then it must be resized and decapped, the mouth must be opened up or flared slightly, a new primer must be seated, and a powder charge must be placed in the case. The wad column must then be placed in the case under the proper amount of pressure, followed by the shot charge. The crimp must be started, and finally fully formed and locked so it will not open under recoil and handling. Since the typical shotshell, whether of paper or the more common plastic construction, lacks the strength of a metallic case and since a great deal of pressure is placed upon it in seating the wad and crimping, it must be supported during those operations or it will bulge. Obviously, a bulged shell won't chamber when the time comes. Provisions are made for all of these operations in a typical shotshell loader.

HIGH-BASE AND LOW-BASE CASES

There are so-called "high-base" and "low-base" shotshell cases, the difference being in the height of the "base wad" or thickness of the case head. High-base cases are used for target loads, and case volume is regulated by the height of the base wad to accommodate the relatively small amounts of shot and powder. Low-base cases are used for heavy loads containing more

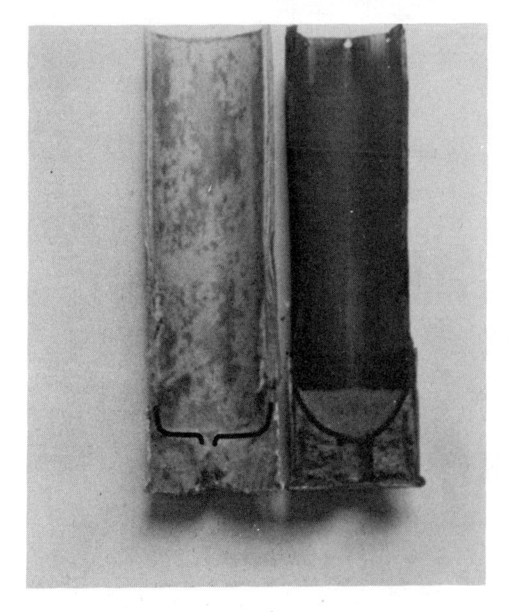

The low-base case on the left has a relatively short base wad which occupies substantially less space than the wad of a high-base case on the right. The smaller base wad allows greater charges of shot and propellant to be placed in the case. The larger wad simply occupies space in the case to compensate for smaller charges of shot and propellant.

powder and shot—the base wad is simply shortened to make more room. To that point, it's simple, but then the confusion begins, for the terms "high-*brass*" and "low-*brass*" are also in common use and have the opposite meaning. *Low-base* cases have *high-brass* metal heads to reinforce the entire case head. *High-base* cases are stronger because of the thicker base wad, so carry *low-brass* heads. Many people get the terms reversed and become confused.

Use high-base/low-brass cases for target loads and low-base/high-brass cases for hunting loads. If you aren't sure, make up a gauge from a length of dowel, with two marks on it—one that comes even with the mouth in low-base cases, the other in high-base. Use this gauge when sorting cases.

SHOTSHELL LOADERS

The typical loader carries two reservoirs, one for shot and one for powder, atop its main structure. A horizontal sliding bar rides beneath these reservoirs and contains a metering chamber for shot and another for powder. Since, as we mentioned under load selection, there is little latitude in powder choice for standard loads, this "charge bar" contains holes into which are placed interchangeable fixed-charge bushings to drop the proper powder and shot charges. Each manufacturer supplies bushings for popular powders and shot combinations for the different standard loads. Thus, in normal loading, there is no weighing and measuring of powder charges. In reality, loading shotshells is far simpler than loading metallics, and there are fewer chances for error. In the beginning, one simply purchases a shotshell loader already set up, with bushings in place for the chosen gauge and load. After minor adjustments (if any) to suit the particular make and model of case being used, it's quite simple.

For our purposes here, we are using a MEC "Versa-MEC" tool, which is representative of the type and one of the most popular for ordinary use. It must be bolted or clamped solidly to a sturdy bench, and the shot (left) and

Most modern shotshell loaders utilize two plastic containers at the top for shot (left) and powder. The bottles sit above a charge bar which moves laterally to meter out the correct amounts of powder and shot.

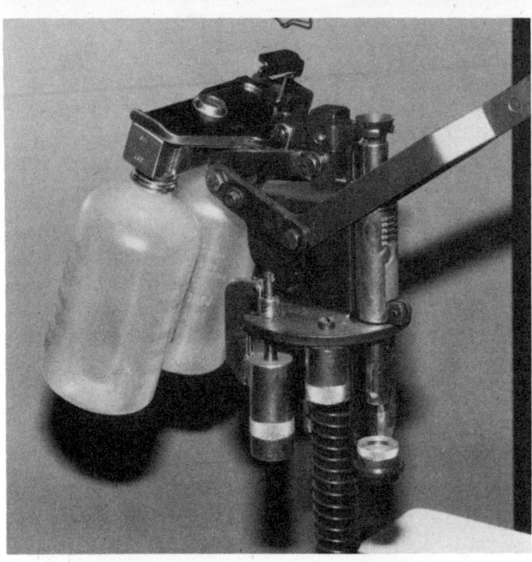

On the "Versa-MEC," as on most other tools, the powder and shot containers may be tipped over in this fashion and then unscrewed from the charge-bar housing to facilitate emptying them.

The charge bar removed from its housing, with the replaceable bushing which permits powder and shot charges to be varied. A wide variety of bushings are available.

powder (right) reservoirs filled. Proper indentification of powder is fully as important here as it is with metallic cartridges. In fact, because of the lesser strength of shotgun actions, excessive pressures caused by the wrong powder or the wrong charge can be more disastrous. The charge bar should be removed and the charge bushings verified. They are stamped with markings; check these markings against the table packed with the tool to determine that they are correct for the load chosen. Make sure the charge bar is all the way to the right.

PREPARING CASES

Naturally, you'll need a supply of fired cases. Since paper cases are rare today, I'll discuss only the plastic variety. Battery-cup shotshell primers are necessary, and they should be chosen to match the case. Shotshell-loading data ordinarily lists the primer by make and model, so stick with the recommended primer. The plastic one-piece cup wad must be matched to the case and powder charges, so do not attempt substitutions.

Prepare cases for loading by careful inspection and sorting. Use only one make and type, or the other components won't fit properly and allow a correct crimp to be formed. Discard any cases that show pinholes or cracks at the front of the metal head, splits or cracks in the crimp area, deformed heads or rims, primer leaks, or loose primers. Any case that is bulged excessively should also be set aside, because it may not resize correctly. Cases with deformed or bulged metal heads can be salvaged, but we'll cover that in another chapter. Stick with perfect-condition cases in the beginning, and you'll save yourself a lot of grief. Plastic cases can be washed, but wiping is usually sufficient.

Unlike metallic cases, plastic shotshell cases do not require lubrication for resizing. The plastic has a slick, smooth surface and will run through good-quality dies smoothly. However, if you should ever decide to load some paper cases, you'll find they may need lubrication, in the form of a bit of beeswax—by no means should conventional lubricants be used on them.

OPERATING THE LOADER

The handle of your loader is spring-loaded in the up position, so simply take a case and insert it into the decapping die (which does *some* resizing) from beneath station #1, right rear, deep enough to be held there, making certain that it is aligned with the die. Bring the handle down smoothly against its stop; you'll feel the added resistance as the case is forced into the die and the decapping pin punches out the primer. Next, bring the handle up with a fair degree of force, but smoothly, and the case will be forced out of the die by a cam working against the decapping rod. The tapered decapping rod reseats the base wad and opens up the case mouth during this operation. Place a battery-cup primer in the priming station (station #2, clockwise from #1) in the tool base, then set a case over it and bring the tool handle down again to the stop. The case will be forced down over the primer, seating the latter solidly. Note whether the primer enters the case snugly or easily. If it goes in too easily, the pocket is probably oversize, and

The decapping station. The rod goes inside the case and punches out the fired primer, while the die body performs some resizing of the case.

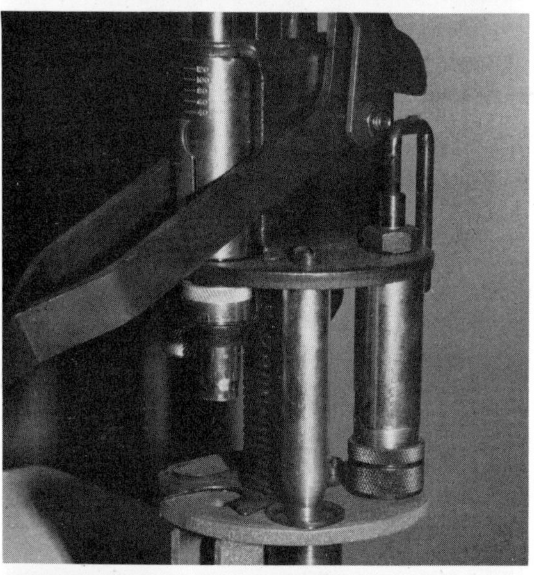

The tool head at the bottom of its stroke against a stop, to decap and resize the case.

When tool head is lowered, the repriming punch forces the case down over the primer, pushing the spring-loaded bushing down so the primer enters the pocket freely.

Typical battery-cup primers. Note the wide flange which seats against the metal head overlay of the case and supports the primer against the firing-pin blow.

that case should be discarded; the primer might fall out in storage and handling, or it might come out in the gun and cause a jam. The primer can be salvaged by punching it out.

Now, to station #3, front center, beneath the powder and shot drop tube. The case rim goes under the metal lip there. Move the handle down partway, the tube entering the case, and smartly flick the charge bar to the left, dumping a powder charge into the case. Raise the handle all the way (leaving the charge bar to the left), and take a plastic shot-cup wad column and start it into the "spring fingers" of the wad guide from the top. Make certain the wad guide is positioned directly over the mouth of the case, and that the inward-tapering fingers will enter the case mouth freely. Now, bring the handle down smoothly and forcefully; the drop tube will push the wad from the guide and into the case and down tight upon the powder. If the load data you're using specifies a particular "wad pressure," verify from the wad-pressure scale above the case that approximately the correct amount of pressure is being applied to the wad. It is not necessary to bring the handle against the stop, just far enough to get the proper wad pressure. While the handle is still in the down position and the drop tube is pressing on the wad, flick the charge bar back to the right, dropping the shot charge into the case. You'll hear the charge fall into position. Then raise the handle and move the case to station #4 for starting the crimp, rim under the lip.

The central station at which powder, wad column, and shot are added. Note the "drop tube" and wad guide above the case. At this and subsequent stations, the rim of the case fits into a shell holder securing it to the base of the tool.

From the beginning, the charge bar should be to the right, in preparation for dropping the powder charge into the case.

The charge bar moved left, dropping powder through the drop tube into the case. Note that the handle has been brought down so that the drop tube enters the case mouth.

With the handle raised, so that the drop tube is above the wad guide, the wad column is placed in the guide.

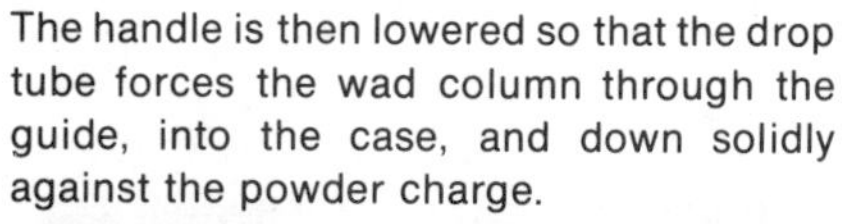

The handle is then lowered so that the drop tube forces the wad column through the guide, into the case, and down solidly against the powder charge.

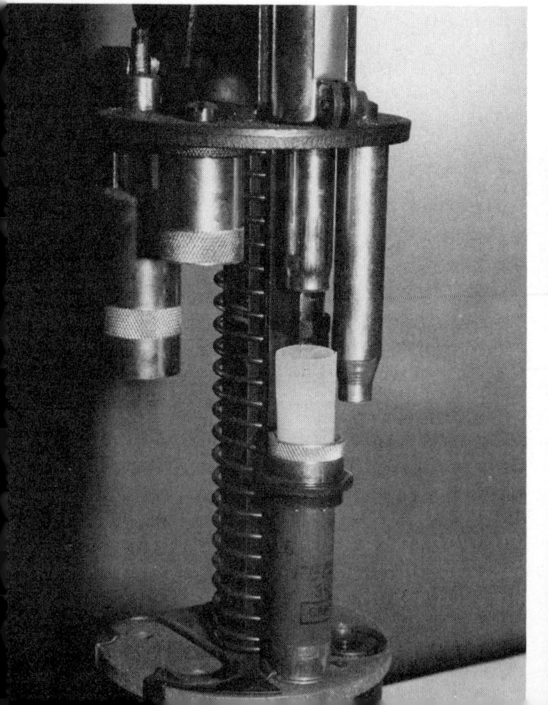

Starting the crimp is a separate operation, necessary so that the six folds of the star-type crimp begin smoothly. Modern starting dies are designed so that they will rotate slightly and automatically align with the residual grooves of the crimp folds. Older tools may require that you manually align the case with the die for this purpose. In any event, bringing the handle down gently runs the crimp-starting die over the mouth of the case, starting the folds and turning the mouth of the case inward to form a truncated cone. Note that no great force is applied to the case in this process.

With the crimp started properly, the case is transferred under the lip of station #5, and the handle is brought down forcefully, running the crimp die over the case. The die is also the final resizing die and further prevents bulging from the considerable force applied in completing the crimp. Performing final resizing as the last operation ensures proper dimensions of the finished shell.

Normally the crimp will be fully formed with a single handle stroke, but there are times when it may be better to raise the handle partway, then come down hard with a second stroke. The object of this is to force the crimp folds down into the shot charge, and to produce the desired depth of recess in the crimp. The entire loaded shell assembly is spongy in a way, being composed of a flexible plastic case and a compressible plastic wad, so a second stroke may be necessary to fully form the crimp. Also, letting the case set a few seconds in the sizing die with the handle fully down will also sometimes improve the crimp. Raise the handle smartly to extract the loaded shell from the crimp die.

Note here that a single case was processed through all the loading operations, whereas in metallic loading, it is standard practice to perform the individual operations on a group of cases.

PROPER CRIMPING

Inspect the loaded shell carefully. The walls should not be bulged, though you may be able to feel slight bumps on its surface over the shot charge. Especially, the case should not be bulged immediately ahead of the metal overlay. Examine the crimp very carefully. It should be recessed about 1/16 inch, the folds should be quite tight and not pushing up at the center, and there should be no significant hole in the middle. A small hole is permissible where the folds meet, but it should be nowhere near as large as the shot pellets used. The outer edges of the crimp—the lips, so to speak—should be slightly rounded to facilitate feeding in repeating and autoloading guns. This is especially true in 3 1/2-inch 10-gauge shells intended for use in the big Ithaca autoloader.

Assuming that the loader was purchased for the load assembled, no adjustments should be necessary, with the possible exception of wad pressure and crimp die. The brochure with the tool describes these adjustments in detail, and the crimp adjustments will be required if the crimp does not hold. Normally, a crimp which *looks* perfect will remain so; however, a marginal crimp may open up hours, days, or even weeks after the shell is loaded. The plastic components of the load are placed in compression by

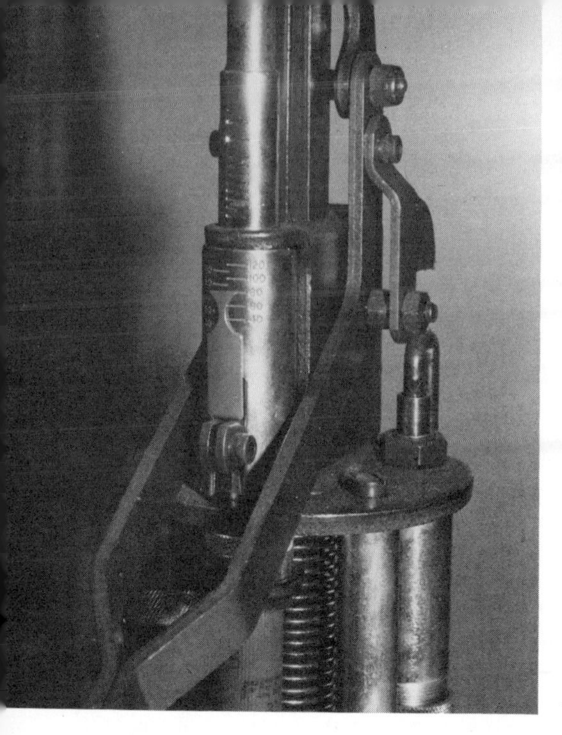

The wad-pressure scale on the loader, showing the amount of pressure seating the wads against the powder.

Shot in the case, showing the approximate correct amount of case above the charge to permit a proper star crimp.

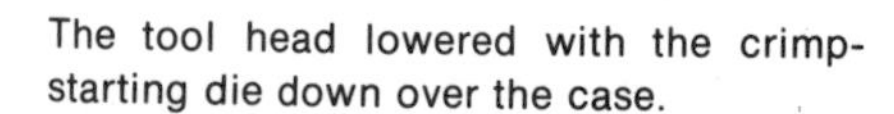

The tool head lowered with the crimp-starting die down over the case.

The crimp properly started, with the folds formed and the mouth of the case coned.

the crimp, and the powder charge to a lesser degree. Both attempt to expand, primarily in length, and if the crimp is slightly weak, this expansion may eventually push it partly open. Once a crimp is loosened, the load will not develop full pressure and velocity because the resistance required by the powder charge for proper ignition and efficient combustion no longer exists. A soft crimp may also open up in the magazine of a repeating gun or in the unfired barrel of a double under recoil. If this happens in the magazine, it only makes a mess and ties up the gun with spilled shot. In a double, though, if the crimp opens up, it spills the shot down the barrel, and this will probably go unnoticed until the barrel is fired. Then the powder will not burn properly, creating what is usually called a "blooper" shot, and may leave the wad and even part of the shot resting somewhere down the barrel. If a subsequent shot is fired into that obstruction, the barrel will at least be bulged or damaged, and it may very well burst. And if the barrel bursts near the off hand, serious injuries can result. I have investigated incidents of this sort where an individual lost fingers or even a major portion of his hand as the barrel split open.

VARYING THE LOAD

The foregoing applies to assembling a single load of any of the standard types. If, say, you've been assembling skeet or trap loads and now wish to put together some more potent hunting loads, you'll need to make some changes. Most likely you'll use a different case, and that will require a different wad and powder charge matched to the new case and heavier shot charge. Don't decide that you know more about it than the guy who wrote the loading-data tables and try to select your own components for such a

The tool head lowered to move the crimping die fully down over the case.

load. Hunting loads generally develop higher pressures and velocity than target loads, so care and attention to detail become even more important. Choose a tested load from existing data, and then obtain a new charge-bar bushing which will drop the proper amount of the chosen powder and the indicated charge of the shot size being used. Be especially careful that these bushings are properly installed in the charge bar, and that the correct powder is placed in the reservoir. If you were to go from a target load to a heavy hunting load, and inadvertently use a target-load powder, its faster burning rate would combine with the heavier shot charge to produce excess pressure and almost surely wreck the gun and injure the shooter. This is not being said to frighten you, but simply to emphasize that you must adhere rigidly to the basic safety precautions.

Many of the popular shotshell loaders may be purchased in one gauge or case length, and then readily converted to another. The manufacturers sell a conversion kit, and it is easily installed by following the directions supplied. Once the conversion kit is in place, loading may proceed as already described.

CASE LIFE

Modern plastic cases have quite a long reloading life. The built-up type does undergo certain deterioration, but if this is corrected early enough its life can be extended even further. Probably the most common problem is swollen and deformed metal head overlays caused by firing in guns that are badly worn or have excess headspace. There are special resizing dies and special tools that will swage the head back to its original dimensions. The newest and best is by MEC. This is a tool employing a type of eight-jaw collet into which the head of the case is placed, then operation of the handle closes the collet around the head, squeezing it back into proper dimensions and relationship with the body and at the same time reforming the rim. Other types of "shell reconditioners" simply employ a close-fitting resizing die that comes down all the way over the head and the rim to swage it back to shape.

Another problem is loose base wads. The churning of powder gases and entry of primer gases behind the base wad can cause it to loosen and move slightly forward in the case. If loading is repeated and this condition is not corrected, the base wad may be thrown out the barrel, or it may come to rest at some point in the barrel, forming an obstruction that can produce dangerous results if a subsequent round is fired. A "base-wad seater" can be employed to force the wad back into intimate contact with the inside of the head, expanding it radially at the same time so that it fits tightly there. The base-wad seater need be nothing more than a punch large enough to fill the case and contoured at the end to match the base wad's shape. If the case, with fired primer still in place, is pressed fully into a hand-type resizing die (available from Lyman) and this assembly is rested on a smooth steel plate, the punch may be inserted in the case mouth and struck smartly with the hammer to seat and expand the base wad. The RCBS "Shell Saver" reseats base wads and reforms the case heads simultaneously.

Case mouths may become frayed and ragged after several loadings, but if they are very carefully trimmed smooth, removing no more than perhaps $^{1}/_{8}$ inch, they may still be reloaded by simply adjusting the crimp die downward until it produces a proper crimp. A slight reduction in shot charge may be necessary, or a slightly shorter filler wad or plastic wad column may also be used.

ADJUSTING FOR PROPER CRIMPING

Crimping-die adjustment will vary slightly from one tool to another, but generally involves moving the crimping die up or down as may be needed to produce the proper crimp. If the crimp does not meet in the center and leaves a substantial hole there, then the die must be adjusted downward; if the crimp meets too much in the center and crumples or bulges, then the die needs to be moved upward so it will turn over less case mouth. However, too much or not enough crimp may also be due to too much or too little case mouth protruding above the shot charge. Most recommended load data will leave the correct amount of case for a good crimp if the load is properly assembled. However, the fact remains that this is not always true, and that approximately $^{7}/_{16}$ inch of plastic case is needed above the shot charge for a proper star crimp ($^{9}/_{16}$ with paper). Unless this amount is available for a crimp, no amount of die adjustment will do the job. So, before disturbing the original adjustment of the crimping die, check to make certain there is neither too little nor too much case mouth. If the occasion for checking this rises often, simply take a piece of $^{1}/_{2}$-inch dowel (smaller for the smaller gauges) and mark it at the proper distance from one end. Then simply inserting the dowel against the shot will show whether or not a good crimp is possible.

You might be forced to use components which are not entirely suited to a particular case that is available, and therefore the proper amount of case will not be available for crimping. If there is too little case remaining, reduce the shot charge slightly. The standard shot bushing in the charge bar isn't adjustable, but simply placing a couple of layers of tape inside it will reduce the amount of shot it drops. If you wind up with too much case for crimping, adding slightly to the shot charge will do the trick. This is harder to accomplish, but you can simply add a certain number of pellets by hand before crimping, or you can make up a simple charge-cup type of

Incomplete and open crimp resulting from too much space left above shot charge.

Incomplete crimp resulting from too little space above shot charge.

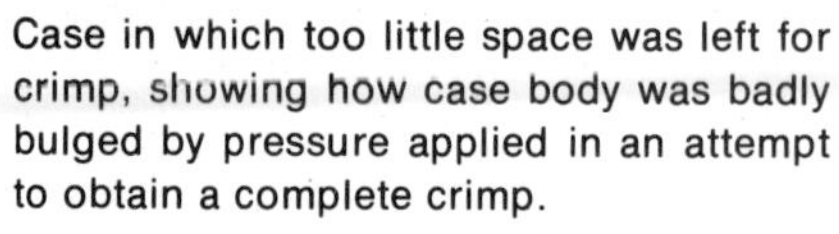

Case in which too little space was left for crimp, showing how case body was badly bulged by pressure applied in an attempt to obtain a complete crimp.

This crimp is fortunately solid and functional, but is off-center and wrinkled around the edge because of improper or incomplete starting.

shot measure from a fired cartridge case and trim it to hold the proper amount of shot. Then just dip shot charges and dump them in the case, instead of using the charge bar.

OLD-STYLE WADS

Thus far we've discussed only the use of one-piece plastic wad columns which incorporate the shot-protector cup. While this type of wad is easiest to use and produces the best all-round results, it is by no means the cheapest. In addition, for some types of shooting—such as short-range quail in close cover—such loads will pattern too tightly. Falling back on the pre-plastic type of over-powder and filler wads reduces cost and will generally open up patterns a bit. Several firms still supply the "nitro-card" (very dense, stiff cardboard) over-powder wad and fiber filler wads. Some of the ammunition manufacturers still offer variations of this type of wad as well.

All the better sources of loading data list this type of load and specify the thicknesses and the type of wads to be used. The proper wads are then just substituted in the loading process for the one-piece plastic wad. Handling three (usually) wads instead of one does slow down the process just a bit, but this really doesn't matter. If the particular thicknesses of wads are not available to make up the wad column, plain fiber wads can easily be split with a razor blade or sharp knife to obtain the proper length of column.

In selecting a load using these cheaper components, note that, other factors being equal, a larger powder charge is required to produce the same performance. This is due to the simple fact that the plastic wad units and cup-type plastic over-powder wads seal the powder gases much better than nitro-card wads, and thus loads with them are more efficient in powder usage. Do *not* attempt to use powder charges recommended for nitro wads with either plastic over-powder wads or plastic wad columns.

Where absolutely maximum economy is necessary, you can obtain a wadcutter punch of the proper gauge and then make your own over-powder wads from heavy cardboard and filler wads from Celotex or similar building board.

This takes care of routine shotshell loading. There are specialized loads you might want, and these are covered in Chapter 12.

Loading for Handguns

WHILE ALL THE BASIC OPERATIONS of handloading metallics apply pretty much across the board, there are still a lot of differences between loading high-intensity rifle cartridges and loading the relatively low-pressure, small-capacity handgun calibers, which generally operate at velocity levels ranging from about 750 to 1,500 fps. Anyway, if you plan only to handload for high-velocity rifles you don't want to wade through a lot of handgun material to get to the meat of your subject, and if you're a sixgunner who shoots only cast-lead-bullet loads by the bushel you don't want to learn all the rifle dope.

As a practical matter, most handgun ammunition is loaded with cast lead bullets and powders that burn very rapidly compared to those used in rifles. Even the primers are different, there being Small Pistol and Large Pistol primers, along with magnum versions of each size. In diameter, pistol primers are the same as rifle primers, but, generally they are slightly shorter. As I'll explain in Chapter 11, under some conditions pistol primers may be used in light rifle loads, but rifle primers are normally considered poison in pistol ammunition, because the greater amount of flame from rifle primers tends to overignite the small charges of fast-burning pistol powder, and the heavier construction of rifle primers may cause erratic ignition. Handgun firing mechanisms are smaller and lighter and don't generate nearly as much firing-pin energy as rifle and shotgun mechanisms. Consequently, they cannot indent the stiffer rifle primer cups adequately to provide consistent ignition. That is just one very important difference between loading for handguns and for rifles, and you'll note others as we move along in these pages.

DIFFERENCES BETWEEN REVOLVER AND AUTOLOADER LOADS

In handguns, we have two quite different sets of handloading problems, because revolvers and autoloaders function differently. A revolver will function correctly with almost any load that will chamber freely and does not protrude beyond the mouth of the chamber, provided the powder charge is sufficient to push the bullet completely out the barrel. Revolvers are *not* dependent upon any particular level of pressure, velocity, or recoil for functioning, nor do they require any particular shape, size, or type of bullet for proper feeding.

On the other hand, the autoloader will function reliably only within fairly narrow limits of recoil energy; and recoil energy is dependent upon the combination of bullet weight and velocity. In addition, autoloaders are more critical of cartridge length than revolvers, there being not only a maximum permissible length but a minimum length that will function reliably through the feed system. To that we must add the fact that almost all autoloaders were designed (and are still being designed) to function primarily with military-type ammunition loaded with round-nose full-metal-jacketed bullets commonly known as "hard ball." There is yet another factor that is more important in some designs than in others, but is

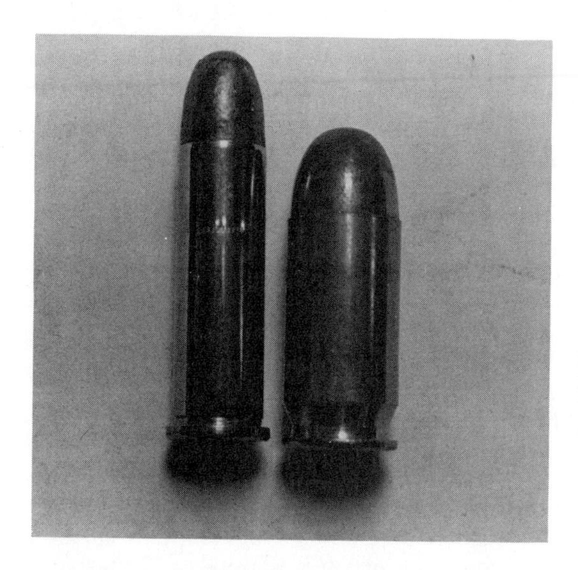

Here can be seen the basic differences in revolver and auto cartridge characteristics. The .38 Special at left is loaded with a lead bullet in a relatively long case with a thick, sturdy rim. The .45 ACP uses a full-jacketed bullet in a short, rimless case.

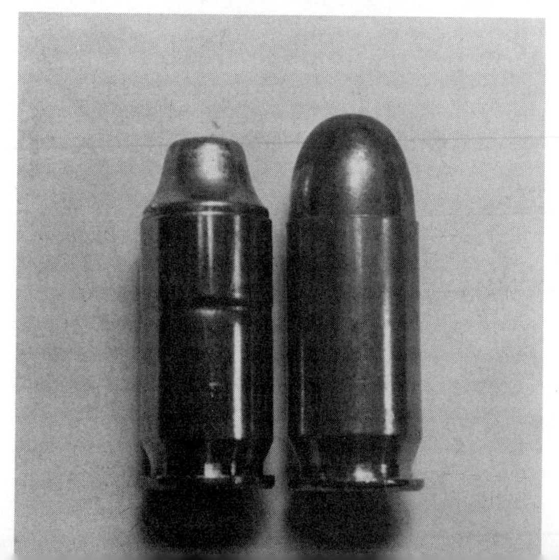

Autoloaders require quite specific cartridge lengths for reliable feeding. At left, a semi-wadcutter target load, and at right, the standard ball load, both in .45 caliber. Generally speaking, no more length variation than this can be tolerated if absolutely reliable functioning is expected.

inherent in most: A trough-like, angled feed ramp guides the cartridge from magazine to chamber, and the upper end of this ramp cuts away part of the chamber wall between five and seven o'clock, reducing support of the case in that area so that well-used or slightly defective cases may combine with relatively high pressures to cause a blown case, damaged gun, and/or malfunction. Autoloader cartridges are also designed to function at higher working pressures than those for revolvers. Generally speaking, only the big magnum revolver loads approach or exceed autoloader chamber pressures, while almost all other revolver cartridges operate at pressures little more than half that of autoloader cartridges.

Then there is the matter of case design. Revolver cases are invariably provided with thick, sturdy rims and are of the straight or only slightly tapered type. A revolver simply cannot function reliably with a case possessing significant taper or bottleneck, which would cause the case to be driven to the rear and jammed against the recoil shield by gas pressure, in-

The feed ramp of an S&W M39 pistol. The upper portion of the ramp intrudes into the chamber and thereby cuts away a portion of the chamber wall, reducing the support given to the cartridge case in that area.

A typical "feed-ramp blowout" of a .380 ACP case. It was fired in a gun whose feed ramp intruded excessively into the chamber, leaving the missing portion of the case unsupported. Had this been a low-pressure load, the case probably would not have ruptured, but would simply have bulged outward into this area. A case failure such as this will not usually harm the shooter, but will wreck the magazine and split the grips of the gun.

terfering with cylinder rotation. Revolver cases are also generally longer than those for autos. On the other hand, autoloaders generally use pure rimless or semi-rimmed cases of relatively short length, and while the straight or slightly tapered types are in the majority, autoloaders actually function *better* with the bottleneck type, because of the funneling action of a bottleneck case into a bottleneck chamber.

There are other differences. Revolver cases are normally crimped upon the bullet, autoloader cases are not. Most existing revolver cases were designed around black powder well before 1900; autoloader cases were designed for smokeless powder of much lesser weight and bulk. Revolver cases were of the balloon-head type in the main until the 1950s, while autoloader cases were of the solid-head type from the beginning. Revolver cases headspace upon the front face of their rims, which seat against the chamber mouth; autoloader cases generally headspace upon the mouth of the case, which seats against a shoulder at the front of the chamber. And you may note other differences as we work our way down the line.

EQUIPMENT FOR HANDGUN LOADS

You set up to load handgun ammunition just as you do to load rifle ammunition, except that you can get by without a powder scale or an adjustable powder measure. Instead, there is the so-called "pistol measure," which functions essentially the same as the bigger rifle-type measure, but has a simple fixed cavity machined in its drum to function as a metering chamber. Drums are interchangeable and low in cost, and by judicious selection of powders and charge weights and loads, one of these low-cost measures with two or three different drums will handle the average pistolero's loading needs without difficulty. Since the metering cavities are fixed at the time of manufacture, there is no need for a scale to check them. A drum made up to throw 3.5 grains of Bullseye cannot change (except by deliberate reworking) and will continue to throw that charge.

Modern handgun-caliber reloading dies consist of three or four units. One should *never* buy an old-style two-die set (no longer manufactured) no

With the exception of the modern magnum loadings, virtually all revolver cartridges were originally designed with balloon-head cases as shown at left. The case on the right (actually a magnum revolver case) illustrates the solid-head design utilized in autoloading-pistol cartridges almost exclusively from the beginning.

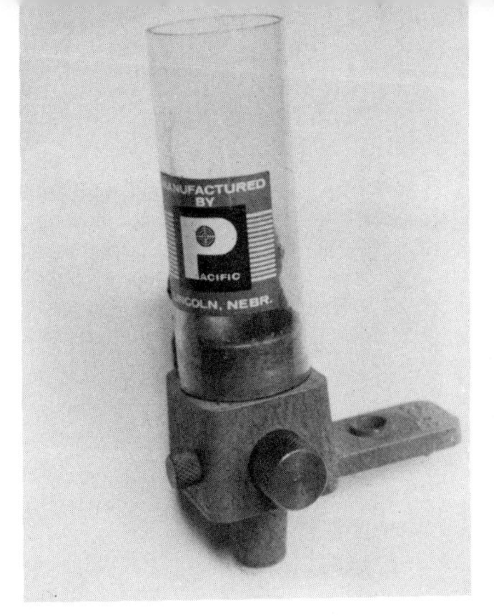

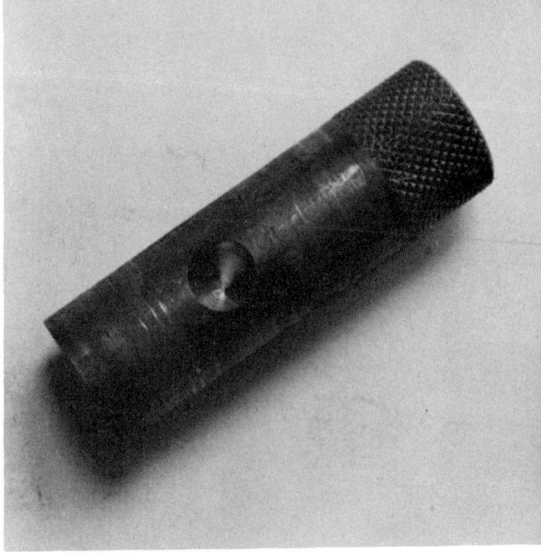

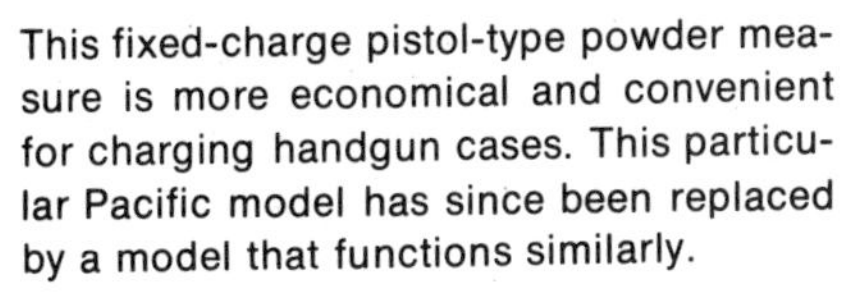

This fixed-charge pistol-type powder measure is more economical and convenient for charging handgun cases. This particular Pacific model has since been replaced by a model that functions similarly.

The charge drum from the Pacific pistol measure shown left. It contains a simple fixed-volume cavity machined into its body and thus is not subject to any change at all during its life.

matter how great a bargain it might be. Two-die sets work fine on bottleneck cases, but drastically reduce the life of straight or slightly tapered cases. While ordinary hardened-steel resizing dies work beautifully with straight or slightly tapered handgun cases, tungsten-carbide-insert dies make loading faster and more convenient and are not likely to be damaged by dirty or gritty cases; they will resize hundreds of thousands of cases without visible wear. I once owned a tungsten-carbide die which had resized over 1.5 million .38 Special cases, and it looked as if it was just getting broken in.

Most rifle loading is done with jacketed bullets and so most people don't really need bullet-casting equipment, but the reverse is true with handguns. You'll be better off to include a bullet-casting setup right from the beginning. A cast-bullet load (assuming you cast the bullets yourself) will cost 3 to 5 cents less than a load assembled with store-bought jacketed bullets. And, even in autos, a properly cast bullet of the correct alloy will function just as reliably as an expensive jacketed bullet. In essence, handgun loading means cast-bullet loading. The subject of the next chapter is casting bullets, so we'll not go into it further here.

CASE INSPECTION

Case preparation and selection is pretty much the same as for rifles except that because of their smaller size, handgun cases are much more easily and efficiently cleaned by running them through a tumbler—similar to a rock-polishing tumbler—in a nonabrasive medium of ground nut hulls or fruit pits. This is especially true for autoloader cases, which are tossed out on the ground and thus pick up grit and dirt. During case inspection, particular attention should be paid to autoloader cases. Look for any significant bulge

Here's a typical four-unit handgun-caliber loading-die set by RCBS. From left to right, resizing die, expanding and decapping die, bullet-seating die, and crimping die.

If you're willing to spend the additional money, a tungsten-carbide die greatly simplifies and speeds up the resizing of your handgun cases. The tungsten-carbide insert is a simple ring fitted into the mouth of an otherwise conventional steel die body. It is visible here as the gray inner ring.

The two most popular types of cast lead handgun bullets are the semi-wadcutter (left) and full wadcutter. Both are easy to cast and size/lubricate, and produce superb accuracy. The semi-wadcutter is generally used for hunting, defense, and similar purposes, while the full wadcutter is used mainly for target shooting.

A typical case tumbler, which saves a great deal of time and cleans cases thoroughly before loading. It is also extremely convenient for removing resizing lubricant and cleaning primer pockets. This model is sold mainly by Gil Hebard Guns.

just ahead of the extractor groove. This bulge is caused by lack of support in the feed-ramp area of the chamber, as mentioned earlier. Any bulge there of more than about .015 inch probably indicates a weakened case, and even if resizing removes all evidence of the bulge, the case does not possess its original strength. If sometime in the future that section again lies in the feed-ramp area of the chamber when it is fired, the case may very well let go.

RESIZING, DECAPPING, AND MOUTH EXPANSION

Again because of their small size, handgun cases are quickly and easily lubricated for resizing by moistening the center of a towel with case-sizing lubricant, then rumbling the cases in it until they pick up a very thin film of lube. Keep in mind, though, that if you are using a tungsten-carbide resizing die, no lubrication will be required; less fuss, less muss, and less time. This alone enables the tungsten-carbide die to justify its cost very quickly.

A handgun-caliber resizing die is set up in the press exactly as is a rifle die. However, while it may contain a decapping stem (depending upon manufacture and design), it will not contain an expander button. Mouth or neck expansion is conducted as a separate operation in all handgun calibers. If the resizing die contains a decapping stem, adjust it so that the fired primer is punched clear but the stem itself does not jam into the inside of the case head. If decapping is accomplished in conjunction with resizing, then all traces of lubricant should be removed before the cases move on to the next operation. Do this by rumbling them in a solvent-moistened towel as described in Chapter 4, or by running them through a tumbler in which the polishing medium has been very lightly moistened with solvent. The tumbler method is best, not only because it is easier and more efficient, but because it will also clean most of the primer residue from the pockets. This isn't considered necessary, but when it can be gotten as a bonus, it is worthwhile.

Case mouths are expanded as a separate operation by a hardened and polished rod threaded into a die body. This body is substituted for the

A typical decapping stem for use in a handgun-caliber resizing die. This one is from an RCBS 9mm Parabellum tungsten-carbide die.

resizing die in the press, and the cases are placed in a shell holder and run up over the expander rod. This rod is of a standard diameter which produces a case neck or mouth of the proper diameter for most general-purpose handgun loads with either lead or jacketed bullets. It also contains a tapered section, and it must be adjusted so that this section enters the case mouth only slightly to produce a visible flaring which will allow the bullet to be started by hand without being gouged by the sharp edge of the case mouth. This flaring must be just enough to permit easy starting of the bullet and no more; excessive flaring greatly reduces the life of the case by overstressing the mouth and causing splits to develop. Also, a case that is flared too much may not enter the mouth of the bullet-seating die. Unfortunately, handgun cases, especially those for revolvers, vary a good deal in length. The result is that with the expander rod fixed in position, some cases will receive more than enough flare, and others may not receive quite enough. This is something you must live with unless you want to go to the trouble—and it is a lot of trouble and not really necessary—to trim cases to a uniform length.

Because handgun cases are relatively soft and have thin walls, no lubricant is required for the expanding operation. It will be easier, though, if the inside of the case mouths are clean, and this is another advantage to tumbling rather than washing. Tumbling gets off the gritty powder fouling and residue of mouth sealer which makes expansion harder.

Some makers of dies incorporate the decapping pin in the expander rod, and thus decapping is done in conjunction with mouth expansion. When this is the case, resizing lubricant should be cleaned off after expansion rather than resizing. The lube should come off after decapping simply because any lube that gets in the area of the primer pocket will then be removed.

REPRIMING

Most presses are designed with the intention that you reprime the case as it is decapped; that is, when the fired primer is punched out, you place a primer in the cup of the swinging priming arm, press it forward into the ram, and then pull the case down over the primer by means of the tool handle. This can't be done if you're cleaning lubricant off the cases after decapping and before repriming. (Of course, if you're using a tungsten-carbide die, no lubricant need be on the cases anyway.) Seating new primers may still be accomplished on the loading press, in the same fashion, but it's a much more lengthy and frustrating process than if a separate bench-type priming tool is used. Because handgun ammunition is generally loaded in relatively large quantities, a semi-automatic priming tool such as the new RCBS is ideal for this purpose. Also, as mentioned in Chapter 4, a bench priming tool offers much greater sensitivity and you're far less likely to crush or deform a primer. This is especially important in handgun primers with their thinner and softer cups. For these reasons, I strongly recommend a bench priming tool at the earliest possible point in the game. Until then, of course, prime on the loading press.

Operation of a bench priming tool, even the very simple Lachmiller (no longer made) or C-H, requires only that you drop the primer anvil-up in the center of the shell holder, then slip a case into the shell holder and press down on the tool handle until you feel the primer seat on the bottom of the pocket. With just a little practice, you can do a very uniform job. With the semi-automatic RCBS tool, you slip the case in the shell holder, press down on the handle, retract the handle slightly, pull out the case, and retract the handle all the way, which cams the primer magazine over the shell holder and deposits a fresh primer therein. By this method and with this tool, cases may be primed many times faster than on the loading press.

Make it a habit as you remove the primed case, from whatever priming tool, to run one finger over the case head, feeling the position of the primer. If it's protruding, you'll notice it instantly, and if it's slightly below the case-head surface, as it should be, you'll be able to feel that instinctively as well. Remember that the surface of the primer should be only *slightly* below the surface of the case head.

CHARGING

After priming, cases should be set mouth-up in loading blocks, ready for charging with powder. Traditionally, the powder measure is screwed or bolted securely to the edge of a workbench, and each case in the block in

A typical handgun-caliber expander plug of RCBS make, used in a separate expander-die body. Note the short section which opens the case mouth, then the tapered portion which produces the flare needed to start bullets.

turn is pressed up into the drop tube of the measure, the handle is rotated in both directions, and the charge is dropped into the case. If you're using a big rifle-type measure, that's about the only practical way to do it. However, with the smaller and more compact pistol measure, I prefer another faster and more convenient method. Fill the measure with powder and double-check the metering drum to make sure it will be dropping the correct powder charge. Then hold the measure in your off hand and its operating knob in your master hand. Set the measure down over the mouth of the first case in the block and quickly rotate the knob in both directions to dump the charge, then move the measure over to the next case and repeat. Continue this, and you can charge a block of fifty cases far more quickly than with a bigger bench-mounted measure.

After charging the cases, *always* visually inspect them under good light for any powder charges that appear to bulk higher or lower than the others. The same rules apply here as detailed in Chapter 4; please do remember that powder charging is the most critical step of the loading process, and that the relative small capacity of handgun cases means that an overcharge will produce a drastic increase in pressure with possible damage to both gun and shooter. An abnormally light charge may leave a bullet stuck in the barrel—big trouble if a subsequent round is fired. Don't play around with powder charges; no beer-drinking, TV-watching, games with girl friend, or playing with the kids. When charging cases with powder, do only that, and concentrate on it to the maximum.

BULLET SEATING AND CRIMPING

Up to this point, what we've said applies equally to revolver and autoloader calibers. Now, though, we come to some division of the ways. Finger-start the chosen bullet in the case mouth while the cases are still in the loading

Charging cases with powder can be greatly speeded up, without any loss in accuracy, by using a pistol-type measure in the mobile mode.

blocks. Get out the seating die, which in revolver calibers will be a crimp/seat die unless you have purchased the more expensive four-die set. It is designed to seat the bullet to the proper depth and crimp the case mouth simultaneously. This is satisfactory for most loads, but may be improved upon where maximum accuracy and uniformity is required.

Anyway, place an empty but resized case in the shell holder and run the ram to the top. Screw in the seating die until it contacts the case, then back off $^1/_8$ turn and secure the die with the lock ring. Place a bullet in the mouth of an empty case and run it into the die carefully, feeling for contact with the bullet-seating screw. If contact is made, carefully seat the bullet in subsequent steps until the mouth of the case is just barely short of completely covering the crimping groove in the bullet. If you don't at first contact the seating screw, turn it deeper into the die until the bullet can be seated to the correct depth. With the bullet seated as described, back the seating screw out of the die about $^1/_8$ inch, then progressively turn the die deeper into the press and run the case into the die until a smooth, uniform, tight roll crimp is formed. It should not be possible to rotate the bullet in the case by hand. Now, with the case and seated, crimped bullet still in the die, turn the lock ring down to secure the die. Turn the seating screw into the die until it makes firm contact with the bullet, then lock it in place as well. Save the "seating dummy" you've just made and give it the treatment described in Chapter 4.

Now you're ready to simultaneously seat and crimp. Take the case with the bullet started in it, slip it in the shell holder, give the bullet a last-minute alignment with thumb and finger so it is as straight as possible in the case,

The entire series of operations performed on the case, this one in .38 Super Auto caliber. From left to right: case resized; resized case decapped, mouth expanded and flared; case charged with powder and bullet started by hand; bullet seated to proper depth as a separate operation; case mouth crimped upon the bullet as a separate and final operation. Note that in this instance I applied a fairly heavy roll crimp to an autoloading-pistol cartridge. This is satisfactory since I was working with the *semi-rimmed* .38 Super case, which at least technically headspaces upon its thin rim rather than the case mouth.

and run the assembly into the die in a single, smooth, reasonably forceful stroke. You'll extract a fully loaded revolver cartridge.

Examine it very carefully. If the case has gouged into the bullet, either the case mouth was not circular, or it was not flared sufficiently, or the bullet was excessively tipped and could not be straightened up by the die in time. If a thin ring of lead is pushed up ahead of the case mouth, it simply wasn't flared quite enough. Stepping back a moment, note also whether there was detectable added resistance as the bullet was forced into the case. If there wasn't, either the inside of the mouth is too large or the bullet is too small. The former may be due either to an oversize expander plug or too-thin case walls. A third and less likely possibility is that the resizing die was oversize and did not reduce the mouth of the case sufficiently.

Generally, with proper lead bullets and modern reloading dies, those problems won't be encountered. High-performance jacketed expanding bullets of light weight are another matter, and we'd best touch on them now. First of all, the seating screw must fit the nose of this type of bullet exactly, or the bullet may be deformed by seating pressure. Second, such bullets are often undersize (deliberately so, for a good reason), and thus a standard expander plug may open up the case mouth too much. The case must be very tight upon high-performance bullets, and this may necessitate polishing the expander plug to a smaller diameter, and perhaps even obtaining an undersize resizing die. It is essential, though, because if the case does not grip the bullet very tightly, powder combustion will not be as efficient as it should, and substandard velocity will be produced. Cases may be crimped on high-performance bullets simultaneously with seating, but I recommend against it. There will be less bullet deformation and a tighter crimp if crimping is done as a separate operation. This means simply that bullets are seated with the die backed out as already described so that the case mouth is just barely short of covering the crimping groove or cannelure. After all bullets have been seated to this depth, the die is readjusted, and the cases are then run through the die again to produce the maximum crimp they will form. The combination of a very heavy crimp and tight bullet/case assembly ensures that there will be sufficient resistance (bullet pull) for efficient powder combustion, and further, that recoil of the gun will not cause bullets to move out of their cases and tie up the gun. This is a fairly common revolver failing in heavy loads with any type or weight of

Bullets representing two different classes of the handgun loads. At left is a lubricated cast lead bullet of standard weight intended for most general-purpose shooting. At right is a light, thin-jacketed, soft-cored, expanding bullet intended primarily to be driven at extra-high velocities for personal defense or hunting nonedible game of no great size.

An expander plug modified to open up the case mouth only to the depth that the bullet will be seated, leaving a slight shoulder there against which the bullet can rest. This shoulder then prevents the bullet from being driven deeper into the case by feeding or recoil forces.

bullet, but especially so with high-performance bullets loaded to the hilt in the magnum calibers.

The bullet-seating problem is different in autoloader cartridges. I'll talk here about cast lead bullets, but the same problems exist with all other types. First of all, since you cannot use a heavy roll crimp to keep the bullet securely in the case, the case must fit quite tightly on the bullet. Where in a revolver the bullet's tendency is to move forward out of the case, when an autoloader is fired, the cartridge being fed into the chamber strikes the feed ramp on its nose, and the tendency is to drive the bullet deeper into the case. To a lesser degree, the same thing occurs to cartridges remaining in the magazine as the gun recoils. The noses of the bullets are smacked smartly by the front of the magazine in recoil, and if they aren't held tightly enough, they'll be driven deeper into the case. With the bullet pushed back in the case, the cartridge will be too short to feed properly, and the loading density will also be increased, resulting in higher pressure and velocity. Bullets should be started in the charged case by hand as already described, then the seating die adjusted so that it *only* seats the bullet to the proper depth, without forming any crimp. Then as a *separate* operation, the cartridge should be run into a "taper crimp" die, which simply squeezes in the mouth of the case on a very slight taper, forcing it into the bullet and thus tying the two together more tightly. Note that in a taper crimp, the mouth of the case is not turned over as in a roll crimp, but is simply reduced in diameter. Since the case must headspace on its mouth, only a small amount of taper crimp should be applied; adjust the die so that the case-mouth diameter is reduced only about .010 inch. When this is done, the mouth is partially buried in the surface of the bullet, forming a shoulder on the bullet which resists its being driven deeper into the case.

The C-H bullet and case-canneluring tool which may be used to roll a cannelure in the case as shown. The bullet is then seated against the cannelure and is supported against any rearward movement.

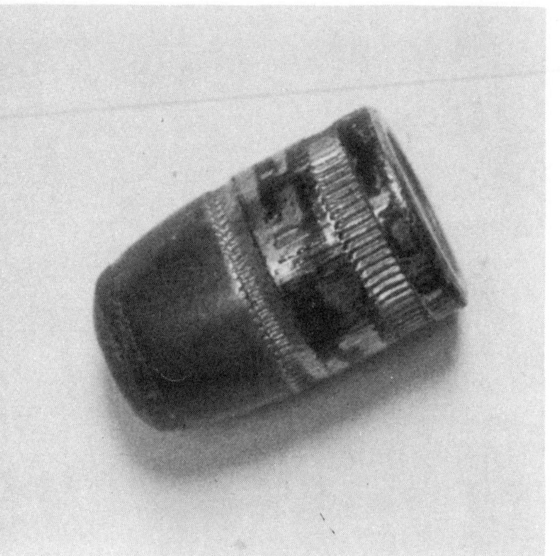

Ammunition factories often use "mouth sealer" compound inside the case mouth to ensure a tighter assembly of case and bullet. Here residue of the hardened sealer can be seen on the surface of the pulled bullet and on the inside of a case mouth. Unfortunately, this mouth sealer is not available to handloaders.

When ammunition is loaded and absolute functional reliability is necessary—as in an autoloader used for defense—finished cartridges should be checked to ensure that they will chamber correctly. The chamber of the gun in which they are to be used makes a very functional "profile gauge," and if cartridges will seat fully of their own weight, they're certain to feed properly.

Even before taper crimping, it should not be possible to rotate the bullet with the fingers. If this can be done, a smaller expander plug must be used to give the case a tighter grip. If even a smaller expander plug doesn't do the job, then it is likely that either the case walls are too thin or the resizing die is too large and you need an undersize die. This is especially likely in the case of high-performance expanding bullets, which often run a bit undersize themselves. In fact, at least one diemaker offers 9mm Parabellum resizing dies in two diameters just to handle this problem.

With some loads and in some guns, it may be that even the tight case/bullet assembly and taper crimp still will not guarantee that the bullet won't be driven deeper into the case. This problem can be solved in either of two ways, one simple and one complex. The simple method consists of shortening the expander rod so that its lower edge enters the case only to a point about 1/32 inch above the final position of the base of the seated bullet. This must be done very carefully, because the expander rod must still go deep enough into the case to flare the mouth very slightly. If the expander rod in question also carries the decapping stem, naturally, you don't just cut off the end. You just reduce the diameter about .040 inch back to the point necessary to obtain case expansion only to the desired level. The altered expander rod will then leave a slight shoulder, which the bullet will strike in seating and actually move down a small amount, resulting in the bullet being held very tightly against the shoulder and the shoulder resisting rearward movement of the bullet.

The more complex alternative to this limited expansion is to use the C-H or Corbin case-canneluring tool to roll a cannelure or groove in the case body to form a shoulder at the same point. The cannelure should be made no deeper than necessary to prevent bullet movement, for if it is too deep, it will weaken the case, especially for subsequent reloadings. Once a case has been cannelured in this fashion, the internal shoulder will remain after firing, and if the expander rod is forced past it in subsequent reloading, the shoulder will be pushed outward and an external bulge will be formed on the case which might interfere with chambering. So, in order to reload cannelured cases, you have to modify an expander rod anyway, so you might as well go that route from the beginning. It's cheaper, faster, and a lot less trouble. While I cannelure a good many cases myself, I don't recommend doing so, unless it is absolutely necessary and nothing less will prevent bullets from being driven deeper into the case.

INSPECTION, PACKAGING, AND CLEANUP

It goes without saying, of course, that freshly loaded handgun ammunition should be inspected carefully, packaged, and then labeled as described in Chapter 4. When using cast lead bullets, you'll find a certain amount of bullet lubricant accumulating in the seating die, and it will be transferred to cartridges passing through it. Thus, you may also have a cleanup job on your hands. A cloth lightly moistened in solvent will serve to wipe off the grease, or it may be removed in a tumbler or by rumbling in a solvent-dampened towel.

8

Casting and Swaging Bullets

WHEN HANDLOADING BEGAN, roughly a century ago, jacketed bullets had not been invented. Lubricated lead bullets were the standard projectile, and while to some extent manufacturers had begun swaging bullets, the handloader had no choice but to cast his own from bar or sheet lead, which was a standard item of trade. As a matter of fact, nearly all rifle manufactures offered some sort of loading tools as accessories to their rifles, and often the tools included an integral bullet mold. In those days, none but the experienced target shooter recognized any shortcomings in the home-cast lead bullet; if it came from the mold looking approximately like a factory bullet and without obvious holes or voids, it was presumed to be "accurate." Shooters cast bullets of necessity, either because loaded ammunition was not readily available or because it was too expensive.

Today, the handloader doesn't necessarily cast bullets because factory-loaded ammunition isn't available. He does so either to save money or to produce loads that are not available as standard factory items. Lead bullets are available from manufacturers, but they are nearly as costly as jacketed bullets. The ever increasing cost of commercial pig lead has boosted the cost of factory-made lead bullets quite substantially. However, the cost of commercial lead seldom has any significant effect on the average handloader. Generally, he employs scrap or salvage lead which costs little or nothing. If he were forced to go out and buy commercial lead from a metals supplier or a plumbing shop (often a good source), he would be paying as this is written $1.20 per pound and upward, and a pound of lead produces only thirty standard .45 ACP bullets or forty-six .38 caliber wadcutter bullets.

WHERE TO FIND LEAD

Scrap lead is suitable, under the conditions we'll describe shortly, and it is available at little or no cost if you know where to look. Most service stations have a bucket, box, or drum into which they pitch cast-off wheel weights, and if your neighborhood service-station operator hasn't already committed himself to some other handloader, you can usually make arrangements to acquire weights from him for 10 to 15 cents per pound (all a scrap dealer will pay for them) or possibly for nothing, just to keep your business. Tire stores are another good source. Usually when they've accumulated a few hundred pounds of cast-off weights, they are sold to a scrap-metal dealer for 10 to 15 cents per pound. You can buy them for no more than that, and probably less by picking them up and saving the store a trip to the scrap yard. A three-gallon bucket filled with lead wheel weights will cast an awful lot of bullets, even after the waste is discarded.

You could also obtain scrap batteries cheaply from service stations, but while it is possible to melt down the plates, they are usually so heavily sulphated that very little usable lead is obtained.

Old buildings often contain lead pipe, and when a building is being demolished, sometimes a fifth of good whiskey or a few cold six packs on a hot summer afternoon will result in several hundred pounds of lead pipe being set aside where you can conveniently pick it up. I've known it to arrive in my driveway shortly after quitting time when the word had been passed that the bar would be open.

Cable sheathing is another source of lead. New cables are sheathed in other materials, but old ones coming out of the ground for repair or replacement can produce lots of lead if you're friendly with the service crew. Print shops using hot type have lots of linotype metal—a hard lead alloy—lying around, and can often be persuaded to part with metal that has been heavily used and is ready to go back to the foundry for reconstitution. If you know of a print shop that is converting from hot type to more modern methods, you can usually pick up hundreds of pounds of linotype at little cost.

Doubtless you'll discover other sources of low-cost lead if you spend just a little time looking around. Actually, the average handloader won't use a great deal. With typical bullets running about forty to the pound, a hundred pounds will last a long time, even if none of the bullets are salvaged for reuse.

PROCESSING SCRAP LEAD

Almost any lead mix from pure pig lead to linotype metal will cast into acceptable bullets for some purposes, but for maximum accuracy, you'll need an alloy of known hardness which you can reproduce as needed. Also, for velocities in the upper ranges and for best feeding in autoloading actions, you'll need a relatively hard alloy you'll be able to reproduce at will. Bullets of typical scrap lead, properly cast, sized, and lubricated, will give good accuracy at velocities up to about 1,000 fps. This makes plain scrap lead—which means essentially wheel weights—good for most handgun applications, and for light, low-velocity rifle loads. Above that level, some hardening will be required. An alloy approximating the hardness of 1 part tin to 16 parts lead will generally suffice up to about 1,500 fps. Above that velocity, a hardness approximating 1 part tin to 10 parts lead is necessary, and for maximum velocity in rifle loads, straight linotype metal will perform best.

Naturally, alloys of these hardnesses can be purchased, and an excellent general-purpose alloy is Lyman's No. 2, which may be obtained through handloading dealers. But it is expensive, as is linotype metal if you must obtain it through normal trade channels.

The main problem, then, is to give your scrap lead the desired hardness for a particular use. If you're going to be loading mainly for handguns and light rifle loads, straight wheel-weight metal will do the job quite well, so let's take a look at processing it.

Wheel weights are generally dirty and greasy, and each weight is cast around a steel clip used to hold it to the wheel rim. Simply melting the weights and fluxing and stirring the molten mixture well will cause the dirt and clips to float to the surface, where they may be skimmed off with a perforated spoon or skimmer. The typical electric melting pot or cast-iron pot (Lyman) set on a gas range will suffice for this purpose. Keep adding weights and skimming off the debris until the pot is full, then cast the metal into ingots and start over. When the pot is emptied, leave at least 1/2 inch or so of molten metal in the bottom, and this will speed the melting of the next batch. Most electric casting furnaces, with the exception of the big 100-pound one offered by Shiloh, will hold at best 20 to 25 pounds of lead, so if you've a goodly supply of weights to process, it may take a long time. If you can lay hands on an electric or gasoline-fired plumber's furnace holding 100 pounds or more of metal, the process can be speeded up a good deal.

If you have other scrap lead, such as cable sheathing, battery plates, pipe, etc., melt it down and cast it into ingots separately, keeping a record of its source. Then, later, when you've accumulated several hundred pounds of ingots, you can blend the different lead alloys together into a single batch of homogeneous bullet material. To do this, separate your wheel-weight metal into pot-size batches, then divide each of the other types of lead you might have equally for each pot batch. Melt and mix, and recast into ingots. The result will be a single large batch of lead that is pretty much of the same content and hardness throughout. This may seem like a lot of extra effort, but it will produce more uniform bullets in the end. If the lead isn't blended, bullets you cast today may be harder or softer than those you cast next week or next month. Variations like this will affect long-term accuracy; a given gun will not necessarily shoot better or worse with one alloy over another, but it may shoot to a different point of impact.

Fluxing is necessary to float the impurities from the metal and to make it flow freely for casting. Consequently, some flux will be necessary even in processing the scrap metal into usable ingots. Almost everything under the sun has been used for flux at one time or another—tallow, beeswax, all manner of greases, and even some exotic chemical compounds. For initial processing of scrap, almost any grease will do, but it will smoke and burn and make a stink. So you'd best either move outdoors to the garage, or use a more modern flux such as Marvelux, which is a chemical flux that produces virtually no smoke or odor and is a great help in producing sharp, clean, perfectly cast bullets.

TESTING AND INCREASING HARDNESS

Once your lead is processed, it will help if you can determine its approximate hardness. To the best of my knowledge, only two tools are available for this purpose. One is the Potter lead tester, which has been around for many years. It utilizes a weight to press a steel ball into a lead ingot, and the depth of the impression is interpreted to indicate hardness. The other tool is the SAECO hardness tester, which works on a cast bullet by forcing a steel point into the lead and permits direct reading on a hardness scale. Either will work well, but the SAECO tool is by far the handiest. Results obtained with the two are not interchangeable; each has its own relative scale with no absolute value.

If you can afford it, by all means get a lead tester and determine the hardness of the batch of metal you've cooked up. If it's a typical mix of mostly wheel weights, with some other scrap added, it will be quite adequate for most handgun loads and low-velocity rifleloads. Nevertheless, *knowing* its hardness will be a great help, especially when you decide to harden some of it for more demanding uses. Gauging hardness by gouging the nose of a cast bullet with your thumbnail—a method often recommended for lack of any other—really doesn't accomplish anything. The lead tester isn't terribly expensive, but it does represent a fair investment, so if you've got a couple of buddies interested in handloading, split the cost

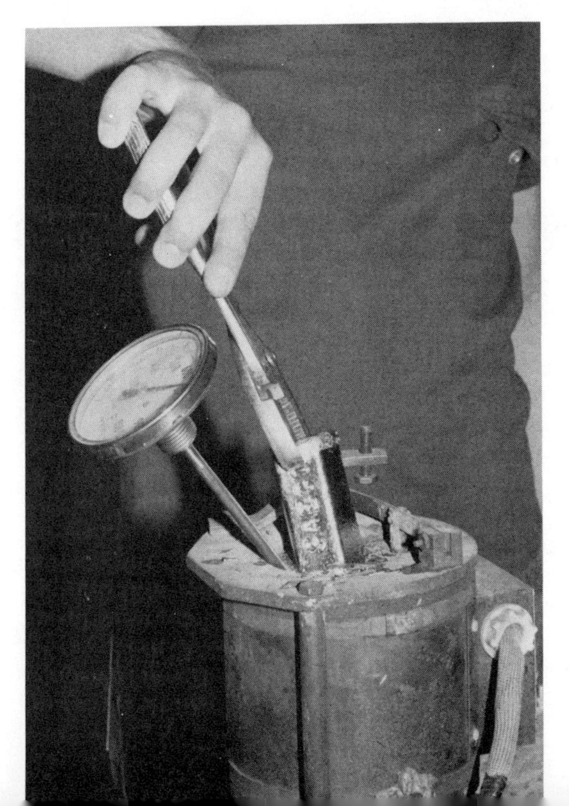

Lead should be added regularly as casting progresses, maintaining a fairly constant head of metal in the furnace. With just a little practice, you'll learn how many bullets to cast to make room for the addition of one ingot. Adding more than one will cool the melt down to the point where you may not be able to get good bullets.

and share its use.

The simplest way of hardening lead is to add tin. Antimony actually does the job better, but the average electric furnace won't get your mix hot enough to melt the antimony properly so it will blend in. Tin melts at a lower temperature, so you'll be able to handle it. Small tin ingots, known as "block tin," are available from some loading-supply houses, but most dealers don't stock it, and in its pure state, it's more difficult to use with ordinary casting equipment. A better, though somewhat more costly, method is to buy 50-50 plumber's solder at your local plumbing or hardware store. This is a half-and-half alloy of lead and tin, and it will melt in molten lead. The trick in adding tin to harden the mix is in determining the amount. If you want a $^{1}/_{10}$ alloy for high-velocity rifle bullets, you can't produce it accurately without knowing the tin content of the lead. Unfortunately, nothing but laboratory analysis will tell you that. So, the lead tester comes in quite handy. Simply add tin a small amount at a time, casting a bullet after each addition, and testing the bullet for hardness. Once you know the bullet is the right hardness, you've got it whipped, and if you started with a known amount of lead in the pot and recorded the amount of tin you added, then you can repeat the process for another potful without more testing. If you started with pure lead, adding two pounds of $^{50}/_{50}$ solder to 19 pounds of lead would give you a $^{1}/_{20}$ alloy. Adding four pounds of solder to 18 pounds of pure lead would give you a $^{1}/_{10}$ alloy. However, as we've already said, wheel weights and other scrap lead already contain some hardening elements, and it will seldom be necessary to add that high a proportion of tin to achieve the desired hardness.

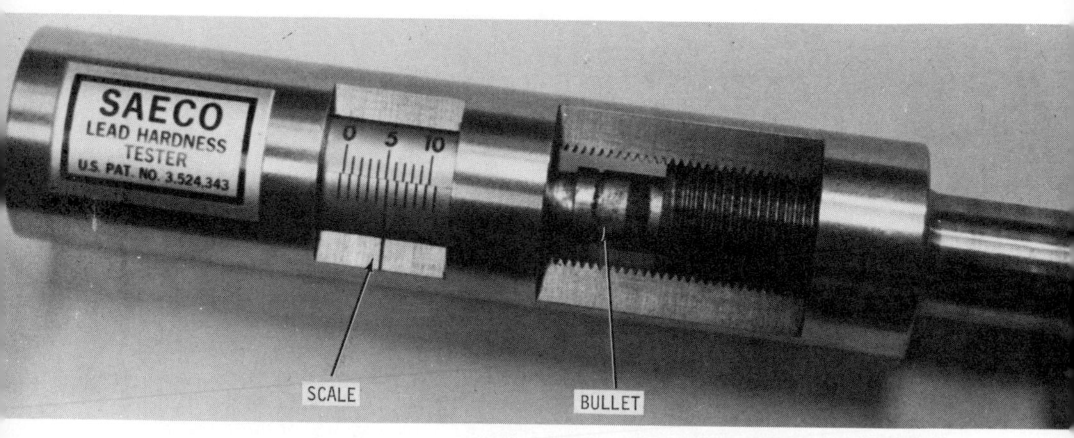

The unusual and very practical "Lead Hardness Tester" by SAECO. A vernier scale registers according to the depth that a hardened, steel point is forced into a cast bullet by a preset spring of known force. Turning in the screw on the right forces the bullet against the spring-loaded point until the single index mark on the body beneath the vernier scale is aligned with the longest mark on the bottom half of the vernier. The hardness value—an arbitrary one—is then read off the upper half of the vernier. Once this is known, hardness is easily duplicated whenever needed. A very useful tool.

Adding the tin is simple enough. Bring your pot of metal up to the highest heat your electric furnace will produce, giving it plenty of time to ensure that molten metal is at top temperature. Then add the bars or rods of solder, and as they melt, add plenty of flux and stir the mixture well. Drop the temperature back down to casting heat, and you're ready to cast.

It is far better to go ahead and make up your bullet metal in batches of the proper hardness ahead of time. That way you can lay in an ample stock that is uniform in hardness. If you attempt to mix the alloy each time you fire up to cast bullets, you'll probably run into far greater variations in hardness.

In any event, once you've made up a batch of bullet metal and cast it into ingots, be sure it doesn't lose its identity. Mark it in some way, right on the ingot; scratch $^1/_{10}$, etc. to indicate its alloy, or use the hardness-scale reading from the lead tester, or if it's straight wheel weights, mark it so. You don't think you'll forget what each batch is, but that can happen easily if the metal isn't marked.

CASTING EQUIPMENT

The actual casting of the bullets has a good deal more to do with their performance, especially their accuracy, than the lead from which they're made. The ideal casting setup is an electric bullet-casting furnace holding at least 20 pounds of metal, with adjustable thermostatically controlled heat selection. While there are several makes on the market, the SAECO has given me by far the best service in both durability and reliability. I have one

Prepared for casting: an old SAECO electric bottom-pour furnace, an RCBS two-cavity mold, a supply of lead ingots and an ingot mold, a coffee can with a perforated spoon for skimming the melt, and a can of Marvelux flux. Don't laugh at the weatherbeaten appearance of this furnace; it has melted over 20 tons of lead for me and still performs correctly.

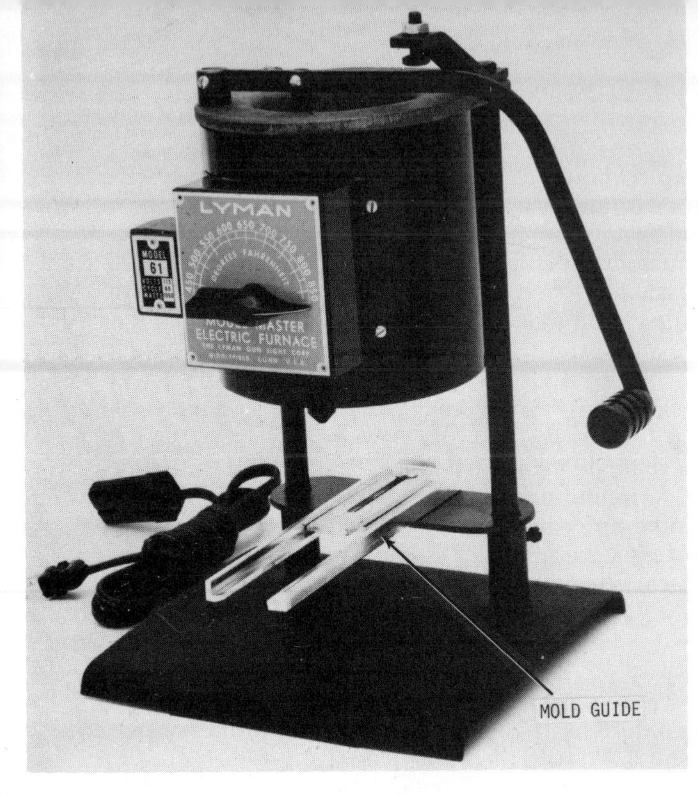

A typical electric lead-melting furnace for casting bullets. This Lyman "Mould Master" model has an adjustable heat control and a bottom-pour spout whose valve is activated by the handle on the right. Note also there is a mold guide, which some casters find a convenience for working with heavy multiple-cavity molds.

A utility electric melting furnace with temperature control by SAECO. This type of furnace is substantially cheaper than the bottom-pour type, and is by far the least expensive choice if you prefer to cast with a ladle.

A simple cast-iron pot in which metal may be melted on a gas range or other high heat source either for blending or purification or for casting with a ladle.

such furnace which is twenty years old, has been overhauled at the factory once, and still performs perfectly after having melted down at least 20 tons of lead. However, if you exercise reasonable care, bullets just as good can be cast from the simple, iron pot and ladle supplied by Lyman, employing a gas burner or kitchen range to melt the lead. An electric range doesn't work nearly as well; gas gives precise and instant heat control.

Of course, you'll need a bullet mold casting the type, size, and weight that you want. Casting is best learned with a single- or double-cavity mold, mainly because they are relatively light and handy. Molds casting a large number of bullets offer additional problems that you don't need. Actually, with a little practice, even a single-cavity mold will allow you to cast a couple of hundred or more bullets per hour, and that's more than enough for most people's needs. Personally, I consider a single cavity the best for starting, but some makers don't even supply them any more, having standardized on the double-cavity size. The new Lee molds are very simple, economical, and easy to use. However, they don't stand up to long service as well as the traditional iron-block type, and not nearly so wide a variety of bullets is available. I prefer to use the traditional cast-iron molds for regular duty, then pick up the lower-cast Lee molds for those bullets I'll not need in large quantities. Learning to cast proper bullets with the cast-iron molds may take a bit longer, but I think it's worth it.

You'll also need some instrument to knock the sprue cutter around. For Lord knows how many years, I have used an old hickory hammer handle for this purpose. A plastic or wood mallet will do just as well, but *do not* use any metal instrument. It will soon batter up the extension of the sprue cutter, and will probably bend it as well, preventing the mold from making perfect bullets.

Always wear gloves, apron, and safety glasses. For the sake of clarity in the photographs in this chapter, we didn't use gloves—but we should have, particularly since the model is my youngest son, Greg.

THE CASTING PROCESS

Before the mold will cast perfect bullets, the cavity must be absolutely free of oil or grease. Traditionally, the oil is simply wiped out, and then the resi-

A low-cost outfit consisting of a cast-iron bottom-pour pot on a stand, combined with a common household propane torch. This outfit isn't for high production rates, but would meet the casting needs of a high percentage of hand-loaders.

The new aluminum-block Lee bullet mold of rather unconventional design, with the blocks made from sections of aluminum extrusion.

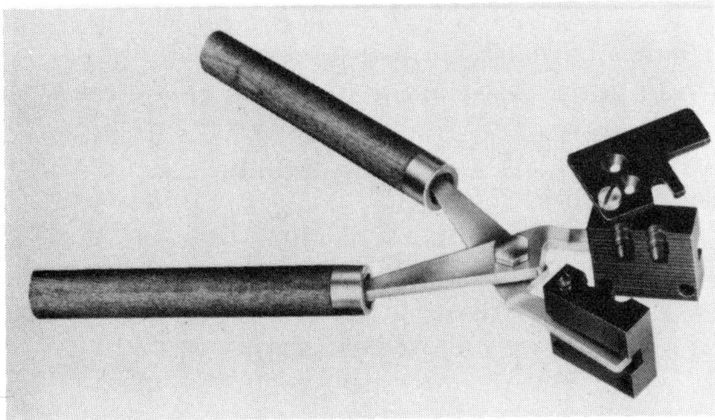

The conventional-type bullet mold with cast-iron blocks. Note the numerous shallow grooves machined in the mating faces of the blocks to permit trapped air to escape. This mold is from RCBS.

due is burned away by casting. This is wrong, because burning out the oil leaves a residue in the cavity which causes trouble. Avoid that by simply cleaning the cavities thoroughly with any good non-petroleum solvent which will not leave behind any oily film. Acetone works beautifully, and a pint bottle obtained from your local pharmacist will last for a year or more if you keep it tightly capped. Use a Q-Tip or similar swab to degrease the cavities thoroughly.

The mold must be brought up to the proper heat before it will drop perfect bullets. This can be done by simply casting and rejecting bullets, but it's simpler to set the mold on the edge of your pot while the lead is melting. When the lead is ready to cast, the mold will also be ready. That's okay on an electric pot, but if you're using a gas burner, don't leave the mold there very long, or it will get too hot and this could warp the blocks or burn the handles.

When the lead is molten, stir and flux it, and turn the temperature control back down to a bit over 600°. If you're using a gas burner, you'll have to turn the heat down by guess until experience teaches you the proper amount. Traditionally, lead is considered to be at the right temperature for casting bullets when it will just barely char without flaming a dry pine splinter. That's a pretty erratic method for determining temperature, but I suppose it's better than none. If you can spare an extra $10 (or a bit more), a thermometer to be placed in the lead is an excellent investment for casting over a gas flame, and it's worthwhile even with an electric pot. Most people never use a thermometer, but I've found it to be especially helpful because different alloys cast best at different temperatures. Also, the temperature scales on the heat controls of many electric pots are often not very accurate. A thermometer is also very helpful when you're casting lots of bullets rapidly and adding fresh metal to the pot often. Without a thermometer, you'll not be able to tell when the metal is back up to casting temperature. It is chilled substantially when cold metal is added and takes some time to get back up to the point where perfect bullets are produced.

With the bullet metal melted, fluxed, and stirred, and the mold degreased and warmed up, you're ready to cast bullets. If you're using an open pot and ladle, submerge the ladle in the lead for about thirty seconds to allow it to heat up. Then, holding the bullet mold in your left hand with the blocks clamped tightly together, the top of the mold vertical and to the right, dip up a ladle of lead and move the mold and ladle together so that the nipple or sprout of the ladle fits into the conical depression in the sprue plate. Then, holding the two tightly together, rotate them 90° to the left so that lead runs from the ladle into the mold. Do this over a piece of canvas or toweling so that any lead you spill won't spoil the floor. Hold the two in that position for five to ten seconds, then sort of "roll" them apart, leaving a small puddle of molten lead in the sprue. If the mold isn't up to temperature, lead will probably have solidified in the sprue hole, and the mold may not have filled.

The traditional ladle method of casting. The egg-shaped ladle (this example by Lyman) is submerged in the molten metal to heat up, filled with lead, and then its nozzle is pressed into the sprue hole of the mold with ladle and mold horizontal; then the two are rotated 90° to the upright position together, permitting the lead to flow into the mold under the pressure of the molten metal remaining in the ladle. After a few seconds to permit the mold to fill fully, the two are rotated back toward the horizontal and the ladle is rolled clear and replaced in the lead. Always wear gloves; they were left out here deliberately to avoid cluttering up the photos.

Many people prefer the bottom-pour electric pot for its greater convenience. The mold is simply held beneath the spout and the valve handle lifted to permit lead to flow into the sprue hole. Some molds will perform better if the spout is seated firmly in the sprue hole, others will react like this one and perform best if the metal is allowed to run free with the mold held below the spout.

After the lead in the sprue has solidified, the sprue cutter or sprue plate is struck forward with a nonmetallic instrument to shear off excess lead.

When the sprue assumes this frosty, crystalline appearance, it has become completely solid, and the sprue cutter may be knocked around.

Put the ladle back in the pot, give the mold just a few seconds for the lead in it to solidify, then knock the sprue plate around, open the blocks, and the bullet should fall out. You should have a pad of folded cloth for the bullet to fall on, because it is still soft and relatively fragile and will be deformed if it strikes a solid surface. That first bullet will probably be lousy, especially if the mold wasn't up to temperature. If the mold or the lead is too cold you'll have a wrinkled mass only vaguely resembling a bullet, so try again. Swing the sprue plate back into position, and repeat the entire process. Be sure the ladle is full of lead so that its weight will help force it into all the sharp corners of the mold cavity. You may have to cast several of these misshapen slugs until the mold becomes warm enough for lead to remain molten in the sprue after the ladle is removed. The molten metal and ladle should both be warm enough that a small puddle of molten metal remains in the sprue after you take away the ladle, then takes a few seconds to solidify. If you watch it, you'll see its color and texture change as it solidifies. Molten, it will be silvery bright and glassy smooth, then suddenly you'll see the surface become frosty and crystalline and you'll know it has become hard or "frozen." As soon as the sprue is hard, strike the sprue plate over and open the mold. If the bullet doesn't fall out freely, rap slightly on the hinge point of the mold handles and it will probably fall free. If it doesn't, rap on the handle up front where the block is pinned to it, on the side in which the bullet is sticking. Unless the mold is defective, this will almost invariably cause the bullet to fall free.

Once you've cast a dozen or so bullets that look reasonably correct, look them over closely. Are the driving bands filled out clean and crisp, with sharp edges corresponding to the inner surface of the mold? Is the base in particular clean and sharp all around? Is there a small hole or ragged depression in the base where the sprue was sheared away? Are there wrinkles or depressions on the bullet's surface?

If the bullet isn't filled out sharply, the mold and/or the metal may still be too cool; if casting a few more bullets to warm up the mold doesn't do the job, increase the heat of the lead. Adding a bit more flux might help as well. If there are wrinkles, there may still be traces of oil in the cavities, or this too may be due to the lead or mold being too cold. If the base isn't perfect, check the underside of the sprue for oil or grease, try filling the ladle fuller, and leave the ladle in the vertical position a bit longer to apply more pressure to the molten lead. If there is an irregular hole in the base of the bullet, you aren't leaving enough molten metal in the sprue to compensate for shrinkage as the body of the bullet hardens. If the base is ragged and

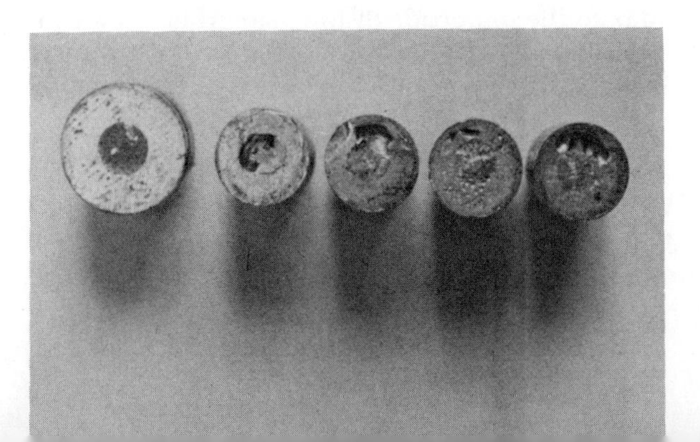

Bullet at left shows a perfect base, while the remaining four all show voids in the base which throw them off balance and will cause inaccuracy. This particular type of void is caused by trapped air or excessive lubricant on the underside of the sprue plate.

Two 9mm bullets cast from the same mold. The one on the right has a perfect base, while the one on the left has a rounded base because of insufficient lead in the mold and perhaps some trapped air as well.

rough where the sprue is cut off, the inner edges of the sprue hole may be dull or burred, or the sprue plate may be loose on the blocks. Its pivot screw should be turned in just tight enough that the plate may be moved easily with the fingers. By correcting these little problems and by gaining experience, you should soon be dropping bullets that are at least externally perfect.

As you progress, particularly if you cast rapidly, you may find the surface of the bullet changing from smooth and glossy to a frosted, crystalline look. This normally indicates that the mold is getting too hot, but it may also indicate that the bullet metal is too hot. Slow down casting at first, and if the condition disappears, you'll know it was a problem of too much mold heat. If it doesn't go away, reduce the metal temperature a bit. Actually, this frosted appearance does no harm at all; frosted bullets shoot as well as shiny ones.

After a while, you may also notice that some of the bullets appear cracked or bent. This is the result of dropping the bullet from the mold too quickly. Even though the sprue has hardened, it may take another three or four seconds for the body of the bullet to harden sufficiently to drop from the mold without damage. This defect may also be due in part to the mold being too hot. This happens most often with large, heavy bullets.

You may suddenly discover that the sprue plate doesn't move easily, and upon looking at its underside, find that molten lead has adhered there (and perhaps to the top of the blocks as well) in thin smears. This is due partly to knocking the plate over before the sprue is completely hard, and also it will sometimes occur if the underside of the plate is not at least lightly lubricated. But *don't* use oil on it. Peel the lead off both the plate and the blocks with a razor blade, being very careful not to mar the surfaces. Then apply just a touch of beeswax to the underside of the plate while it's warm enough to melt the wax. Don't let any get down in the cavities, just a trace on the plate. Just a touch of mold release will often accomplish the same goal.

CORRECTING CASTING IMPERFECTIONS

Bullet casting is by no means a science, and often it will be necessary to juggle several variables in order to obtain perfect bullets. A bit more or less tin may enable you to obtain bullets that are filled out better. Raising or lowering the temperature may help (another place where that thermometer can be very useful). Raising or lowering the temperature of the mold by varying the speed of casting will sometimes help. In some instances, a different flux will produce better bullets. Even the manner in which you hold the mold can have an effect; squeezing the blocks too tightly together might trap air inside and prevent filling out, so try relaxing your grip a little, so long as the blocks don't separate and allow lead to escape. With bottom-draw electric pots, varying the distance between the spout and the sprue hole can make a difference. In fact, casting perfect bullets is pretty much an art, and if you don't get perfect bullets after satisfying the basic requirements we mentioned earier, it's just a question of shifting one or more of those variables around untill everything comes together. Two molds for the same bullet from the same manufacturer and apparently identical may react quite differently to a given set of casting conditions. One may produce perfect bullets with ridiculous ease, while the other will require juggling a half-dozen variables and coddling like a newborn babe if top-quality bullets are to be produced.

Sooner or later, you'll look down into that pile of freshly cast bullets and notice one with fins sticking out around it. If those fins are simply thin slivers of lead that have flowed out into the vent grooves on the mating faces of the mold blocks, they won't cause any problem. You can either brush them off, or they'll be wiped off when the bullet is sized. However, if the fins are solid, no matter how thin, it means that the mold blocks were held apart for one reason or another and that the bullet is substantially egg-shaped. It *can* be trued up by sizing, but may then be off-balance. Often a small fragment of lead will get between the blocks and prevent them from being closed completely, thus causing these fins to develop. Another cause is that you don't hold the handles tightly enough, and there is a tiny gap between the blocks and the lead flows into it. Any lead (or other foreign material, for that matter) which gets on the faces of the blocks will cause fins, and should be removed immediately. When the fins are only from the vent grooves, it follows that you have a casting alloy/flux/temperature combination that flows extremely well, and it will normally produce perfect bullets with ease. Once you encounter this, it's worth some time and effort to determine exactly what the combination is and record it for fu-

Light-colored smears on top of the mold blocks are traces of molten lead resulting from knocking the sprue cutter around before the sprue and base of the bullet have completely hardened.

Lightweight 9mm bullets containing fins caused by tiny fragments of lead on the surface of one of the blocks, holding the blocks very slightly apart.

ture use. After all is said and done, the secret of perfect bullets is an alloy and related conditions such that the lead flows very freely and fills even the tiniest nook and cranny in the mold cavity. Incidentally, when all else fails, sometimes the addition of a very small amount of finely powdered arsenic will solve the problem by reducing surface tension on the lead so that it fills the mold better.

However, bullets that simply *look* perfect aren't necessarily so. They often contain voids, sometimes called air holes or air pockets, resulting from air trapped as the lead splashes around upon entering the cavity. There may also be a void near the base, caused by shrinkage, but not visible from the outside. If the metal isn't well mixed and fluxed and skimmed, there may also be small bits of foreign material suspended in it, and these can wind up inside a bullet, having the same effect as a void. This is especially likely to occur if you're using dirty, greasy wheel weights and melting them down for casting directly, rather than processing them ahead of time as already described.

Regardless of the cause, any void or foreign material inside the bullet will throw it off balance. This means simply that the bullet's center of gravity will not coincide with its center of form or mechanical centerline, and thus it will travel in a spiral after it leaves the muzzle. Obviously, this isn't going to help its accuracy.

Since voids are not visible and the average handloader certainly doesn't have access to industrial X-ray equipment, the only way they can be detected is by weighing bullets. Naturally, it would be highly impractical to weigh every perfect-looking bullet that you cast. However, in the learning process, it's a good idea to weigh, say, 10 percent of each batch. Once you've gained experience and refined your technique so that great weight variations don't show up, you'll know that you aren't producing voids very often—if at all—and you can forget about weighing bullets routinely. Instead, just weigh them whenever you have a particular use for which you want the bullets as perfect as possible. When doing that—perhaps selecting bullets to use in a match—it's a good idea to select for uniform weight as well. They need not be exactly uniform, but discard those at the top and bottom of the scale. Don't throw away those that are off in weight; just reserve them for less demanding uses like plinking.

While we are on the subject of weight and the voids which affect it, it's a

This bullet was cast with the mold blocks slightly out of alignment, but the defect was not noticed until after sizing and lubricating. After passing through the sizing die, the obvious difference in width of lubricating grooves shows that the bullet halves are out of register; the bullet is badly out of balance and will not shoot accurately.

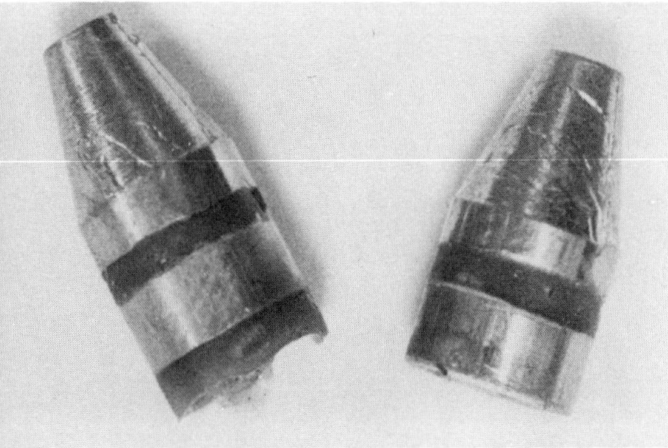

The 9mm bullet at right has a perfect base and was run through the sizing die correctly. The one at left has a slightly rounded base, and was not forced all the way into the die and held there firmly while the lubricant screw was advanced. Consequently, a thick layer of lubricant was forced between the base of the bullet and the top of the base punch. Very messy.

This 9mm bullet was tipped slightly to the left as it was forced into the die. Consequently, the nose is no longer aligned with the bearing surface and its accuracy will be reduced.

good time to compare home-cast and factory-swaged lead bullets. As mentioned in a previous chapter, factory lead bullets are swaged from sections of lead wire under great pressure. The lead slugs are cut just a wee bit heavier than the finished bullet is intended to be, then pressure placed upon them in the die forces the excess out through a bleed hole. This brings the bullets to more consistent weight than can normally be achieved by casting, and the tremendous pressure involved eliminates any voids that there might be in the wire. Thus, generally speaking, swaged lead bullets

A conventional cast bullet at left, compared with the new Hornady swaged bullet of the same type and caliber, substituting knurling for lubricant grooves. Formed under tremendous pressure, the swaged bullet simply can't contain unseen voids as may be found in perfect-looking cast bullets.

are more uniform in weight and density than those you might cast yourself. Only the most expert bullet casters, with many years experience, can cast bullets that will be as uniform as the swaged variety.

CASTING HOLLOW-POINTS

For hunting or defense, it may be desirable to cast hollow-point bullets. A hollow-point mold is the same as any other except that a hole is drilled into the nose of the cavity centered on the meeting line of the blocks. Then a hardened steel rod is made to fit this hole closely, with its end shaped to form the cavity desired. A lug is formed on the rod, and a screw is set into one of the blocks. The rod is thrust into this hole with the blocks closed, then rotated so the lug goes under the head of the screw, and thus holds this "nose pin" in place. Casting is then conducted in the normal manner, except that before the blocks are opened, the nose pin must be rotated and withdrawn. The insertion and removal of the pin makes casting hollow-points rather slow, but otherwise doesn't present any problem. Hollow-base bullets are cast in essentially the same manner, but it is often difficult to produce fully filled and formed bases. The base cavity is quite large in respect to bullet diameter, leaving only a relatively thin wall of lead at the base. It is difficult to get this thin wall to fill out fully; it may require a lot of juggling of temperature, flux, alloy, and casting techniques. Actually, with the single exception of Minié bullets for muzzleloaders, there is little reason for using the hollow-base type. In my opinion, they simply aren't worth the trouble of casting them. If you feel you do need hollow-base wadcutter bullets for target ammunition, it's simpler and more convenient to simply buy the superior factory-swaged variety.

LUBRICATION AND SIZING

Once cast, bullets always require lubrication, and usually sizing. Generally, the two operations are performed simultaneously in a "lubricator-sizer."

A mold for hollow-base bullets; molds for hollow-point bullets are similar. The pin which forms the cavity fits in a groove between the blocks, and a pin on its shaft engages under a screw head in one of the blocks to hold it in place during casting.

Essentially this tool forces the bullet into a cylindrical die of the proper diameter, containing holes which permit the passage of lubricant that is carried in a reservoir under heavy spring pressure. A base punch fills the die when the tool is not in use and keeps lubricant from squirting out, though the spring pressure should be relaxed when the tool is not in use. A bullet is placed base-first in the die and forced into it by a nose punch shaped to fit the point of the bullet, and the die brings the bullet to size (diameter) and roundness. As the lubricating grooves in the bullet pass the holes in the die, grease squirts in to fill them. Then, on the reverse stroke of the handle, the base punch ejects the bullet out the top of the die, and everything is ready for the next bullet. Lyman, SAECO, RCBS, and Star all offer lubricator-sizers. The Star differs in that bullets are pushed straight through the die and fall out the bottom. This is a far faster method of processing bullets, but the tool is also substantially more costly. The other three all do an excellent if slower job and for less money.

Alternatively, bullets can be lubricated without sizing by simply standing them on their bases in a shallow pan of melted lubricant deep enough to cover the uppermost lubricating groove. The lubricant is then allowed to harden, and the bullets are removed with a gadget called a "cake cutter." This is generally nothing more than a cartridge case of the same caliber with its head cut off. Its mouth is pressed down over the bullet, separating it from the lubricant but leaving the grooves filled. The cake cutter is pressed down over bullets in succession; each new bullet ejects the previous one from the top. You can buy a cake cutter for a few bucks, but a cut-off cartridge case works just as well. After being thus lubricated, bullets may be sized by forcing them through a hole of the proper size in almost any piece

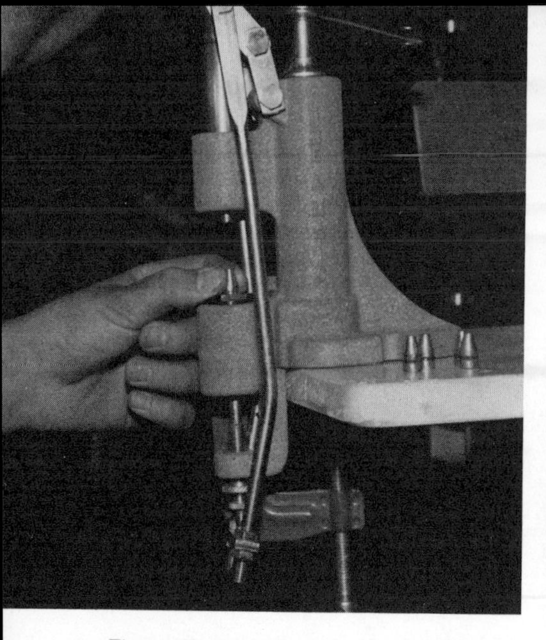

The cast bullet is placed in the mouth of the die, with the lubricator-sizer handle up, and aligned as vertically as possible. Completed bullets are shown at right.

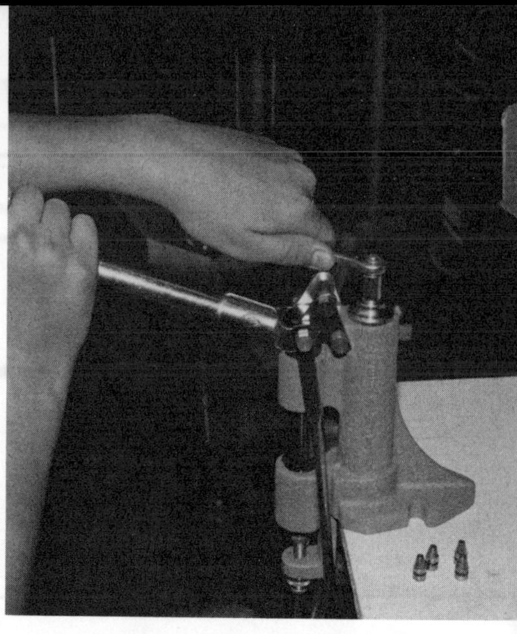

The bullet is forced into the sizing die by pulling the handle down, then held there while the ratchet wrench on top of the lubricant reservoir is advanced a tiny fraction of a turn to force lubricant through holes in the die into the bullet grooves.

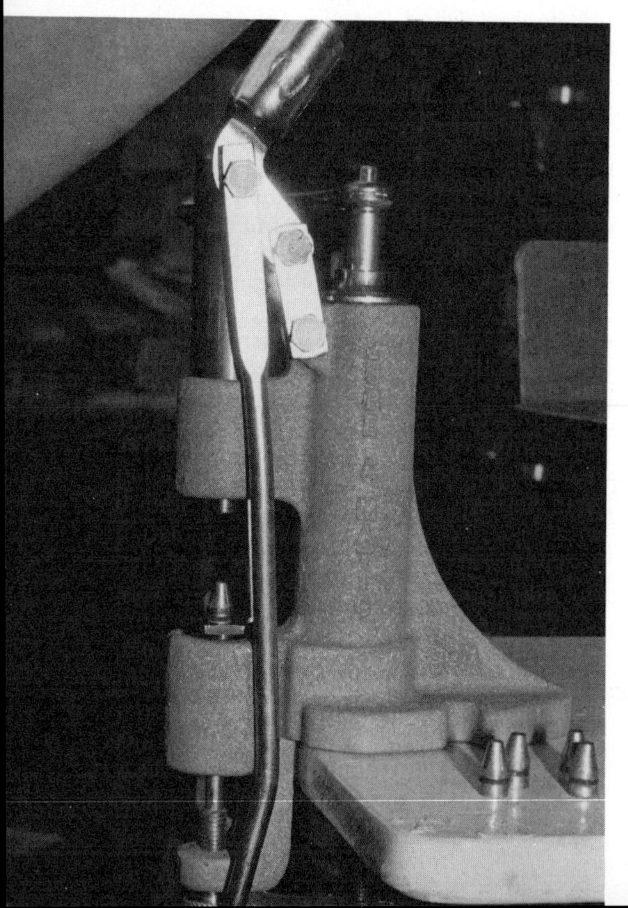

The handle is then elevated, and the base punch inside the die forces the bullet back up out the die, ready for seating.

of metal. The cheapest sizing die available is the Lyman "310 Tool Sizing Die." It may be used in the Lyman tong tool, the Lyman "Tru-Line Jr." loading press, or any loading press with a $^{7}/_{8}$-14 adapter. Actually, in the beginning, a cake cutter and the Lyman die in your loading press will be entirely adequate, and will avoid the necessity for spending $45 or $50 for a lubricator-sizer.

Regardless of the sizing method used, bullets should always be pressed into a die base-first, and by a punch that fits the nose very closely. A poor-fitting nose punch will deform the bullet, and if it is pressed through the die nose-first, irregular fins are formed on the base, and these are deleterious to accuracy.

GAS CHECKS

Gas checks are not as widely used on cast bullets today as they once were. A gas check is simply a shallow copper cup (sometimes brass) pressed on the base of a lead bullet to insulate it from the heat of the powder gases and also to prevent leading. The bullet must be designed for use with a gas check, containing a reduced-diameter section right at the base which will fit inside the cup, since the cup must be of finished-bullet diameter. Most lubricator-sizes (except the Star) allow placing the gas check on the base punch in the sizing die, then the bullet is started in by the check hand, and seated in the course of being forced into the die. Alternatively, and when another sizing method is being used, the gas check can simply be placed over the base of the bullet and fully seated by tapping it into place with a dowel. In any event, the gas check goes on the bullet *before* sizing in order that the slightly tapered edges of the cup will be forced inward and the check sized at the same time.

Actually, I see no need at all for gas checks in handgun bullets, if the bullet is cast of a sufficiently hard alloy, properly lubricated, and sized correctly. They do serve a useful purpose, though, in rifle bullets driven at higher velocities.

JACKETED BULLETS

You may also "swage" jacketed bullets at home with a relatively small investment. Half-jacket or three-quarter-jacket handgun bullets are made quite easily in low-cost dies fitted to your loading press. This is one reason for thinking carefully about the press you buy initially; a heavy-duty press with compound leverage will swage bullets much more easily than the typical plain-leverage C-type press. Principal suppliers of low-cost dies for this type of bullet are C-H, LLF, Forster, and Corbin. The job is done exactly as the factory would assemble a jacketed bullet, first placing an undersize lead core of the proper weight in a slightly undersize copper jacket cup, then forcing the two into a die which expands the core to fill the jacket and the entire assembly to fill the die. When fully formed, the bullet is ejected by a rod or pin in the die. This ejector pin may also be shaped to form a hollow point, and the base punch may be shaped to form a hollow base. The same type of dies may be used to form similar bullets for use in rifles, but they

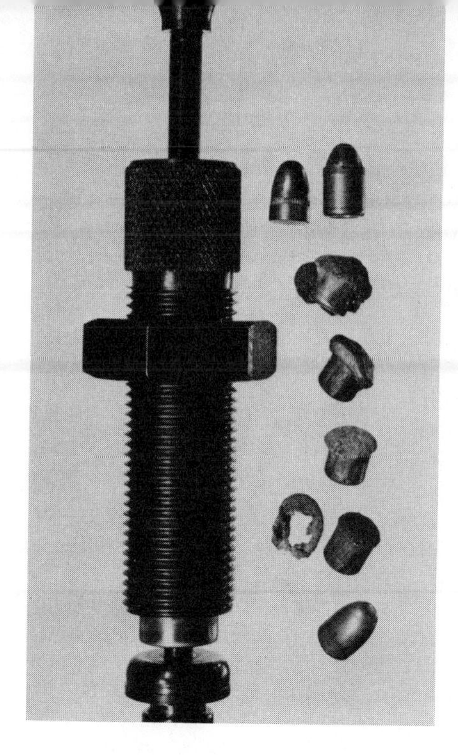

This simple bullet-swaging die set by Corbin is of the least complex design. The die body screws into a conventional loading press, and the bottom punch slips into the press ram. The plunger protruding from the top is a combination punch and ejector rod. Recovered bullets at right show the type of expansion that can be obtained from home-swaged bullets made in simple dies of this sort.

These are more complex Corbin dies used for producing jacketed rifle bullets in a conventional loading press.

are generally suitable only for low to medium velocities because of their light construction.

Whether used in rifles or handguns, the half-jacket bullet is notorious for leading bores. A portion of the core is exposed ahead of the jacket, and it contacts the bore; not being lubricated, lead rubs off on the bore. In addition to that, when driven at very high velocities, the forward portion of the bullet upsets to increase the mount of core in contact with the bore. As a result, I don't recommend the use of half-jacket bullets, even though many people do, and they are the cheapest and simplest type you can make. You'll be far better satisfied if you make three-quarter-jacket bullets whose jacket extends far enough forward to prevent any core contact with the bore.

In addition to the swaging dies, you'll need a supply of jackets, an adjustable core cutter or core mold, and a supply of lead. Lead wire is the most convenient to use, and it must be cut to length in a core cutter. However, wire is expensive, and it is more economical to cast cores in an adjustable mold.

The die and ram are installed in your press in accordance with the manufacturer's instructions, then a core is inserted in the jacket, and the two are placed in the mouth of the die. Then the ram is run up, carrying the assembly into the die. Compression between the punch and die expands the core in the jacket and the entire assembly in the die, producing the correct diameter. The nose of the die, or in some types a separate nose punch, controls the form of the bullet point. When the operations are performed smoothly and uniformly, surprisingly consistent bullets can be produced. Actually, the procedure just described applies primarily to the half-jacket type of bullet, and core-seating and expanding operations may be required with the three-quarter-jacket type, depending upon the particular make and type of dies you are using. The manufacturer's instructions are specific for each make and model, and I can't really cover them all here.

The swaging of conventional jacketed expanding bullets for use in rifles at high velocities involves essentially the same operations, but thicker, heavier, and longer jackets are employed. In addition, it is often necessary for the lead core to be swaged to near-final shape and weight as a separate operation before being placed in the jacket. Then, some dies also require that the core be seated and expanded to a tight fit in the jacket as another separate operation before the bullet is brought to final form in the finish die. With experience, proper techniques, and first-class dies and materials, exceptionally good bullets can be produced in this fashion. As a matter of fact, many bench-rest shooters make their own bullets and achieve remarkable accuracy, almost one-hole groups at 100 and 200 yards. However, the bench-resters employ additional operations and degrees of finesse that make the process very lengthy. Probably the most practical tool for making swaged rifle-caliber bullets for hunting and other ordinary use is the "Mity-Mite" made by Corbin. This is a self-contained tool and does not employ a conventional loading press as its base. It is not a particularly cheap tool, and unless you plan to make a good many bullets it's hard to justify its cost.

While much has been written on the subject of swaging jacketed bullets, Corbin has recently published an excellent and well-illustrated *Bullet Swage*

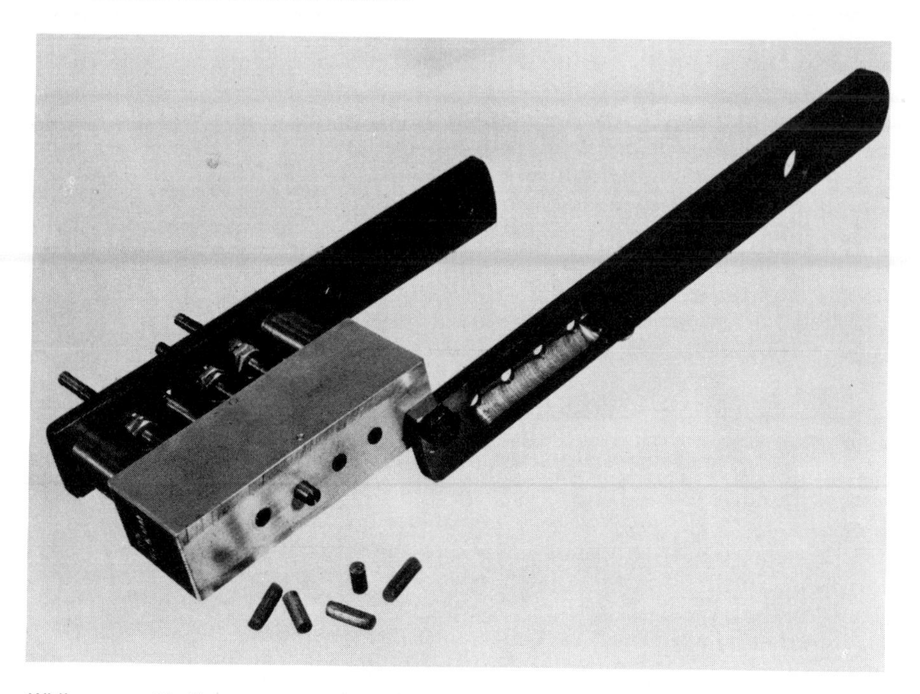

While swaged bullets are generally made with cores cut from expensive lead wire, an adjustable core mold such as this example from Corbin allows casting the cores much more economically.

Manual. Anyone contemplating swaging any type of bullet will probably save himself a good deal of frustration, and perhaps grief, by investing a few dollars in this book and studying it before buying equipment or even attempting to make that first bullet.

Swaged jacketed bullets offer nowhere near the degree of economy that can be had with cast lead bullets. It is not practical to make your own jackets, so they must be purchased commercially, and their cost alone will substantially exceed materials cost for a lead bullet. Then, too, some bullet designs and some die types require the use of expensive lead wire, and so the cost increases. Even so, one can make, for example, a 180-grain .30 caliber JSP rifle bullet for one-half to two-thirds what it will cost across the counter as a factory product. If your labor is considered as a cost, home-swaged bullets of this type are no bargain. However, most of us have more time than money, so that really isn't a significant factor.

In any event, making your own bullets can be not only profitable, but a source of pleasure in and of itself. I suspect that a good many people cast or swage bullets more for pleasure than for economy. And in either case, making you own will broaden your shooting horizons and increase your knowledge of just how firearms work.

9

Pressure

MANY HANDLOADERS, even those of long experience, think of "pressure" as a somewhat evil entity which is going to sneak up and stab them in the back someday. In a firearm, pressure alone is not dangerous; in fact, without pressure, and lots of it, a firearm could not function. High pressures within the chamber and barrel are an absolutely essential part of firearm's operation. The entire firearm, whether it be shotgun, rifle, or handgun, is designed specifically to take advantage of pressure and to utilize it to perform the function of hurling a missile toward some distant object. Pressure and heat go hand in hand, one hardly ever existing without the other, at least in a relative sense, and so in effect the gun is actually a "heat engine."

Let's compare your automobile engine, which is also a heat engine of a different type, to a firearm, and perhaps some of the witch's tales about pressure can be cleared up. In your auto engine, a tube closed at one end forms the cylinder, and a block of metal fitting closely within that tube forms the piston. With the piston at the top of its stroke, near the closed end of the cylinder, a fuel-air mixture (gasoline being the fuel) is ignited and burns, producing a large volume of high-temperature gas at high pressure. This gas attempts to expand in all directions in typical fluid behavior, and since the piston is movable, it thrusts the piston toward the open end of the cylinder. The piston is not free to be pushed out of the cylinder completely, and another means is provided for exhausting those hot gases, after which the piston returns to its original position, and eventually another charge of fuel and air is burned to repeat the process.

That's not much of an explanation of how an automotive engine works, except as necessary to correlate it with the function of a firearm. In a firearm, we have a long tube (barrel) closed at one end, and this compares to the cylinder of the auto engine. In that tube we have the projectile (bullet) near the closed end of the tube, trapping there a fuel mixture (the powder), which contains its own oxygen (air). At this point, the only difference between the auto engine and the firearm is that the fuel is solid while that in the auto is liquid; and that the fuel in the firearm contains its own oxygen while the auto engine draws its oxygen from the atmosphere in the form of air. In the firearm, then, the fuel is ignited (by the primer) and burns very rapidly (more so than a gasoline/air mixture) and generates a great volume of high-temperature (sometimes as high as 3,500°) and high-pressure gas (as high as 50,000 CUP), which expands rapidly and seeks to escape through the path of least resistance. That least-resistant path is by forcing the bullet down the barrel.

Up to this point, our firearm heat engine has functioned in exactly the same fashion as the automobile heat engine. At this point, they part company, because the automobile piston cannot escape, while the bullet in the firearm is free to be forced completely out the barrel. The auto piston returns to its original position and a new charge of fuel and air is burned to again force it the length of the cylinder. In the firearm, the bullet/piston is lost forever as it travels away from the gun, and thus it becomes a single-cylinder expendable-piston heat engine. In the automobile, the piston performs work by transmitting its own linear motion to rotary motion through a connecting rod and crankshaft and eventually to the wheels to move the auto through appropriate gearing and other devices. The piston in the firearm performs its work by traveling far beyond the confines of the barrel and striking a distant object and transmitting considerable energy to that object. Thus in both cases, we burn a fuel/air mixture inside a closed tube behind a piston, driving that piston down the tube to accomplish work.

Thus, we can see that pressure—pressure produced by burning fuel and air—is essential to the functioning of a firearm just as it is to the automobile engine. If the gas pressure inside the cylinder of an automobile engine becomes excessive, something breaks and the engine is damaged. In the firearm, if the gas pressure produced by the burning fuel/oxygen mixture becomes excessive, something breaks and the high-pressure gas escapes into the mechanism to cause damage.

So, it should be quite obvious that pressure is essential to the function of both heat engines, and that both will fail if that pressure becomes excessive. The handloader should, therefore, consider pressure as an essential and desirable element of the firearm's system, and should realize that it poses no threat whatever as long as he takes necessary measures to keep it within the strength limitations of the firearm.

PRESSURE LIMITS

So, now, let's look at the gun itself and find out just how it resists chamber pressure and why there are different limits in different guns beyond which we cannot go safely. The barrel, receiver, and bolt of a rifle can be made of steel sufficiently thick and strong to withstand pressures several times as great as can be tolerated in a typical firearm. Those components are not the major limiting factor in the gun's ability to withstand pressure. Modern firearms, with the exception of shotguns and some military arms, utilize a self-contained metallic cartridge whose case or envelope is made of brass. The case contains the bullet, propellant powder, and primer. The case is given the job of sealing the breech against the pressures generated when the propellant burns. It is the cork in the bottle, so to speak, and plugs the gap between the bolt and the open rear of the barrel. Even the best cartridge brass is quite ductile, relatively soft and weak. There are gaps in the breech mechanism, necessary to feed cartridges, for the functioning of extractors and ejectors, and because of manufacturing tolerances; and this *weak* brass plug closes those gaps. When chamber pressure exceeds the strength of the brass, the limit of the entire mechanism has been reached, in spite of the fact that the strength limit of the steel components might not even be closely approached. The result is that the brass ruptures into and through the unsupported areas, releasing high-velocity jets of very hot gases. Gas in motion is capable of doing far greater damage than when simply developing static pressure, as inside the closed chamber. These jets of gas rip off extractors, split stocks, bulge or rupture the thinner steel sections, and melt both brass and steel in their path. Once released, gas will find its way back through all the crevices and openings in the action, and unless the design prevents it, some of that gas—carrying incandescent particles of metal—will strike the shooter in the face.

The cartridge case is the weakest link in the chain, and when it lets go, the chain is broken, and everything comes all unglued. Rifles, which are very carefully designed and made and fitted up tightly, may stand pressures approaching 100,000 CUP with brass cartridge cases. With closely fitted *steel* cases of greater strength, such actions have experimentally withstood far greater pressures. Shotguns, because of their weaker plastic or paper cases and lighter and weaker construction, may let go at pressures of 20–25,000 CUP. In handguns, there is a greater spread in the excessive pressure range, with some of the simpler blowback autoloading pistol designs letting go at as little as 20–25,000 CUP, while locked-breech designs like the Browning High-Power withstand pressures up to 75–80,000 CUP. Some revolvers in circulation in the larger calibers may let go at 25,000 CUP, while others operate normally at 40,000 CUP, and will withstand a great deal more before failing.

In any event, though, with the exception of some revolvers where the very thin chamber walls rupture first, failures from excessive pressures are generally due to plastic deformation of the case in or near the head. At very high pressures, the brass begins to flow, just as will a ball of clay when squeezed. As it begins to flow, it oozes out into the gaps in the breech, with gas pressure accelerating the flow, and eventually breaking through. As the brass gives way, the gas escapes also, and at high velocity literally melts away the brass that is in its path.

Some gun designs yield more to chamber pressure than others, and this yielding encourages case failure by opening up the spaces into which the case may rupture. The Colt .45 Auto pistol is a classic example, with the feed ramp cutting away a portion of the chamber wall and leaving the case unsupported there. In rifles, the Springfield M1903 is another classic example; the rear portion of the barrel is funneled to facilitate feeding, thus reducing case support. Some lever-action rifles, locking at the rear of a long bolt, stretch a bit under load and thus make it easier for the case to fail.

DETERMINING MAXIMUM PRESSURE

Theoretically it might be possible to predict the pressure at which a particular gun and cartridge case will fail, but there are so many variables that such computation is not a practical reality. It is for this reason that it is impossible to answer such questions as "What is the maximum pressure I can load to in my Mauser rifle?" We just can't answer that for a specific gun, though Mauser rifles of good quality are ordinarily chambered for cartridges with working pressures in the 50,000 CUP range, and in Europe, those same rifles are generally proof-tested at over 70,000 CUP. A particular rifle and cartridge case might withstand 100,000 CUP, or it may very well come unglued while being proofed at 70,000 CUP. This is exactly the reason that ammunition for use in bolt-action sporting rifles of Mauser type is generally loaded in the 50,000 CUP range. We know that generally the gun will withstand greater pressures than that, but some individual rifles and cartridge cases will not. Establishing that 50,000 CUP working pressure gives us a safety cushion.

HOW PRESSURE DEVELOPS

Now, let's take a look at *how* pressure is developed inside the chamber and barrel of any firearm. Modern nitrocellulose propellant powders, whether they be single-base or double-base (the latter with nitroglycerin added), burn very slowly when unconfined. You can demonstrate this to your own satisfaction by simply pouring a teaspoon of propellant on the sidewalk and igniting it with a long taper from a safe distance. It will flare up in a brief, very hot flame, but there will be no explosion and no report, just a loud rushing noise. Unconfined, smokeless powder is simply a highly flammable solid, *not* an explosive. The reason it does not burn well unconfined is that the gases generated by its burning dissipate into the atmosphere almost as rapidly as they are formed.

When the same powder is confined in the chamber of a firearm, initial ignition of the primer produces a large volume of hot gas which we might say "pressurizes" the cartridge case at the same time it ignites that portion of the propellant charge next to the flash hole. The gas first given off by the primer and that given off by the first granules of powder to begin burning increase the pressure inside the chamber, and this in turn accelerates the rate of burning, which produces a larger volume of gas, thus increasing the pressure in the chamber, and further accelerating the burning of the propellant. Thus, for the very brief time during which the volume of the chamber remains constant, the propellant feeds upon itself and burns with ever-increasing rapidity, producing ever-increasing amounts of high-temperature gas. But this lasts only a very, very short period of time, because the increasing gas pressure forces the bullet from the case and into the barrel, increasing the volume of the chamber. This volume increase bleeds off some of the pressure being produced, as the gas expands into the barrel space behind the bullet. For a very short period of time after the bullet begins to move, pressure and gas volume continue to rise, but shortly the bullet has moved far enough down the barrel that gas expands into the space behind it at a rate greater than new gas is being generated. Also, this very hot gas is being cooled quite rapidly by the steel walls of the chamber and barrel, which act as a heat sink. Once gas is expanding into the space behind the bullet more rapidly than it is being generated by the burning propellant, pressure and temperature begin to drop very rapidly. In a high-power rifle barrel of about 24-inch length, gas pressure will have dropped well under 10,000 CUP by the time the bullet leaves the muzzle; and instantly thereafter, the gas remaining in the bore expands into the atmosphere and pressure drops to virtually zero.

The effect of all this is that the maximum chamber pressure is reached very shortly after the bullet begins to move, rising at a very steep angle, and then drops off less rapidly as the bullet leaves space into which the hot gases can expand. The rate of pressure decrease drops off as the bullet moves farther down the barrel, and approaches a fairly gentle slope by the time the bullet reaches the muzzle.

It is because combustion "feeds upon itself" that increasing the powder charge increases the maximum pressure, but the pressure increase is far greater in proportion than the increase in the amount of powder. Consequently a relatively small increase in powder charge of an already-heavy load may very well produce excessive pressures.

POWDERS

Essentially, all single-base propellant powders have approximately the same energy content. They become double-base powders with the addition of nitroglycerin in varying amounts, and while this increases the energy content somewhat, it also increases the heat of combustion. This means that we trade greater energy for greater heat, and the point of dimishing returns is reached very quickly. Whether single-base or double-base, the propellant is ignited by the primer and burns on the surface of the individual, cylindrical kernels. Most sporting propellants are perforated, so that the area for combustion is increased, and also so that as the outer surface burns away and decreases in area, the inner surface burns away and *increases* in area. Overall kernel size and perforation size are regulated in individual powders to produce the desired burning rate. Generally speaking, the smaller the individual kernels, the higher the burning rate. And the higher the burning rate, the higher the peak pressure and the quicker it will be reached, all other factors being equal. An exaggerated comparison in this respect may be made between Bullseye pistol powder in its very thin discs and IMR4350 powder with its much larger cylindrical kernels. Bullseye is formulated to burn very quickly and to be suitable for use in very small amounts in small-volume cases and short barrels to produce maximum velocities with light, large-diameter bullets of handgun type. Hardly more than a pinch of it will drive a 60-grain .32 caliber pistol bullet at 1,000 fps from a 3- or 4-inch barrel. On the other hand, nearly 60 grains of 4350 is required to drive a 180-grain bullet of approximately the same diameter at about 2,800 fps from a 24-inch barrel. If Bullseye were substituted for the 4350 in the latter example, it would burn so quickly and maximum pressure would be reached so rapidly that the gun would burst like a grenade before the bullet could be moved far enough down the bore to bleed off that excess pressure.

The general rule of thumb for selection of propellants is that small-kernel, fast-burning propellants are required for light bullets in short barrels, while slow-burning, large-kernel propellants are required for heavy bullets in long barrels. There are many, many powders available, suitable for cartridges from .25 ACP up through the heaviest magnums such as the .378 Weatherby. Since these powders come from a variety of makers, they cannot be rated precisely by burning rate except under laboratory conditions. Even if it were possible to do so, such a rating would be valid only within a very narrow application. Burning rate changes according to the application, and in a given caliber, the burning rate of a given powder will change with the bullet weight and type, and to a lesser degree with other factors. Thus, there is no single "best" powder for anything except a *single application.* It simply isn't possible to answer the questions often put forth by readers—"What is the best powder for loading my .270 Winchester?" There can be a most efficient powder for 150-grain bullets within a certain velocity range, but 100-grain bullets within a different velocity range may call for a different "best" powder.

PRESSURE AND VELOCITY

It is a popular misconception that the greater the chamber pressure the greater the velocity will be given the bullet. With powders reasonably efficient for the load, this is generally true. However, it is not the maximum or "peak" pressure that determines bullet velocity nearly as much as it is what ballisticians call "the area under the curve." The "curve" referred to is the time/pressure trace covering the time from primer ignition until the bullet exits the muzzle. The greater the area under the curve, the higher bullet velocity will be. One powder might produce a peak pressure of 50,000 CUP and a velocity of 2,800 fps; while another powder more efficient for that particular application may produce a peak pressure of only 45,000 CUP and a velocity of 2,900 fps. The second powder has more area under the curve, even though its peak pressure is less. Thus it is the total amount of pressure applied to the base of the bullet while it is in the barrel that determines velocity, not the maximum pressure produced at any point in time. The classic explanation of this is the "closing door" analogy. A sharp, hard blow against an open door will not necessarily close it, while a lesser impact applied over a longer period of time will close it easily. In the final analysis, the propellant which produces maximum velocity most efficiently will be the one with the greater area under the curve, not the one with the highest peak pressure.

VARIABLES THAT AFFECT PRESSURE

Though the choice of propellant has most to do with maximum pressures, pressure in general is affected by several other factors. Temperature, a factor completely outside the gun/ammunition combination, has a substantial effect. A powder charge which produces normal velocities and pressures at the standard testing temperature of 70° may not produce sufficient pressure to even function an autoloading action at temperatures below 0°; at temperatures above 70°, pressure will be above normal. There are several factors in the gun which affect pressures. An oversize bore will reduce pressure, an undersize bore will increase it. A tight chamber will increase pressure, a loose chamber will decrease it. A short throat (sometimes called "leade," the origin of the rifling) will increase pressure, while a longer one or "free boring" will decrease it. A weak firing-pin blow may decrease pressure, while an abnormally hard blow may increase it. A cartridge remaining in the chamber for a few minutes after a string of rapid fire which heats the barrel will have its propellant heated enough so that pressures will increase substantially.

In the ammunition, there are also many factors aside from the propellant that affect pressures. An oversize bullet will increase pressures, while an undersize one will reduce them. Variations in bullet-seating depth will alter pressures, but not necessarily predictably so, because of its relationship with the leade in the barrel, tight bullet/case assembly will increase pressure, while loose assembly will reduce it. A case with a thick head and walls will produce higher pressure than one with less brass in that area. Among bullets of the same weight, the one with the longer bearing surface will produce the higher pressure. A bullet with a thick, hard jacket and hardened core will produce higher pressure than one with a thin, soft jacket and soft core. Bullets have an especially strong effect on pressures, and laboratory tests conducted for the NRA a good many years ago show quite clearly that different makes and types of bullets of the same weight may cause as much as 10,000 CUP spread in average maximum pressure with an otherwise standard load. This is the principal reason that when choosing a load from a manual published by a bullet manufacturer, you should not attempt to use a bullet of a different make or type. In the extreme, substituting one 150-grain .30-06 bullet for another—with the same case, primer, and powder charge—may produce either an increase or decrease of up to 10,000 CUP in chamber pressure. With that 10,000 representing an *average* figure, the *peak* difference might well be 15,000 to 20,000 CUP. That much difference under some conditions is sufficient to convert a safe working load to a dangerous load.

I think we've dwelled long enough on the why and how of chamber pressures. Pressure is not dangerous in and of itself—in fact, it is absolutely essential to the functioning of any firearm. It is only when we permit excesses that any danger exists.

10

Lead-Bullet Loads for Rifles

THERE ARE SEVERAL CATEGORIES of loads for rifles which may be assembled with cast lead bullets. The lightest is the "ultralight" load discussed in Chapter 11, which, while it serves admirably for some purposes, is not sufficiently powerful or accurate for ordinary hunting or target work. The next step up the ladder is the so-called "light load," which can be made to perform quite well for hunting small game and for target shooting at ranges not generally exceeding 100 yards. Then we have what used to be called "midrange" loads, used mainly for practicing target shooting at 200 to 300 yards. Top of the line in lead-bullet loads is the full-charge loading employed in rifle calibers generally above .30, and in which the velocity of factory, jacketed-bullet loads is equaled or approached very closely with a lead bullet.

Ultralight and light loads are of practical value and may be assembled in virtually any caliber. Midrange loads have traditionally been more or less limited to those calibers used in organized rifle competition—.30-40, .30-06, .308/7.62mm, etc. Full-charge loads may be assembled as a practical matter in only a very limited number and range of calibers. Obviously, we aren't going to drive a lead bullet at over 4,000 feet per second to match the performance of the factory .220 Swift load; nor can we reach over 3,000 fps claimed by many other factory loads. However, by using the proper techniques and methods, we can drive cast bullets as fast as 2,500–2,700 fps in calibers from about .30 upward. This means that we can easily duplicate the performance of the ubiquitous .30-30 Winchester, the .30-40 Krag, some .30-06 loads, and the .45-70 and .458 Winchester.

Light loads will fall in the 1,500-fps range. Since velocity of factory loads varies a great deal among calibers, light loads would probably better be defined as those which produce less than half the standard factory-load velocity. Midrange loads would then be categorized as those which produce from half to three-quarters of that velocity, and full-charge loads those

Cast bullets weighing from 120 grains (left) to 175 grains in .308 Winchester caliber—a range to suit almost any use you might wish to make of this caliber, though top accuracy will probably be obtained more easily with the longest bullet because of its long bore-riding front section.

which produce virtually all of it.

But the first question to be answered is "Why bother with lead-bullet loads at all?" Economy is, of course, the most tangible reason. You can produce a full-charge lead-bullet load for 5 to 6 cents less than it would cost you to assemble the same load with a jacketed bullet. The saving is even greater in midrange and light loads. The second reason—and it exists entirely independent of economy—is that the ammunition factories simply do not offer any loadings producing less than full power in rifle cartridges. If you want to shoot a .30-06 rifle with ammunition producing less than the factory-standard 3,000 foot-pounds of energy, you are simply out of luck unless you or someone else handloads it.

In any event, the basic operations in producing the lead-bullet loads we'll

The handloaded .30-06 at left, with its lead bullet and minuscule charge of pistol powder, costs only a few cents to load, as opposed to the factory load at right with its costly jacketed bullet and large powder charge.

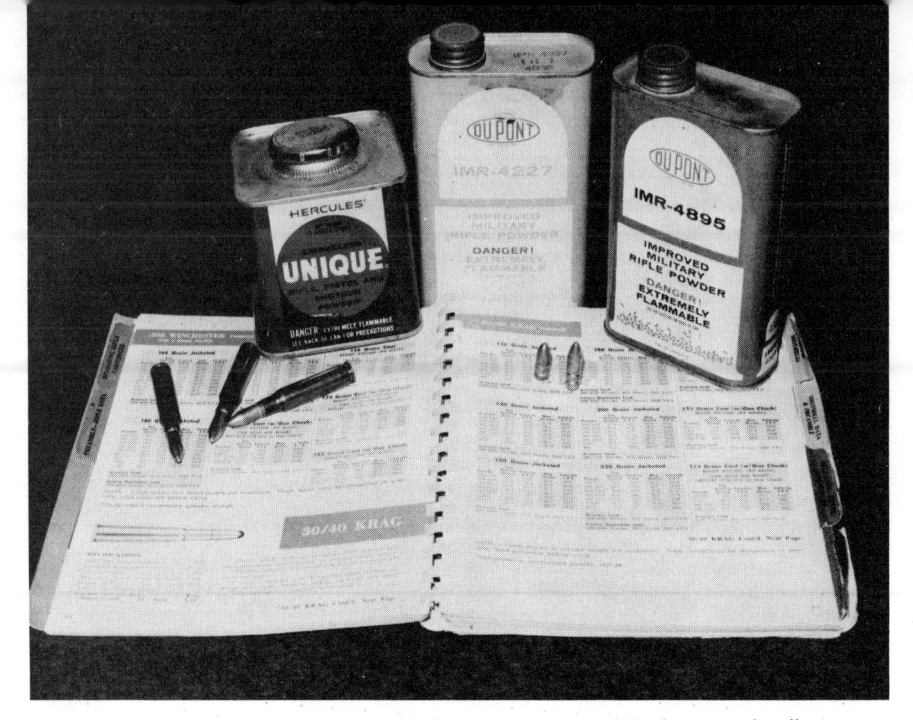

This assortment of powders, good cast bullets, and a copy of the Lyman reloading manual will allow you to assemble cast-bullet handloads economically that will cover a much broader use range than factory loads.

cover here are essentially the same as for jacketed-bullet full-charge loads. Cases must be thoroughly inspected, segregated, and cleaned and then resized. Chamfering of the case mouth is especially important with lead bullets. If this isn't done, the mouth will have a tendency to dig into the bullet and deform it unless it is excessively flared, and that reduces case life. Case-neck expansion differs because lead bullets are normally sized to a diameter greater than that of jacketed bullets. Traditionally, lead bullets have been sized to a diameter as much as .003 inch greater than barrel groove diameter. Many rifles produce best accuracy under these conditions, though some will do better with smaller bullets. The effect of this is that necks should be expanded to a larger diameter, and most die manufacturers can furnish the larger expander button when it is requested. In addition, lead bullets are softer, and if the neck is too much undersize, the bullet will be deformed in seating. A number of years ago Lyman introduced a unique two-diameter expander plug for use with lead bullets. Its lower portion, a bit longer than the case neck, is of the correct diameter to produce an adequately tight assembly of case and bullet; the upper portion is of just slightly greater diameter than the sized bullet. The two sections are joined by a polished bevel so that the case will not be deformed. This expander is forced into the neck until the enlarged portion has penetrated about $^{1}/_{16}$ to $^{3}/_{32}$ inch, then withdrawn. Consequently, neck expansion must be accomplished as a separate operation (as in handgun calibers) rather than simultaneously with resizing. The considerable advantage offered by this two-diameter form of neck expansion is that it allows the bullet to be started in the case by hand without excessive flare and further that it aids in accurately aligning the relatively long bullet with the case neck. This prevents tipping in the seating die, ensuring that the axis of the bullet when

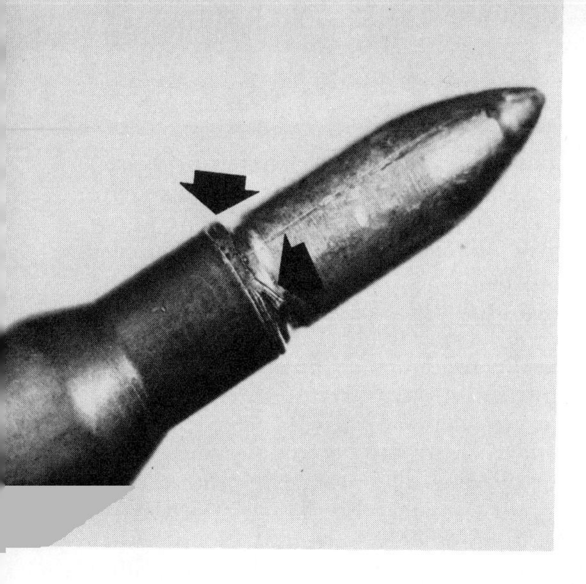

Failure to chamfer the case mouth properly or to expand or slightly flare it may very well result in lead being shaved from the bullet-bearing surface (arrow) and thus distort the bullet to the point where it may not give worthwhile accuracy.

seated is more likely to coincide with the axis of the case and chamber. Because of the superiority of this type of two-diameter expander plug for lead-bullet loads, it should always be used; the added time and effort it requires are quite justified. It should be used for all lead-bullet loads except those which do not require any resizing of the case.

CASE SIZING

Traditionally it has been recommended that with most lead-bullet loads the case should be neck-sized only. For the purist rifleman whose main concern is maximum accuracy (and I don't mean to imply that the rest aren't concerned with accuracy), this is quite satisfactory, especially in Mauser-type bolt-action rifles which can easily chamber snug-fitting cases. It is also quite practical for straight rimmed cases like the .45-70, but the greater the amount of case-body taper and the greater the degree of bottleneck, the

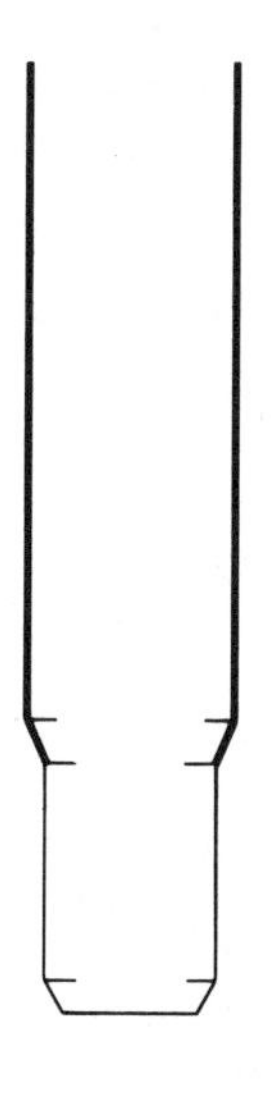

This two-diameter type expander plug (which must be used as a separate operation rather than combined with resizing) was introduced by Lyman a number of years ago and makes for much better lead-bullet loads. Its lower portion expands the neck so that it will be tight upon the bullet, while the upper portion opens up the case mouth sufficiently to permit easy starting of the bullet and to prevent shaving lead.

less practical it becomes. It also becomes less practical as chamber pressure rises and produces greater case expansion. So-called "springy" actions such as that of the Winchester M94 lever gun and some autoloaders will require full-length sizing with any midrange or full-charge cast-bullet load. Actually, there are many variables affecting whether or not your gun will function freely and easily with cases sized only at the neck. Personally, I prefer to resize full-length for everything except the very lightest loads. By doing so, I make certain that the cartridges can be used in any rifle of the appropriate caliber, and also that an aberrant round won't refuse to chamber or cause some other malfunction.

Quite a bit has been written about neck sizing and "partial resizing." The neck *alone* cannot be resized in an ordinary full-length sizing die; this is simply because forcing the full length of the neck into the neck portion of the die automatically means that the case body is also resized. Neither can necks be resized properly by running the case only partially into a full-length die. In fact, attempting to do this causes another problem. If the full-length die is backed out about 1/8 inch, as is fairly common practice for partial resizing, the rear 1/8 inch of the neck will not be resized. That probably isn't of great importance, but what happens to the shoulder of a bottleneck case is. Even though the case lacks 1/8 inch of entering the die fully, the major portion of the body will be reduced somewhat in diameter. That's fine, but this has the effect of moving the case shoulder *forward.* Think about that for a moment: As the diameter of the case body is reduced, the brass must move somewhere. The only direction in which it can move is forward in the shoulder area where it is *not* in contact with the shoulder of the die. Thus, the distance from the head to the shoulder of the case is increased. As long as this condition exists, the case will not chamber properly, even in the rifle in which it was originally fired. It will enter the chamber easily enough, but its shoulder will contact the chamber shoulder too soon, and the action won't close. *If* there is enough power available, the shoulder will be resized by the chamber, and the action will close; but it won't be easy.

You may ask why this doesn't happen in ordinary full-length resizing. The answer is simply that it does, but after the shoulder has moved forward from the initial reduction of the body, it is forced against the shoulder of the die, which shoves the brass back toward the head, and establishes the correct head-to-shoulder length.

Necks may be resized properly without dislocating the shoulder only when a pure neck-sizing die is used. A die of this type has the body portion of the cavity cut oversize, but with the shoulder of the die properly located and only the neck portion of the cavity small enough to produce any reduction of the case. This type of die is then adjusted in the press just like a full-length die, and when cases are run into it, it changes the dimensions of *only* the neck.

Purists have yet another objection to resizing full-length, and it applies to all types of bullets where the absolute maximum accuracy is to be obtained. It is that a case of less diameter than the chamber will invariably lie on the bottom of the chamber, and this results in the axis of the case neck and bullet being *below* the axis of the bore. Then, when the cartridge is fired, the bullet is forced to move upward a bit to align itself with the bore and may thus be slightly deformed and travel less accurately than if it were perfectly aligned. Bench-rest shooters have proved that this is at least technically true. However, in the average hunting rifle, I do not believe the difference in accuracy can be detected by any but the most expert shooters. Consequently, until you become an advanced handloader and a superb marksman, there are more advantages than disadvantages to full-length resizing for all but the lightest cast-bullet loads.

PRIMERS

Many suggestions will be found in other references concerning the use of pistol primers for cast-bullet loads in rifle calibers, but I have always obtained quite satisfactory results from rifle primers. On several occasions, I've experimented with both types in the same load, esspecially when using relatively large charges of pistol powders, and was unable to identify any provable and repeatable accuracy improvement with pistol primers. Since the primer pockets of rifle cases are designed specifically for rifle primers (with their thicker cups and slightly greater length) and rifle firing mechanisms are designed for optimum ignition with less-sensitive rifle primers, I am of the belief that one should use them unless he is able to prove conclusively that an improvement is gained with pistol primers. There is also the quite provable fact that at the pressures of full-charge loads pistol primers flow, extrude, flatten, and leak more easily than the rifle type because of their lighter and weaker construction. So, if you feel you must, go ahead and try pistol primers in the lighter loads, but *never* use them in full-charge loads or any loads known or suspected to produce pressures above about 40,000 CUP.

POWDERS

With the exception of full-charge loads, powders for use with lead bullets should generally be of substantially faster burning rate than those used with jacketed bullets. Even in the case of full-charge loads, powders a step or two faster in burning rate than those used with jacketed bullets are an excellent choice, because the lead bullet generates less resistance as it is forced into the rifling, and somewhat less friction as it moves down the bore. In this respect, we should point out that a jacketed bullet and a lead bullet, otherwise as similar as possible and driven at the same velocity under identical conditions, will differ measurably in the chamber pressure generated. Pressure will be less with the lead bullet.

Generally speaking, pistol or shotgun powders or very fast-burning rifle powders are best with light lead-bullet loads; midrange loads are served best by the faster-burning rifle powders; and full-charge loads require powders burning only slightly faster than comparable loads with jacketed bullets. In years gone by, there has been a considerable tendency to use large charges of very slow-burning powders such as 4831 with cast-bullet loads simply because this propellant was available quite cheaply as military surplus. One ardent shooter I know worked up loads in an 8mm Mauser rifle using a 190-grain gas-check bullet and a compressed charge of 4831 powder. He was delighted that this load performed rather well with a powder that he was able to stock up on at only a fraction of the price of commercial powders. The load produced excellent accuracy, and functioned the autoloading mechanism of his favorite rifle properly. Almost immediately, though, he encountered an unusual problem: Occasionally the fired case would be minus its neck and part or all of the shoulder. Close examination showed that the case was literally pulled apart at the point of separation, and that the missing portion was either blown out the barrel behind the bullet or stayed with the bullet. On one occasion, part of a bullet was recovered from a gravel backstop which showed some evidence that the case neck had stayed on the bullet during its passage through the bore; however, the evidence wasn't entirely conclusive. We conjectured that partly because of the bullet's light resistance, the forward portion of the powder charge was jammed into the neck and shoulder area of the case—like a wedge—by initially poor ignition of the base of the charge, and that initial combustion forced this portion of the charge into the bore, the abrasive powder granules generating enough friction on the inside of the case to drag it along, tearing it away from the case body. As mentioned elsewhere in this book, availability and/or low cost is a very poor reason for using a particular powder unless it is actually suitable for the load at hand. Generally speaking, light loads perform well with powders in the Hercules Unique–Hercules 2400 burning-rate range. Using a faster powder simply boosts pressures, and using a slower one simply requires a good deal more propellant. Full-charge loads are probably most efficient with powders whose burning rate is quite similar to IMR3031 and IMR4895. Midrange loads are handled well by powders such as 4198 and 4227.

When the powder charge occupies less than half the case volume, more consistent ignition and velocities will be produced if the charge is in the same position for every shot. It probably wouldn't make any difference whether this position is up against the case head, against the bullet, or spread evenly along the bottom of the case; however, the easiest *consistent* position to obtain is back against the case head next to the flash hole. Balls of Teflon fluff or kapok (see Chapter 11) serve this purpose very well, with Teflon being the lighest in weight, and therefore having the least effect upon chamber pressure. When used in ultralight loads, these balls of fluff hold the minute powder charge in place simply by friction against the walls of the case. However, with charges weighing up to 30 grains or so, that isn't sufficient, so the wad of fluff must be large enough and somewhat elongated so that it fills the balance of the case interior. With a little practice, you'll be able to pinch off enough of the fluff to do just that, and then roll it out into an elongated shape so that it can be forced through the neck and expand to fill that portion of the case above the powder charge. Of course, in straight cases like the .45-70 and .458, a card wad seated against the powder is simpler and easier. Nothing is to be gained by using this method when the powder charge occupies more than one-third to one-half the case; under those conditions, at least part of the charge will be plenty close to the primer to ensure consistent ignition.

For all but full-charge loads, powder charges may be *safely* measured out in a charge cup made from a cut-off cartridge case fitted with a handle. The

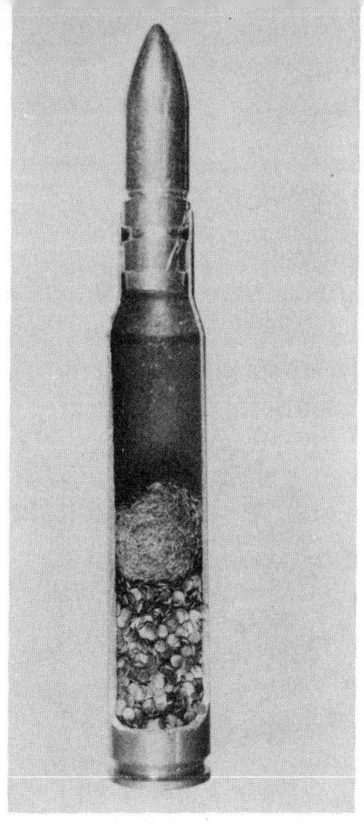

While by no means actually necessary (as some writers have indicated), use of a ball of kapok or Teflon fluff to hold small charges of powder at the rear of the case may well improve accuracy if you are a sharp enough marksman to detect it. As a practical matter, I don't use fluff, but quite a few shooters do. The powder shown here is Hercules Unique.

cup is made and used as described in Chapter 11. The amount of powder it holds must be verified by means of a good scale. Once a load has been chosen, from whatever data source, the charge cup should be cut and filed to hold just that amount of powder. However, the use of a charge cup is just an economy measure, and a good adjustable volumetric measure will usually give more consistent results. Such a measure, with charges properly verified on a good scale, must be used with full-charge loads. Remember that while moderate charge variations may be safe enough in the lower-level loads, really good accuracy cannot be expected unless powder charges are as uniform as possible. Don't use a charge cup simply because it's quick and easy if you have a good measure and scale available; use the best you have.

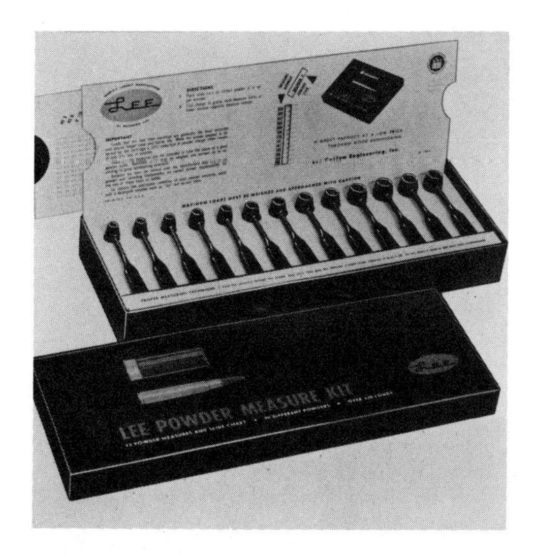

If you'd prefer to use charge cups and thus avoid the expense of a scale and/or powder measure, this graduated set from Lee is a worthwhile investment. It costs little and comes with a slide-rule device that is used to determine exactly how much of each powder each charge cup will hold.

BULLETS

Cast bullets that are less than perfect may shoot fairly well in ultralight rifle loads and in handguns. However, in rifle loads above that level, nothing less than the most perfect bullet you can produce will deliver good accuracy at the longer ranges. This requires meticulous care in casting, utilizing all the tips and gimmicks mentioned in Chapter 8, and careful sizing and lubrication. Bullet bases must be perfect and the entire bullet must be as concentric as you can make it. In sizing bullets, it is entirely possible to change accuracy from lousy to excellent. First of all, make certain that the sizing die you have is of the modern type where the "start" and "finish" diameter portions of the bore are joined by a smoothly polished taper. This type allows the bullet to be reduced concentrically, while the old style with a sharp transition might very well shear lead off one side, creating a serious imbalance.

Short bullets can be aligned with the die with ease, but long, heavy bullets are prone to tipping as they begin to enter the die, and if sizing is completed in this fashion, the bullet will be out of balance and thus deliver poor accuracy. Perfect sizing requires that the nose punch fit the bullet very closely, and that the punch be concentric with the die. Since the nose punch is normally carried in a movable member that is raised and lowered by a handle while the die is fixed in the base of the lubricator-sizer, any sloppiness between the two is likely to produce unbalanced bullets. If the punch and the member carrying it can be wobbled back and forth by hand, it obviously can't produce bullets that are sized concentrically.

Note also that the less a bullet must be reduced to proper diameter, the more likely it is to be concentric and properly balanced. If you must have a bullet of .310 inch diameter, ideally it should drop from the mold with a diameter of about .311 inch. If the bullet comes from the mold measuring .314 or .316 inch diameter, it is less likely to size perfectly.

Choice of bullet lubricant is also more important than many people believe. While many different makes and formulas are available, and

Here is an example of what can happen if a poor-fitting nose punch is used to seat lead bullets. Note the deformed ring around the bullet nose at the arrow; it would not be quite so prominent if this bullet had not been an especially tight fit in the case neck.

various references also contain instructions for making several types at home, extensive tests by the NRA over the years prove conclusively that those based on Alox are quite superior both in accuracy and in preventing barrel leading.

Many bullets intended for rifle use are of gas-check design. They have a reduced-diameter section at the base over which the copper or brass gas check fits. It is generally intended that the gas check simply be thumbed on the base of the bullet, and then seated home by the pressure of sizing. That doesn't always work, because any base irregularity is likely to prevent the check from seating perpendicular to the bullet axis. And if it is not perpendicular, accuracy will suffer just as if a plain-base bullet had an angular base. Examine the base carefully, and if there are raised irregularities left by the sprue cutter, either scrape them off with a sharp knife blade or toss that bullet back in the pot. Even then, better results are likely to be obtained if the gas check is tapped solidly into place before the bullet is sized. Once this is done, then sizing the bullet only crimps the gas check in place, though it's still a good idea to put a little extra pressure on the handle at the bottom of the stroke to ensure that the gas check hasn't tipped in passing through the die.

Assuming a perfectly cast and sized bullet, accuracy depends to a large degree upon that bullet entering the rifling concentrically. Consequently, bullets with a fairly long bore-diameter nose perform best under average conditions. Even though the chambered cartridge may lie so that the bullet is not perfectly aligned with the bore, this long nose portion will enter the bore and tend to align the bullet properly. A bullet of similar weight with a long radiused nose won't have the advantage of this pilot effect, and is less likely to enter the bore concentrically. A bullet of this type must be fairly long, and that means heavy. For this reason, light bullets are not consistently as accurate as the longer and heavier ones.

BULLET SEATING

Generally speaking, cast bullets will deliver best accuracy when they are just touching the beginning of the rifling, or no more than $^{1}/_{16}$ inch rearward of

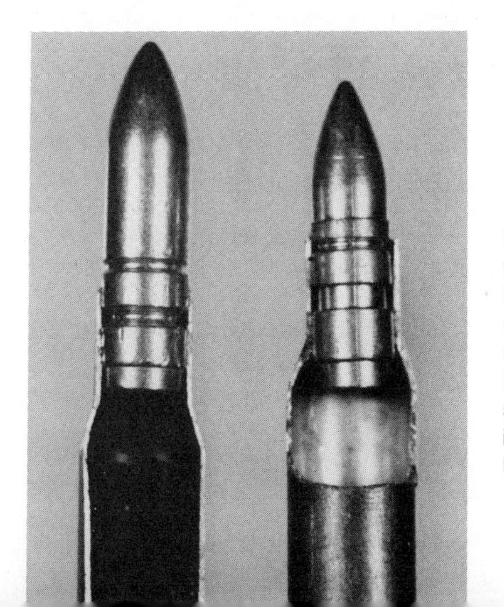

When gas checks are used, the probability of the check coming off the bullet from handling is far less if the base of the bullet does not protrude past the end of the neck as at left; as seen at right, if the bullet base moves into the enlarged area of the shoulder, the gas check is retained only by its grip upon the bullet, and thus it could be jarred loose.

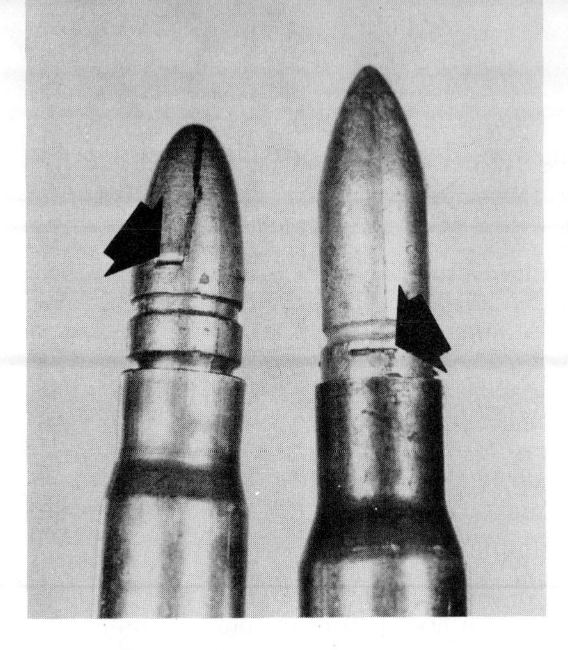

The .30 caliber bullet at left is full diameter until the ogive begins; therefore, note at the arrow that it runs into the rifling without any guidance except that given by the chamber and the case neck. On the right is a bullet with a bore-diameter pilot section ahead of the bearing surface. Note at the arrow that it contacts the rifling only at its bearing surface, after the front portion has entered the bore for a substantial distance. The latter provides improved guidance to the bullet and thus increases accuracy potential.

that point. Some bullet/barrel combinations will do their best when the bullet is actually pushed slightly into the rifling, the lands cutting into the surface of the bullet. The latter is usually impractical for field use, because if an unfired cartridge must be extracted at any time, the bullet may stick in the barrel, and the powder charge will foul the action as the case is pulled from it. Then the gun will have to be cleaned up, and the bullet will have to be knocked out with a cleaning rod. Bullets seated out to the rifling may make cartridges too long for magazine feeding, so you must single-load.

Since we can't see inside the chamber, a bit of care is necessary when first adjusting a seating die unless the bullet is known to not touch the rifling when seated to normal depth. To save trouble, it's best to make up a seating dummy right at first, just as described in Chapter 4. Seat a bullet shallowly in an unprimed and uncharged case, then drop it into the chamber and observe the position of the case head in comparison with an empty case. Seat the bullet progressively deeper until the case head approximates the position of an empty case. Then, *very gently* close the action on the dummy, feeling for any additional resistance caused by the bullet engaging the rifling. If none is felt, then seating depth is correct. If resistance is felt, extract the dummy and seat the bullet just a tiny bit deeper. Once this has been accomplished, adjust the seating die on the dummy cartridge, then identify and preserve the dummy for future use.

Incidentally, the case mouth should not be crimped on the bullet unless the cartridges are intended to be used in a tubular-magazine rifle. The one exception to this is those big-bore cartridges with considerable recoil that are intended to be run through the magazine. For example, a .458 Winchester rifle with full-charge lead-bullet loads will pound those bullets deeper in the case unless they are securely crimped in place. Though cases are traditionally crimped on lead bullets in conjunction with the seating operation, I prefer to seat first to the proper depth, and then readjust the die to form the crimp, just as described in Chapter 7 for loading for handguns. Unless the case mouth, die, and bullet are perfectly matched, simultaneous seating and crimping will result in lead being plowed up ahead of the case mouth.

LEAD ALLOYS

Bullets for velocities up to about 1,000 fps may be cast of almost any alloy, though some barrels will deliver better accuracy with a particular alloy or a harder bullet. Bullets for velocities on up to 2,000 fps should be of a $^1/_{10}$–$^1/_{15}$ alloy or the comparable Lyman #2 metal. Above 2,000 fps, best results will be obtained with a harder metal, and I have yet to find anything better than fresh linotype metal. Gas-checked linotype bullets in .30 caliber have been driven as fast as 2,700 fps with excellent accuracy and without any significant leading.

LOADING DATA

Since most loading manuals are published by bullet manufacturers, data for jacketed bullets is far more common than data for lead bullets. Consequently, the largest single source of up-to-date *tested* lead-bullet loading data for rifles is the series of Lyman reloading manuals, particularly the *Lyman Cast Bullet Handbook.* This reference contains the most extensive listing of loads with recent powders that may be had. It covers light and midrange loads quite well, with the one exception that it does not list any powders burning slower than 4198 and 4227. The result is that many of the midrange loads listed for large- and medium-capacity bottleneck cases produce higher pressures than necessary. The older Lyman reloading handbooks, No. 44 and earlier, contain more loads with slower-burning powders, especially including the midrange and full-charge loads utilizing powders in the IMR3031 and 4895 class. Consequently, for the heavier loads, the older manuals are often a better source.

The foregoing isn't meant to imply that the faster-powder loads in the cast-bullet handbook aren't good ones. They're not only good, but because they require less powder, they are more economical. Nevertheless, when approaching 2,000 fps and above, I prefer the slower powders simply because in the past they have always given me better results.

LEAD-BULLET LOADS FOR AUTOLOADERS

The increased popularity of autoloading hunting rifles these days prompts many shooters to ask whether it is possible to make up lead-bullet loads that will function in them correctly. Many shooters use gas-operated autos in the .308/.30-06 cartridge class, and they'd like to take advantage of the lower cost of lead bullets for small-game and fun shooting. Fortunately, loads can be produced which will cycle the actions of rifles such as the Remington M740/742, Winchester M100, M1 Garand, and the like. The basic requirement for functioning of a gas-operated autoloader with *any* handload is the production of adequate "port pressure." All of these designs are operated by gas escaping through a small port in the barrel and expanding against the head of a piston, which is driven rearward to cycle the action. Unless the piston is driven rearward far enough and rapidly enough, the gun won't function; and this means that the pressure of the propellant gas at the time the bullet passes over the gas port must be above a certain minimum level. Light loads won't do the job, no matter what type of powder or bullet is used, and we must at least approach the pressures of full-charge factory loads in order to make the gun function. Generally, this means using one of the heavier cast bullets available for the caliber, combined with a powder in the 3031–4895 burning-rate range. Taking the .30-06 as an example, we see that Lyman lists a 220-grain gas-check bullet (#311284) at velocities up to 1,827 fps, and a chamber pressure of 32,000 CUP, produced by 24.0 grains of Hercules 2400 powder. That is the heaviest load shown, and partly because of the relatively low chamber pressure, it will not reliably cycle the typical gas-operated action.

So it's time to look elsewhere for a load more suitable. The logical place to look is in jacketed-bullet loading data, and in another Lyman manual, we find the 220-grain jacketed bullet driven at just under 2,100 fps by 38.0 grains of 3031 or 40.0 grains of 4895. These are the lowest charges listed with those powders, and because they are relatively fast-burning, we may expect them to produce a bit more velocity with a lead bullet than with a jacketed bullet of the same weight. This gives us a good starting point. Assemble five to ten rounds of either load, and fire them in your autoloader. The load may function the action and it may not. If it does not fuction reliably, then increase the powder charge in increments of 0.2 grain until either proper functioning is obtained, or you have approached the maximum charge listed with that powder for bullets of that weight. If the latter point is reached without obtaining reliable functioning, then switch to the next- slower-burning powder shown in the same table. In this case, directly after the loads already listed, we find 41.0 grains of IMR4064 listed, so this would be the next one to try, again working up in small increments of powder charge if the initial load doesn't produce proper functioning. Switching to a slower powder increases the port pressure, and thus it may function the rifle where the faster-burning powder did not.

Working in this fashion, you'll eventually find a load that will function a gas-operated autoloader chambered for a bottleneck case of 7mm or greater caliber. Often we must use the heaviest lead bullet available to provide greater resistance to powder combustion and to help keep the port pressure at the highest level. Theoretically, we could obtain proper functioning with a lighter bullet, but we might have to drive it so fast that all semblance of accuracy would be lost. Even with the heaviest bullets, the casting alloy should be straight linotype metal or something equally hard. Anything softer may fuse or melt at the base under the pressures and velocities needed to cycle the action correctly.

In any event, we know that best accuracy is not likely to be obtained at highest velocity. Therefore, the powder charge should not be increased beyond the amount which will produce reasonably reliable functioning of the mechanism.

It may work out the other way, with the first load tried producing proper functioning of the gun. In this case, it's wise to reduce the powder charge in increments of 0.2 grain until you determine the point at which the gun will no longer function properly. Then boost the powder charge back to the lowest level that will ensure reliable functioning. In this manner, you'll hold velocity down to the minimum necessary, and you won't be wasting powder.

As we've indicated, the foregoing applies to autoloading rifles of 7mm and greater caliber and reasonably modern gas-operated design. The recently developed class of light autos chambered for .22 centerfire cartridges such as the .223/5.56mm simply cannot be made to function reliably and shoot accurately with cast bullets by any methods I've tried. The problem is simply that these designs are far less tolerant of varying loads, and that you simply can't obtain the necessary velocities with cast bullets and still obtain any practical degree of accuracy. You can drive a 55- or 60-grain linotype-metal bullet at 3,000 fps, and with it could probably function the gun. However, you wouldn't be able to hit anything with it. When working with autoloaders, keep in mind that they are generally designed to function best with pointed bullets. Avoid choosing a lead bullet with a very blunt nose, or you might encounter some feeding problems.

Within the range of calibers we've indicated, you should always be able to arrive at a functional autoloader load by starting with the heaviest cast bullet available and the lowest charges recommended of powders in the 3031–4064 burning-rate range. Modest charge increases from those starting levels will normally produce reliable functioning well before any dangerous pressures might be reached. Even the M1 Garand will work well with cast-bullet loads, particularly with a bullet of about 180-grain weight and a charge of 38 to 40 grains of IMR4895.

As I'm sure you've surmised, cast-bullet loads are not the simplest and easiest to assemble. Certainly casting, sizing, lubricating, and perhaps attaching a gas check is a lot more work than simply taking a factory-made jacketed bullet from its box and seating it in the case. However, in the end, by using cast bullets, you'll be able to shoot loads that are more suitable for your purposes, not available commercially, and a lot cheaper than what you can buy across the counter.

11

Ultralight Loads

THE VERY TERM "ULTRALIGHT" connotes to many a sort of creampuff performance simply not associated with any danger or lethality. This is an impression one must *not* work under when assembling and using such loads. Every one of the ultralight loads mentioned—containing even the slightest amount of propellant–is certain to produce quite serious and painful wounds on humans as well as other animals, at the ranges at which it will normally be employed, and beyond. In addition, they are quite capable of killing if such a wound occurs in vital areas. As a matter of fact, virtually all of our ultralight loads possess more energy and penetration (in animal tissue) than the .22 Short, and many of them exceed those values for the .25 ACP pistol cartridge. It is well known that those two calibers are often carried for personal defense in the form of hideout guns. I have personally examined more than a few deceased persons who succumbed to one of those tiny bullets in a shooting scrape or accident. The same can easily occur with ultralight handloads.

In addition, the fact that such loads have less maximum range than full-charge loads must not lead you into thinking that they can be handled like shotgun target loads with their 300-yard pellet travel. A good many ultralight loads will hurl their bullets 500 to 1000 yards when fired at moderate elevation; they aren't intended for use at such long ranges, but the bullets will *travel* that far. And, upon striking, they can produce serious injuries, not to mention property damage. You—and anyone else who shoots your loads—*must* always keep in mind that ultralight loads are just as dangerous as the full-charge variety.

One other factor is pertinent to safety in this same regard and perhaps should be emphasized here, even though we'll touch upon it farther in later pages. Ultralight loads use such miniscule charges of propellant that it is almost impossible to detect a double charge or even a triple charge by any practical means. The usual method of holding a loading block under strong light and looking down into each case just doesn't work when there is only a pinch of propellant way down on the case head. A multiple charge isn't dangerous in the sense that it will produce pressures high enough to damage the gun. But it is dangerous because it will give the bullet much greater velocity and energy, with the inevitable result that it may penetrate an otherwise suitable backstop or bullet trap and travel on to cause injury or damage. Unwanted multiple charges are avoided by simply paying attention when placing propellant charges and by starting the bullet in the case immediately after the charge has been dumped. This procedure may slow you down a bit, but it insures against accidents that can cause you untold grief and cost.

PREPARING CASES FOR LOADING

The exceedingly low chamber pressures of ultralight loads produce so little case expansion that resizing becomes hardly ever necessary and this not only results in extremely long case life, but it eliminates the need for dies and consequently the need for a loading press. All you need to assemble such loads is some means of decapping and repriming the case; the bullet can be seated with the fingers or tapped in place with a small stick. Decapping the case can be done with a length of dowel or rod, of the largest diameter which will fit through the neck easily, containing a headless nail or piece of stiff wire 1/16 inch in diameter. I've seen several decapping punches of this sort made by simply filing down about 1/2 inch of the point of a large nail to a diameter that will enter the flash hole. A 1/4-inch hole is drilled in a block of wood or metal, the fired case is set over it, and the punch is inserted and rapped smartly with a stick of wood or plastic hammer to punch out the fired primer. Repriming can be done by placing a primer anvil-up on a hard, smooth surface, then placing the case head over the primer, and tapping it down to seat the primer by means of a dowel or stick or light hammer. A hundred cases can be decapped and primed in less than an hour. However, repriming can be done more rapidly and efficiently on the very low-cost Lee priming tool, which is held in the hand and squeezed to seat the primer.

Cases to be used for ultralight loads should first be fire-formed with a full load in the rifle in which they are to be used. Thereafter, they should require no resizing whatever. The fire-forming serves to center them in the chamber and place the neck and shoulder in close relation to the chamber walls.

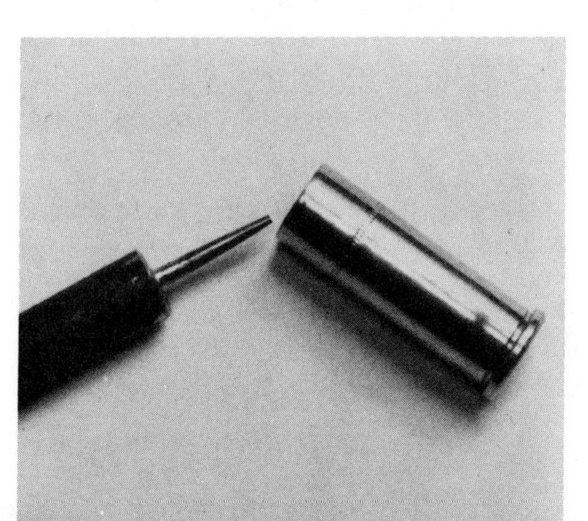

Since resizing is not required for subsequent loading, decapping can be done with the simplest of hand tools. This decapping punch was filed from a piece of scrap steel, but a large spike nail will serve just as well.

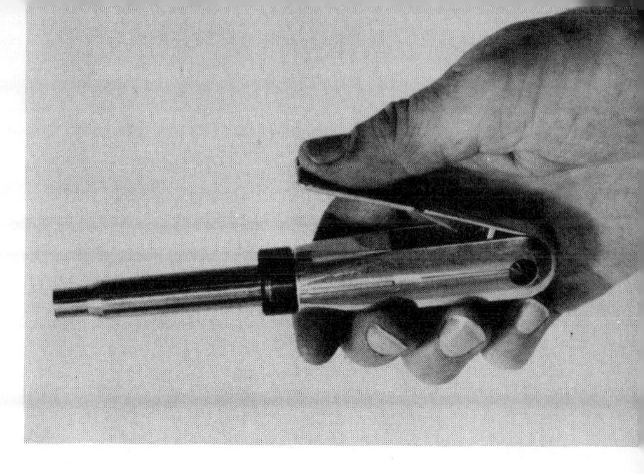

Considering its low cost, the most practical means of repriming for ultralight loads is this simple priming tool made by Lee.

The very light pressures generated by ultralight loads will not expand the case sufficiently to seal the chamber against powder gas leakage if there is any significant clearance. Some loads may not do so even then, and in that case, the neck and shoulder of the case should be well annealed. This may be done by the molten-lead method described near the end of Chapter 14, or simply by heating the neck and shoulder area with a propane torch until the brass just barely begins to glow, then plunging the case in cold water. This will make the neck and shoulder dead-soft, so it will expand more rapidly. However, annealing of this type produces a neck that is really softer than desirable for full-charge loads, so reserve it for loads of this type. Incidentally, it has often been said that rimless cases used for very light loads should not later be used for full-charge loads. The rationale behind this is that the forward thrust by the primer will drive the case deeper into the chamber, setting the shoulder back, and thus producing a condition of excess headspace. Theoretically this is true, but I have found that only rarely does it occur to a significant degree. You can easily determine if the shoulder has been set back by noting the fired primer; if the primer is protruding significantly above the case head, then you know that the case shoulder has been set back, or that the rifle chamber has excess headspace. This primer condition is a positive indicator of excess headspace, but its absence does not necessarily indicate that headspace is correct. The only way to be absolutely certain is to use a case gauge of the type manufactured by Forster and others, but in the long run it's really simpler and cheaper to follow the old warnings and keep ultralight-load cases separate.

Much has been written about the use of pistol primers for light loads in rifle calibers. There is no economic or other advantage to using them. They may be used in small-volume cases, but in the larger cases, they will not ignite powder uniformly unless it is held to the rear by a wad or ball of fluff.

ULTRALIGHT CHARGES

With the cases primed, we must consider the powder charge. Since only a very small amount of fast-burning pistol powder is used, it will occupy perhaps no more than 2 to 5 percent of the case volume. Obviously, such a tiny charge will be ignited a bit differently if it is positioned up in the neck of the case than if it is back near the head or strewn along the bottom. No trouble will be encountered in ignition or combustion, but velocity will vary somewhat according to the position of the powder, and this will reduce consistency. In straight cases such as the .45-70 and .38-55 Winchester, a thin, light cardboard wad that fits snugly in the case can be pressed down to hold the powder against the case head. This won't work in typical bottleneck cases, so use a small ball of kapok or Teflon fluff. Pinch off a bit of the fluff and roll it into a loosely compacted ball that is about the size of the case head. Then squeeze it through the case neck and seat it with a dowel down on the powder. (A cutaway view of this is shown in Chapter 10.) The ball of fluff will expand and cling to the inside of the case tightly enough to hold the powder in place. An alternative is to simply elevate the muzzle of the gun immediately before firing each shot, causing the powder to fall back to the head of the case. This is practical for most fun shooting, but not necessarily for hunting.

Powder charges are not critical for ultralight loads. I've used Bullseye and Unique for this work exclusively, in virtually every rifle caliber from .22 Hornet up to .458 Winchester and in all handgun calibers. In cases ranging in capacity from .22 Hornet up through .223/5.56mm, 0.5 grain of Bullseye is an excellent starting charge; cases up to the capacity of the .308 Winchester need a starting charge of 1.0 grains of Bullseye; in cases of greater capacity, start with about 1.5 grains of Bullseye and work upward until a satisfactory level of performance is obtained. If you'd rather use Unique powder, simply increase the charges mentioned by 40 to 50 percent.

These are starting charges, and represent the smallest amount of powder I've found it practical to use. They'll produce loads which are quite adequate for shooting in the garage or basement and for a good deal of outdoor plinking. You'll be able to increase those charges to meet your particular needs, but I suggest doing so in increments of only 0.1 or 0.2 grain. Certainly no more powder should be used than that necessary to drive the bullet fast enough for your particular use and to produce the degree of accuracy desired. Personally, I feel that ultralight loads in rifle calibers are restricted to a range of about 25 yards. Using more than 2.0 grains of Bullseye in the smaller cases and 5.0 grains in the larger cases removes the load from the ultralight class. Except in the largest calibers, a good ultralight load should penetrate cleanly a single dry pine board nominally 1 inch thick (actually only 3/4 inch). Penetration of two boards takes it from the ultralight class.

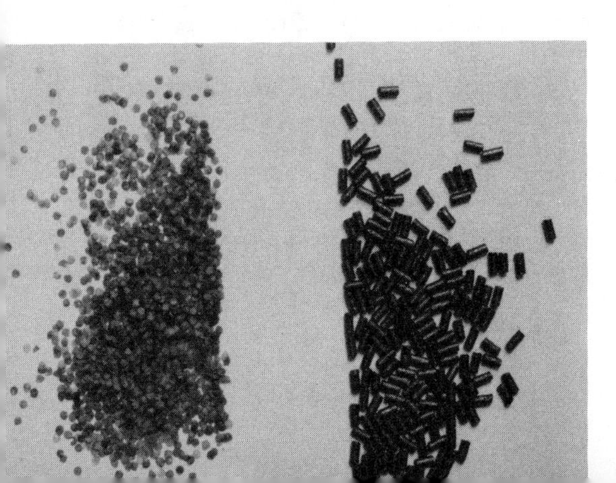

At left is a sample of Hercules Unique powder, commonly used for ultralight loads. This is a fast-burning pistol/shotshell powder, very different in appearance from IMR 4350 shown at right, which is ordinarily used in full-charge loads in many rifle calibers.

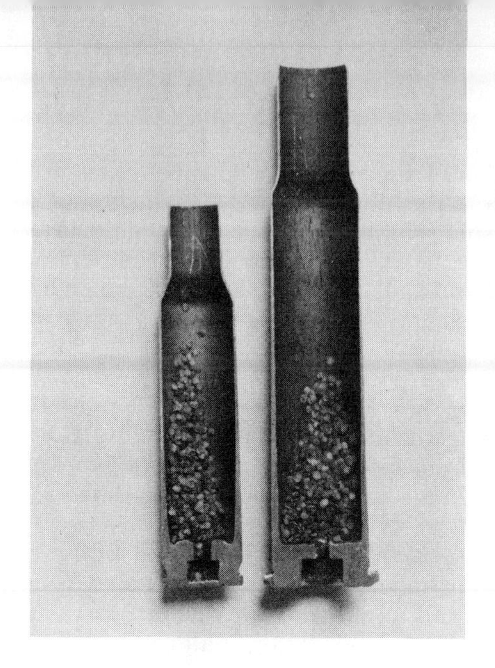

Powder charges for ultralight loads occupy only a very small percentage of the case volume. At left is 1 grain of Unique in a .223 Remington case, at right 3 grains of the same powder in a .30-40 Krag case. Note that the small kernels of this powder will readily pass through the flash hole to lie beneath the primer. This will sometimes produce flattening of the primer and give a false indication of high pressures.

BULLET WEIGHTS

Bullet selection is not particularly critical, nor is the alloy from which bullets are cast. Ordinary scrap lead works quite well, for there is no problem with leading at the velocities produced. Bullets should be as light as practical for the caliber, and the following is what I've found best in rifles: .22, 35-40 grains; .25, 50-60 grains; 7mm, 80-100 grains; .30, 90-110 grains; 8mm, 90-125 grains; .35, 100-150 grains; .45, 185-230 grains.

Actually, bullet selection will be simplified if you use the ones we've found quite practical, listed in the *Lyman Cast Bullet Handbook.* They are as follows: .22, #225353; 6mm #244203; .25, #25720; 6.5mm, #263314; 7mm and .270, #287202; .30, #311227, #31133, #311255; 8mm, #32360; .35, #357443, #357446; .375, #37582; .45, #45467, #454309.

POWDER MEASURES

The very small charges of pistol powder required cannot be metered accurately by the typical rifle-size powder measure, nor can they be weighed accurately on the average powder scale. They are simply too small. An adjustable pistol measure or a fixed-charge pistol measure will do the job much more accurately. However, charge cups made from .22 rimfire cases (with a paper clip handle soldered or cemented in place) are quite adequate for the job if handled correctly, and they cost nothing. A fired .22 Short case will hold 2.2 grains of Bullseye and 2.7 grains of Unique; the LR case will hold 3.0 grains and 3.6 grains respectively. Other charge weights may be obtained by simply filing the case shorter, or if more is needed, using a larger case.

Use of the charge cup is simple, but it must be done uniformly from charge to charge. Pour out enough powder to fill a coffee cup, then submerge the charge cup in the center of the powder a good $^1/_2$ inch or so, allowing the powder to run into it. Lift the cup straight up, then with any

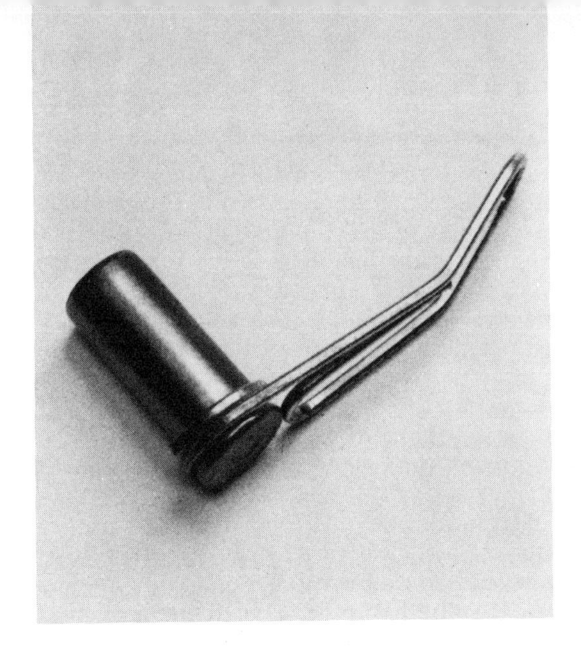

This charge cup is made from a fired .22LR case and a common paper clip. For some calibers, this case may be used unaltered, and for others filed to a shorter length. Charge cups are quite satisfactory and safe for use with ultra-light loads.

handy instrument, such as a small knife blade, strike off the excess powder.

PREPARING AND SEATING BULLETS

Cast the best bullets you can, and then lubricate them by dipping the bearing surface in molten bullet lubricant and setting them on their bases to drain and dry. They need not—in fact, should not—be sized. The excess diameter helps seal the bore better, and also helps prevent them from coming out of the case in normal handling.

Seating the bullet is a simple hand operation. Hold the charged case in one hand, start the bullet in the chamfered case mouth with the other, and twist it about $^1/_2$ turn as it goes in to center it. The oversize condition and the coating of lubricant will hold it snugly in place. Seat bullets to a reasonably uniform depth. Bullets aren't held tightly, so such loads must be single-loaded and handled carefully.

ROUND BALLS

Incidentally, it is quite practical to usc round lead balls in ultralight loads. Factory-made balls are available in diameters that will fit some standard cal-

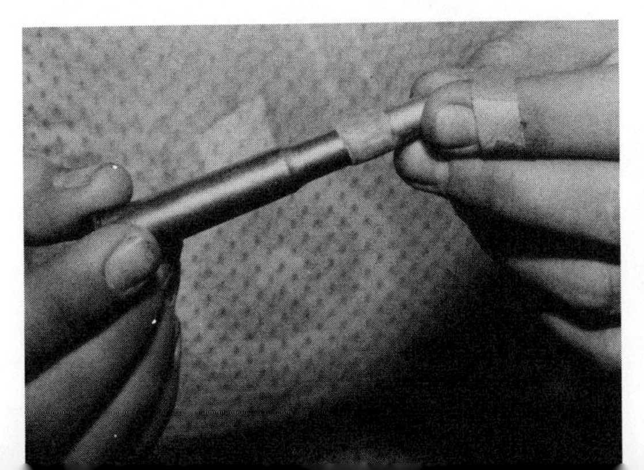

Seating dip-lubed bullets is done by hand, and the excess lubricant is sheared off by the case mouth. After the bullet is pressed in place with the fingers, the excess lube is easily wiped off the case.

ibers, and the bullet-mold manufacturers offer a wide enough variety of round-ball molds to meet almost any need. Ideally, balls should be of such a diameter that they may be pressed by hand into the fired case neck and fit snugly. Most references suggest seating the ball half its depth in the case neck, and providing lubrication in the form of a grease wad or disc of bullet lubricant beneath the ball. However, I find it simpler to seat the ball fully inside the neck, then simply smear bullet lubricant over the ball. A slightly oversize ball may be used by simply tapping it into the case mouth with a stick; if the mouth hasn't been overchamfered, it will shear off a thin ring of lead, reducing the ball to the correct diameter. When doing it this way, make certain that the ball isn't bulging the case mouth to the point that it will not chamber freely.

Round balls require the lightest powder charges, and if one attempts to drive them too fast, the very limited bearing surface will strip in the rifling, and accuracy will be lousy. If your chosen caliber can be suited by commercial lead balls, loading becomes exceedingly simple. I recall one particular summer when I rid a farm of an excess of barn pigeons using 0 buckshot balls (lubricated with Vaseline smeared in the case mouth) driven by 2.5 grains of Unique in a Lee-Enfield No. 4 .303 rifle. At 50 to 60 feet, the combination was accurate enough for a high percentage of head shots on pigeons, and good accuracy was needed to avoid puncturing the roof or breaking windows.

ULTRALIGHT HANDGUN LOADS

Ultralight loads in handgun calibers are really no different, except that there is no need for holding powder to the rear of the case. Decapping and

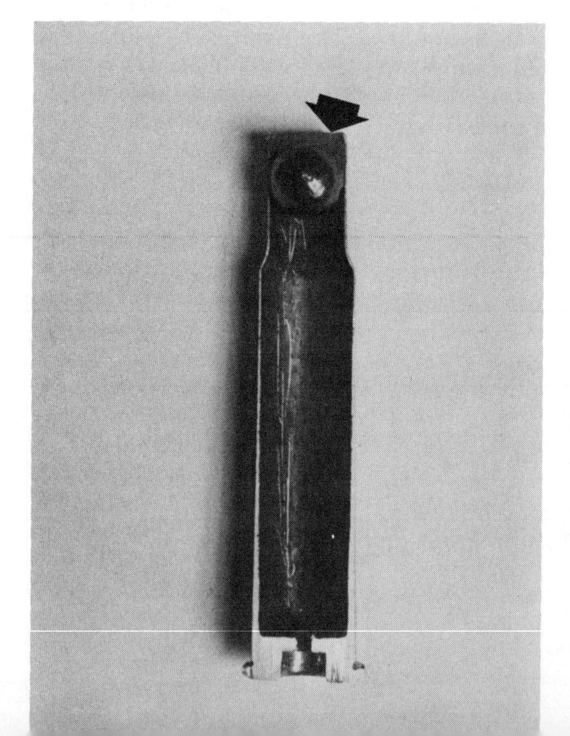

For the very lightest in rifle-caliber loads, round balls are satisfactory. I have had best results by seating the ball fully inside the case mouth, then smearing lubricant over the ball. The lubricant shown here (arrow) is Vaseline, but any common bullet lubricant will do just as well.

repriming are even simpler and quicker because the cases are shorter and easier to handle, and no resizing is required unless you're starting with fired cases that won't chamber in the gun to be used. Normally the best bullet is the lightest wadcutter type to be had in that particular caliber. In my experience, those are the following Lyman bullets: .32, #313492; .38/.357/9mm, #35887, #358101, #35425; .41, #41026; .44, #429348; .45, #450225, #452389. Bullets may be cast of almost any soft alloy, lubricated by dipping, and loaded without sizing. Here you may find that the bullets cannot be pressed easily into the case by hand, so simply tap them in with a stick or plastic mallet. Bullets should be seated deeply in the case, and I've gooten best results by seating them flush with the case mouth. This reduces case volume, increases loading density, and permits more efficient powder combustion.

Round balls may also be used; in fact, my best ultralight .38 Special load many years ago consisted of a 000 buck ball seated inside the case mouth over a .22 short case full of Bullseye and lubricated with softened beeswax (melted and mixed with petroleum jelly) finger-smeared in the case mouth over the ball. I shot thousands of this load in the woods with complete satisfaction.

Bullseye is the best powder, and no more than 0.75 to 1.0 grain is required in .32 and .38 caliber to produce a workable load. In .44 and .45 calibers, use a starting load of 2.0 grains. In handguns, and especially in revolvers, make certain that the first round fired with the starting charge actually pushes the bullet all the way out the barrel. If not, punch it out with a cleaning rod, and increase the starting charge by about 0.2 grain. Repeat if necessary, because quite wide variations will be found in revolvers in the amount of powder required to get the bullet out of the barrel. As with

Round-ball revolver loads. From left to right, ball simply thumbed snugly into the case mouth over a grease wad; ball tapped into the case half its diameter, thus securing it tightly enough to stay in place during normal handling and rapid fire (note case mouth is shearing off a thin ring of lead); ball seated entirely within the case, as I prefer, with lubricant (arrow) smeared over it.

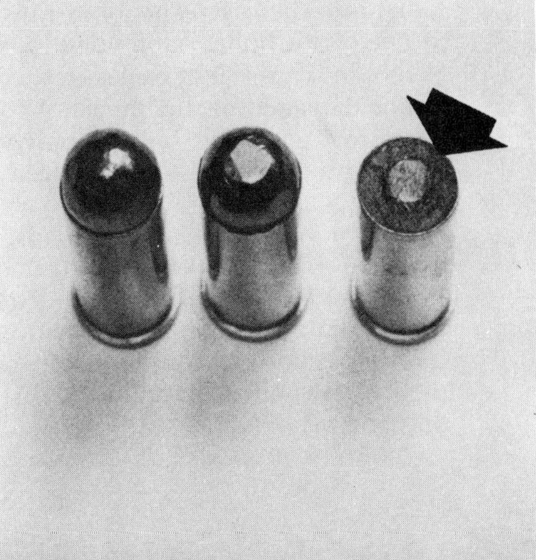

rifles, don't use any more powder than necessary to obtain practical results.

Ultralight handgun loads are at their best in revolvers, which function normally with them. They must be single-loaded in autoloaders, because they will not normally feed from the magazine and they do not generate enough recoil to cycle the action. The best method I've found for using them in autos is to put a magazine in the gun so that the slide stop will hold the action open automatically each time the slide is retracted. Then it's simple enough to lower the muzzle, drop a cartridge in the chamber, thumb the slide stop down so the gun closes, fire, then yank the slide back smartly to extract and eject the case and to be caught and held by the slide stop.

If any significant amount of unburned powder is found in the bore (especially in the larger calibers), substitute a magnum primer for the standard variety. This will usually cure the problem, though if the load is too light, even that may not help and the powder charge will require upward adjustment. Actually, as long as the load does the job, unburned powder presents no problem at all. Each bullet sweeps out any left by the preceding shot, so there is no buildup or functional problem.

When using round balls, performance may sometimes be improved with a snug card wad seated over the powder to hold it to the rear. This is simply because the bearing surface of the ball is so small that it may not offer sufficient resistance for efficient powder combustion. Crowding the powder against the case head improves its ignition, which offsets this problem.

PLASTIC AND WAX HANDGUN LOADS

There are two other forms of ultralight load which are applicable only to handguns, and revolvers in particular. One is the plastic bullets and cases currently offered by Speer, though others have made them in the past. This ammunition system is unique in that it does not utilize any propellant powder; the only propulsive force is the primer. The Speer cases are of molded plastic, adapted to the Large Pistol primer size, and contain an oversize flash hole. Case walls are rather thick, and the rear portion of the plastic bullet is reduced so that the two may be assembled easily by hand. To load these cartridges, simply seat a primer in the case and thumb the bullet into the case. The job is finished.

The plastic bullet is intended to be reusable, but only to a limited extent. If shot into a resilient backstop such as strips of carpeting or canvas, it will not be damaged by the impact. A solid backstop will damage the bullet too much for reuse. The bullet is only very lightly engraved by the rifling, and if recovered otherwise undamaged, may be reused until its accuracy falls off.

Accuracy of plastic-bullet loads, with unfired bullets, is usually quite good up to about 20 feet. With the primer providing the only propulsive force, the bullets will penetrate two or three sheets of heavy corrugated board at that range. The addition of a very small charge of Bullseye powder, as done by some shooters but not recommended, greatly increases their power, but without any particular other advantages. I prefer to use only the primer.

The Speer plastic-bullet ultra-light load offered in .38 (.357) and .44 revolver calibers. Bullets are reusable to a limited extent, and no tools are required for loading.

Even though quite light and slow, plastic bullets are capable of producing painful if not serious injuries. They must not be regarded as a toy, and shooting must be done with all the usual safety precautions.

The plastic bullets may also be used in conventional brass cartridge cases, in which instance they should be seated as deeply in the case as possible. When brass cases are used, the flash hole should be enlarged; if this is not done, the primer will back out of the case and may jam against the recoil shield, preventing cylinder rotation. For Small Pistol primer pockets, the flash hole should be opened up with a #31 drill, and the hole should not exceed .120 inch diameter; if the hole is larger, there will be insufficient shoulder against which to seat the primer in the bottom of the pocket. Large Pistol primer pockets may have the flash hole opened up to #20 drill size. Some makes of primers will produce better results than others; magnum primers seem to perform best of all. It's a good idea to try different primers.

At left is a standard .38 Special case with its flash hole drilled out for use with wax or plastic bullets; at right is a case with standard-diameter flash hole.

Wax bullets are formed and seated simultaneously by simply pressing the mouth of a case completely through a 1/2-inch-thick cake of paraffin wax. Other fairly hard waxes are suitable, but paraffin is the cheapest and is widely available.

The "wax-bullet" load was popularized quite a few years ago by some quick-draw shooters. Cases are prepared with enlarged flash holes as already described, and then are simply pressed mouth-first through a 1/2-inch-thick cake of paraffin (from the home-canning section of your market), leaving a full-wadcutter wax bullet seated flush with the case mouth. Note that the bullet is formed and seated *before* priming; this is done to avoid compression of air inside the case, which makes bullet seating more difficult and, in some instances, might force the bullet back out.

In my experience, wax bullets are not quite as accurate as the plastic type. However, they are substantially cheaper. Wax bullets are destroyed upon impact, but the fragments are easily recovered, melted down, and recast into 1/2-inch-thick blocks for reuse. Five pounds of paraffin will provide a lot of shooting when recovered and reused. Plastic bullets for the same amount of shooting will cost many times more.

One last word of reminder, and it *must not* be ignored. Ultralight loads with lead bullets are lethal, and any of them striking an animal or human being will produce a serious wound. Plastic and wax bullets are not ordinarily lethal, but can cause quite painful injuries, and are capable of destroying any eye or penetrating the softer parts of a human body. Consequently, no matter how weak loads of this type might appear to be, they must always be fired with safety and concern for bystanders uppermost in mind.

The completed wax-bullet load in .38 Special. Occasionally a small amount of wax may cling to the outside of the case and should be wiped off.

12

Special-Purpose Shotshell Loads

LOADING CONVENTIONAL SHOTSHELLS is really the simplest of all handloading, using the modern self-contained multiple-station loader of the type that has developed over the past two decades. However, shotshell loaders have been so highly developed for conventional loads that they don't really have the capability or the versatility for producing the special-purpose loads that a great many people require. For example, the modern loader won't turn out buckshot or rifled-slug loads, and scatter loads are barely within its capabilities. Ultralight and extra-high-velocity loads are also a problem. Don't misunderstand—the modern shotshell loader is a great boon to the conventional scattergunner. But it is nowhere near as versatile as the older and less sophisticated equipment with which we were forced to get along before the late 1950s.

Cases can be prepared for the special-purpose loads on your regular shotshell loader. Run them through the resizing, decapping, and repriming stations. If you can obtain or make a powder bushing for the charge bar to drop the appropriate charge, you may also do that on the loader. After that, though, the operations become different, and you'll need other equipment.

SLUG LOADS

With the great proliferation of whitetail deer over the past fifty years, virtually every state now offers a deer season, and many of them in the East restrict hunters to shotguns with rifled-slug loads. So let's take a look at that particular load. First of all, you'll need the rifled slugs. They can be purchased, ready to load, or you may cast the hollow-base slug in a mold obtained from Lyman, and then swage the rifling into its outer surface with a punch-and-die set from the same source. However, the rifling really has very little effect on the slug's flight; it derives most of its stability and accuracy from its hollow base, which shifts its center of gravity up near the nose, giving it what is generally called "arrow stability." Consequently, quite adequate results (compared to the *rifled* slug) may be obtained from the same slug without rifling. These slugs are cast just like hollow-base bullets as mentioned in Chapter 8; a good bit of juggling and practice may be necessary to produce slugs with perfect bases.

Both paper and plastic cases may be used for slug loads, provided they are in first-class condition. Since one seldom uses a great many slug loads, I think it is wise to buy new cases for them. Killing your fall deer for meat certainly shouldn't take more than a handful of loads, and allowing an adequate number for practice and zeroing still won't add up to more than forty or fifty, and their cost is cheap enough insurance for the hunt. Low-base cases should always be used. The loads can be assembled in high-base cases, but there will be too little space between powder and slug for an adequate wad column. Too little filler wad means that there is very little compensation for the shock of initial acceleration of the slug, and this can reduce accuracy by deforming the base. As with regular shot loads, the wad column absorbs that initial kick by the rapidly expanding powder gases.

Once you have the slugs at hand, drop one in the case, and you'll note that it is a very loose fit. Don't worry about that for the moment, because the final crimp will center it in the case so that it is aligned with the bore of the gun.

Back now to the sized, primed, and charged case. An over-powder wad is essential, and the traditional thick nitro-card wad .125 or .200 inch thick will do the job. It simply requires a slightly larger powder charge than the cup-type plastic wad, which seals the bore better. Regardless of the type, the wad must be seated tightly against the powder. Various loading manuals recommend specific wad pressures for different powders, and if your ordinary shotshell loader has a wad-pressure indicator, use it for the seat-

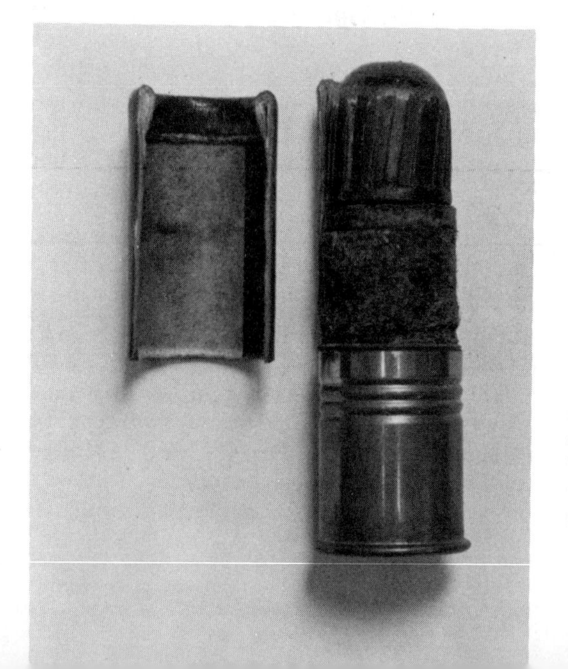

This slug handload with the case cut away shows the slug rifling, the hard nitro-card seated directly beneath the slug for best accuracy, and the long wad column which reduces shock to the base of the slug and thereby improves accuracy. Note how the edge of the roll crimp tucks down tightly between the slug and the case wall to center the slug and secure it in place.

While both of these cases have relatively low base wads, the one on the left has a longer metal head overlay and is therefore more suitable for slug loads, which are usually loaded to maximum pressures.

ing operation. Ordinary composition filler wads go on top of the over-powder wad, and for best results, the wad column is topped off by a nitro-card wad. With some loads and guns, a bit better accuracy is produced by two card wads, so try it both ways. The purpose of the card wad directly under the slug is to reduce base deformation and to prevent fragments of the relatively soft filler wads from being driven up into the hollow base and remaining there during the slug's flight. Any material remaining in the base hollow is likely to throw the slug off balance and reduce its accuracy.

Once the wad column is assembled, it can be seated in the proper station of an ordinary shotshell loader, but as a separate operation. Otherwise, seating may be done in a "Lee Loader" die, or in one of the older-type wad-seating dies. If you don't have any specific tool for the purpose, wads can be seated with a dowel fitting closely inside the case by hand pressure, or light taps of a plastic mallet. Once the wad column is completed, there should be approximately 1 inch of case remaining to accommodate the slug and a proper *roll* crimp. Depending upon the combination of case, powder charge, and wads available, it may be necessary to slice filler wads to a lesser thickness to make the column come out right. A thin, sharp knife or razor blade will cut the wads easily.

MAKING THE ROLL CRIMP

Simply drop the slug into the case, and for the last operation, you'll need a "roll-crimp head," available from Lyman. This tool must be rotated rapidly, while pressing down with moderate force on the case. A drill press is ideal for this, and the crimp head has a round shank for fitting into a chuck. If a drill press isn't available, an ordinary portable electric drill will do a good enough job if you hold it in proper alignment. This is rather difficult to do freehand, so a drill-press attachment for your portable drill will be a worthwhile investment.

You'll need some means of holding the case securely, since simply holding it in your hand on the drill-press table isn't really good enough. The hardwood tongs shown in the sketch work quite well, and when aligned and clamped to the press table, they serve not only to line the case up with the crimp head, but to prevent it from spinning.

With the slug in the case and the case in the tongs, bring the spinning crimp head down over the case mouth, applying moderate pressure, and move it down slowly so that it turns the case mouth over 180 degrees and forces it down against the slug. This will center the slug in the case, and will also hold it down tightly against the wad column. Do the first case by feel, forming the crimp gradually until it fits snugly against the slug and holds it firmly in place. Then stop the press and bring the head down firmly on the crimp, and set the drill-press quill stop at that position. Thereafter, you'll not need to feel for the crimp—just bring the spinning head down smoothly to the stop. Any variation in the load or a change in make and type case will make a new adjustment necessary.

If excessive pressure is required to form the crimp, then you haven't allowed quite enough case above the wad column; and if the case tends to crumple and fold, rather than turn over smoothly, you've allowed too much. If there isn't quite enough case, applying more pressure to the wad column may shorten it up enough to get by; and if there's too much, seating another thin card wad on top may solve the problem. However, you won't have either problem if you adjust the height of the wad column carefully before preparing a batch of cases. There is always the temptation to apply just a little bit more pressure to make the crimp a little tighter, but too much pressure will bulge the sides of the case, and this leaves you set up for a jammed gun in the field. The least pressure that will turn over a smooth crimp and secure the slug tightly against the wad column is best.

Plastic cases may be crimped without additional attention, but paper cases will crimp more smoothly if a bit of beeswax is applied to the mouth. The easiest way to do this is to melt a bit of wax in a small container, and then dip about 1/8 inch of the case mouth into it just before putting the slug in place. It will penetrate the paper to some degree, and then the friction of the spinning crimp head will melt it again and force it into the paper, reinforcing and waterproofing the crimp and lubricating the crimp head. Paper cases that have been around quite a while or have been fired a few times (and I don't recommend several-times-fired paper cases for slug loads) may not form a satisfactory crimp under any circumstances unless wax is added.

BUCKSHOT LOADS

Probably the second most popular special-purpose shotshell load is buckshot. Buckshot differs from lead birdshot only in that the spherical balls are larger in diameter, and therefore fewer of them may be accommodated in the space available in the case.

Technically, "birdshot" and "buckshot" divide at size "1" which appears near the bottom of the first column of the shot-size table on page 144. Actually, sizes B and BB are often used for waterfowling, and for fox hunting, but they are still in the buckshot range. Due to the similarity of the terms "BB Gun" and "BB" shot size, it is often assumed that pellet diameters are the same; this isn't true, as can be seen in the table where "BB Gun" size is listed as "Air Rifle" and a diameter of .175 inch, while BB shot size has a .18-inch diameter. In any event, as a practical matter, the smallest birdshot is size 1 with a diameter of .16 inch, while size B begins the buckshot range with a diameter of .17 inch.

Buckshot size designations are more than a little bit confusing. The system simply "grew" over the years and doesn't represent any single, coherent pattern. On the accompanying table, buckshot sizes begin with "B." and from there on up, there is no rule of thumb by which pellet diameter can be determined from the size designation. About all that can be said is that among the alphabetical designations, pellet diameter increases along with the increase in the number of characters in the designation. Thus "BB" is larger than "B;" and "TTT" is larger than "TT", which is larger than "T". Numberical buckshot sizes follow the logic of birdshot sizes, with the smaller number representing the larger pellet diameter, so that of the entire range, "4" is the smallest, and "1" the largest. Then, in ascending order of pellet diameter, we get into the "0" sizes where the pattern of alphabetical buck designations is repeated; "00" being larger than "0" and so forth, with seldom-seen "0000" (not included in the table) being the largest.

Sizes 0 and 00 are probably the most popular for hunting, especially for deer and other big game in the deep south; they, along with 000, are also popular these days for law-enforcement use, though many departments prefer Number 4 for use in built-up and heavily populated areas where its lesser penetration does not pose as great a hazard to bystanders and property while still being quite effective on human targets at reasonable ranges.

Because of their size, buckshot pellets of the 0 series cannot be dropped from a shot measure of any type, and the pellets must be placed in the case individually in a set pattern. The load is no longer designated by the *weight* of the shot charge, but the number of pellets. Placing those little lead balls in their individual layers in the case can be a bit frustrating, but it isn't all that difficult, and it *must* be done or the case will not accommodate the full number. Just taking the specified number of pellets and dumping them into the case won't work at all; the pellets will jam or bridge, and there won't be enough space left for a proper crimp. So don't try to do it that way; align the pellets properly.

Cases are prepared in the usual manner up through the seating of the wad column, and this may be done on the ordinary shotshell loader. At that point in the process, the shot pellets are added individually. Size 000, commonly known as "triple-ought," is placed in four nested layers of two pellets each. Size 00, "double-ought," fits in three layers of three pellets each; and size 0, "ought," is positioned in four layers of three pellets each. Incidentally, this information applies only to 12-gauge; the smaller gauges do not have space enough to contain enough of these larger pellets to form an effective load, and also, the original sizes were probably developed around the 12-bore. Magnum loadings usually contain one extra layer of pellets.

Traditionally, buckshot is simply placed in the case without any other attention. However, in recent years, granulated plastic fillers have been introduced to reduce pellet deformation produced by acceleration forces and scrubbing against the bore surface. Much better patterns are produced if

SHOT SIZES

Size No.	Diameter (inches)	Pellets in 1 Ounce	Size No.	Diameter (inches)	Pellets in 1 Ounce
12	.05	2385	Air Rifle	.175	55
11	.06	1380	*BB	.18	50
10	.07	868	BBB	.19	42
9	.08	585	T	.20	40
8	.09	409	TT	.21	35
7½	.095	345	TTT (or F)	.22	30
7	.10	299	TTTT (or FF)	.23	27
6	.11	223	4 Buck	.24	21
5	.12	172	3 Buck	.26	18½
4	.13	136	2 Buck	.27	15
3	.14	109	1 Buck	.30	11
2	.15	88	0 Buck	.32	9
1	.16	73	00 Buck	.33	8½
B	.17	59	000 Buck	.375	8

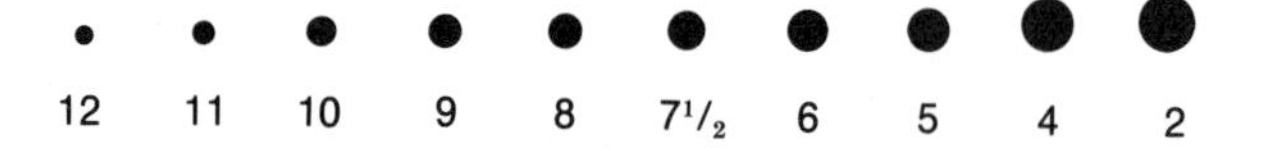

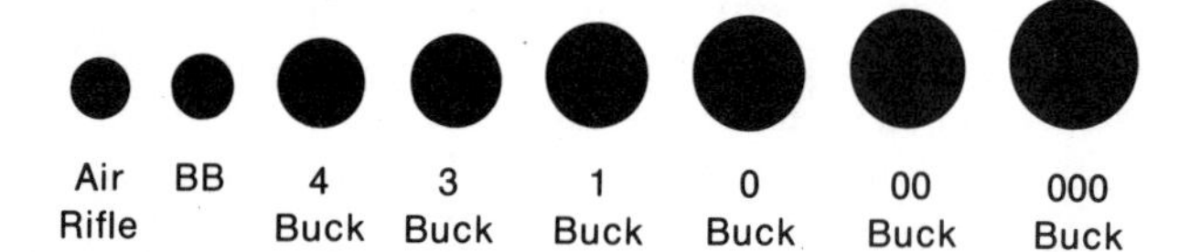

At left, size O buckshot in a cut-off 12-gauge case shows how four layers of three pellets each are stacked for the standard 12-pellet load. At right, size 00 buck shows how three layers of three pellets each nest almost perfectly to yield a nine-pellet load. (Note: a three-inch magnum case would hold 12 pellets of 00.)

the space between pellets is filled with finely granulated polyethylene or some other inert filler. The granulated plastic filler is often difficult to obtain, but an acceptable and reasonably effective substitute is cornmeal or Cream of Wheat. Its addition slows up the loading process considerably, but the improved patterns it permits are well worth the effort. Place a very small amount of the filler in the case first, position the first layer of pellets, and then trickle in a bit more filler, enough so that the pellets are thinly covered and the space between them is filled. Then add the second layer of pellets, tapping them into position with a dowel so that they are bedded in the filler. Sprinkle in a bit more filler, and add the third layer, repeating the process. When all the pellets are in place, tap the side of the case a bit to settle the filler and the pellets, then add enough filler to bring it flush with the top of the upper layer of pellets.

Once the shot charge—and filler, if used—is properly in place, there should be $^7/_{16}$ inch of case remaining for a proper roll crimp. A roll crimp is needed simply because the shot charge does not offer the flexibility needed to make the individual folds of a star crimp. Thumb a card over-shot wad into the case mouth, and then apply a roll crimp as already described for slug loads. Minor adjustments of crimping pressure and/or wad-column height may be necessary to secure a firm, tight crimp. The crimp must hold the shot charge tightly in place by pressing down firmly against the over-shot wad. However, it must not press down so heavily on the wad that imprints of the pellets bulge through. Care must also be taken that too much crimping pressure is not applied; the large individual buckshot pellets will form individual bulges in the sides of the case and interfere with chambering. As heavy pressure is applied, the pellets in each layer exert a wedging affect on those of the layer beneath them, forcing them outward to bulge the case. If you wind up with any bulges whatever, each individual load should be checked by dropping it into the chamber of the gun in which it will be used. If it will not chamber fully and freely of its own weight, it may produce functional problems in the field. You don't want a jammed gun when there is a fat and sassy eight-point buck scarcely 30 yards away.

Since buckshot loads are used mainly in the field under all sorts of weather conditions, it's a good idea to waterproof those which you'll actually use in hunting. The over-shot wad can soak up water, even though the plastic case is waterproof. The simplest way to waterproof is to take a small brush and clear lacquer, brush a thick coat over the wad, then when that is dry, run a bead of lacquer around the junction of the crimp and wad. This won't make it absolutely waterproof, since the lacquer won't adhere to the plastic, but it will seal the cardboard, and it will plug any gaps between the wad and crimp. This will protect the load from anything except complete immersion.

SCATTER LOADS

Upland Game

Taking upland game in thick cover at short ranges requires a wider and looser pattern than is generally available in today's factory loads. In fact, the typical modern load with its one-piece plastic shot-cup/wad-column

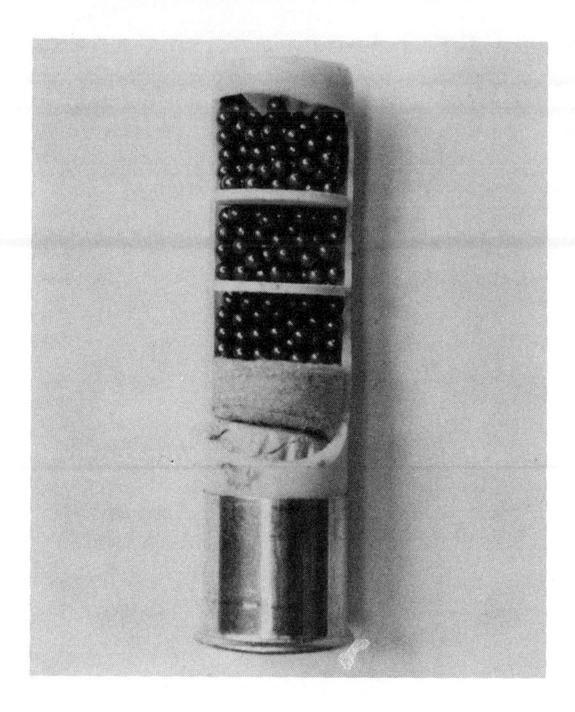

In this form of scatter load, a 20-gauge 3-inch case houses two thin over-shot card wads to divide the shot charge into three equal segments. This load works well, but loading is slow and laborious.

unit often produces patterns that are too tight and too dense for some game shooting. To go the other way and take care of those fast, short-range shots, we have what is called the "scatter load." It is produced by reloading with the old-style nitro-card and composition wad column, then dividing the shot charge into segments.

Cases are prepared in the usual fashion up through the seating of the wad column. Then we have two options for the shot charge. It may be divided horizontally with thin, circular card wads into three or four segments, or by two rectangular cardboard separators slotted to fit together like an X. The latter is the easier to use, because it is placed in the case and the shot charge simply dumped in and then shaken a bit to level it and equalize the four segments. The former type requires that you dump in one-third or one-quarter of the shot charge, seat the separator wad, dump in the next segment and seat the next wad, and so on until the entire charge is in place. That takes a lot more time.

The wads or separators take up space themselves, and thus reduce the amount of space available for shot. If a normal wad column is used, this will require reduction of the shot charge. However, this shouldn't present any problem in the type of close-range shooting for which such loads are used. Nevertheless, if you want the full amount of shot, then it's necessary to reduce the wad column a bit to make extra space for the separators. The separators should be made of very thin but relatively tough card. Though I've used the word "cardboard," ordinary business-card or filing-card stock works fine. In the form of file cards, it's readily available almost anywhere. Once the shot charge and separators are in place, it's a simple matter to in-

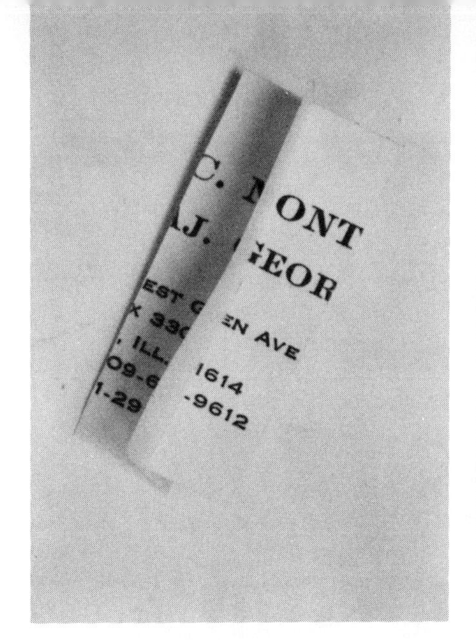

For faster dumping of the shot charge, you can make up cruciform wads from slotted rectangles you've cut from note-card paper, as shown at left. The cruciform then fits neatly into the case and the shot is simply dumped and then shaken a bit in order to level it.

sert the over-shot wad and form a roll crimp as already described.

Those are the most useful and practical special-purpose shotshell loads that you'll be able to assemble from readily available components. There are others, of course, but their use is so limited that we'll not eat up any space with discussion of them here. In any event, the ability to produce these special loads, some of which are not available commercially at all, and the others only at very high prices, will enable you to enjoy a good deal more shotgunning by handloading.

Waterfowl

As noted in Chapter 3, components for handloading of steel shot are not yet available. Undoubtedly they will be someday. But until then, don't experiment with components designed for other purposes.

13

Loading for Black-Powder Guns

THERE WAS A TIME when people shot black-powder guns simply because that was all they had, or all they could afford. However, since WWII, there has been an ever-increasing blossoming of interest in the restoration and shooting of nineteenth-century black-powder breechloaders. There has also been a tremendous upsurge of interest in shooting muzzleloaders, but we are concerned here only with cartridge guns in reloadable calibers.

While it is possible to load most black-powder calibers with smokeless propellant, that takes most of the romance from the game, and there is also the problem that even in modest quantities, smokeless powder burns so differently from black that it can overstress those nineteenth-century guns. Even the heaviest of the original black-powder loads produce chamber pressures under 20,000 CUP—and even duplicating the relatively modest performance with smokeless powders generates not only higher pressures, but greater stresses in the form of more rapid pressure development. Some of the older designs, like the Winchester High-Wall single-shot and the Model 1886 lever gun, are capable of handling smokeless-powder loads without difficulty. But many aren't, so you must stick with black powder.

Black powder is a mechanical mixture of charcoal, sulfur, and saltpeter. It is mixed wet, pressed into hard cakes, then broken up into small particles, and those particles are screened into four standard granulations used in the sporting guns. From largest to smallest they are Fg, FFg, FFFg, and FFFFg; the last is not normally used in metallic cartridges. FFFg, commonly known as 3F, is used mainly in handgun calibers and the small rifle calibers such as .32-20. Calibers up through approximately .45-70 are best served with FFg powder, while the bigger .50 calibers can make good use of Fg. However, as a practical matter, FFg granulation is suitable for virtually all the more common black-powder calibers you might decide to reload.

Original black-powder caliber designations included the weight of the

A pair of typical 1870s-vintage black-powder cartridges of medium power—the .38-40 Winchester (left) and the .44-40 Winchester.

A pair of Sharps bottleneck black-powder cartridges intended for use in single-shot rifles. Note paper-patched bullets and lack of any case-mouth crimp. Left is the .40-50, right the .40-70. Cases were not crimped on bullets for use in single shot rifles.

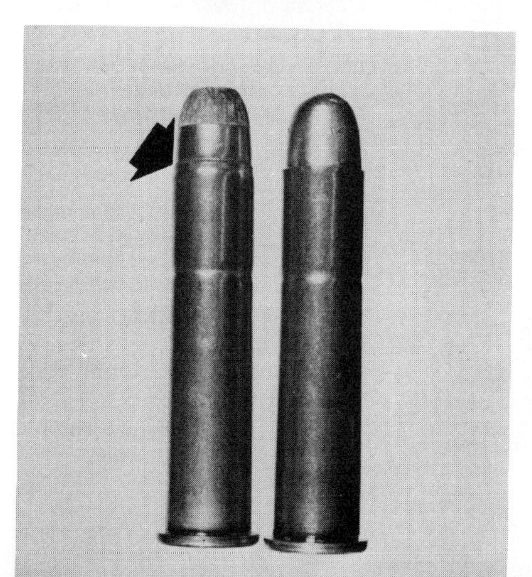

Doubtless the one black-powder cartridge that remains more popular today than any other, the .45-70 U.S Government. At left is a current factory load utilizing a jacketed bullet and smokeless powder, with heavy roll crimp applied so that it may be shot in the many tube-magazine repeating rifles still in service in this caliber. At right is a full-charge black-powder handload utilizing a cast lead bullet.

powder charge as the second set of digits in a compound numerical designation—for example, the .44-40 Winchester was a .44 caliber cartridge containing a charge of 40 grains of black powder. A third set of numbers was *sometimes* included, indicating the weight in grains of the standard bullet. Under that setup, the same cartridge was identified as .44-40-200. Generally, though, the bullet-weight designation was ignored in everyday use, even if it was originally applied at all. At the time those designations were applied, cartridge cases were of much thinner construction than now; modern cases have less capacity and will not hold the full original charge. Thus, today's .44-40 case will hold only 35 grains or a bit less of black powder. Reformed cases and modern thick-wall cases such as those offered by Brass Extrusions Laboratory Limited (BELL) may hold even less.

Don't try to use old fired cases that still contain black-powder fouling; the brass will be heavily corroded and weakened beneath it. Wherever possible, use new cases, either reformed from modern brass or the new basic cases as discussed in Chapter 14, and clean them as described later in this chapter as soon as they are fired.

Though the black powder of today may be of better quality and more consistent in performance, it is the same mixture of charcoal, sulfur, and saltpeter that it was a century ago. Though it's technically "better," its energy content remains essentially the same, and under given conditions, a charge of 40 or 70 grains today will produce the same performance it always did. Black powder burns well without confinement, and for this reason, it makes an inefficient but simple and cheap bomb. For this reason, its sale has been controlled in recent years by federal law and regulation, but it is still generally available in most communities, provided you are willing to go through the paperwork involved in making a purchase.

Black powder burns most efficiently in ammunition when it completely fills the available powder space. Thus when black-powder cartridges were

Old fired black-powder cases which were not thoroughly cleaned of fouling shortly after firing will be heavily corroded inside and consequently weakened, so they should not be used. Note heavy caked fouling in the cut-off case head at left, beneath which the brass is badly pitted and eaten away. At right is a modern case fired with black powder and not cleaned for a few days; thus the fouling in it is less, but will eventually weaken the brass. All black-powder cases were originally made in either the balloon-head design shown or in the much weaker folded-head design.

originally designed, the case was made to hold the chosen amount of powder, no more and no less. But modern cases have thicker walls and heads, so they simply won't hold the original amount of powder with the bullet seated to the same depth. In fact, some of the cases being made around the turn of the century would not hold the full original powder charge because as the case designs improved and manufacturing methods changed, case volume became less. However, the amount lost doesn't reduce performance significantly. The .45-70 may hold only 60 to 65 grains of powder, and the .44-40 may hold only about 35 grains—but when the cases are loaded to full, 100 percent density, velocity won't be noticeably different.

A full charge of black powder fills all the available case volume under light compression. Though smaller charges may be used, little is to be gained in doing so. To determine the proper charge for a modern case, first mark the case with the location of the bullet base when the bullet is seated to the correct overall cartridge length. Then pour powder into the case, settling it by tapping the case with a brass rod or extra case, until it is filled to about 1/16 inch above the location of the bullet base. That extra 1/16 inch of powder produces the proper amount of compression when the bullet is fully seated.

Once this has been done, weigh the amount of powder, then set your measure for that amount. Record the charge weight for that particular caliber and you'll be ready to duplicate it by simply setting the measure at any time in the future.

Some old-timers suggest using pistol primers with black powder because it ignites very easily. Pistol primers of the proper size will ignite black powder quite readily and consistently, but to avoid confusion and mixups, I prefer to use rifle primers. The loads shoot just as accurately with them as with pistol primers, and both types cost the same, so there's no real advan-

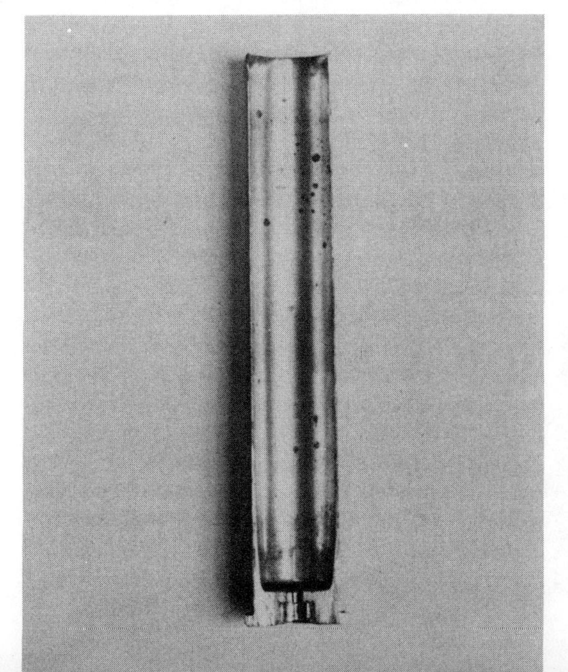

This is a modern solid-head case, the .45 "basic" made by BELL to be shortened and resized to produce cases in all of the old black-powder calibers based upon the .45-70 head. It allows nearly a score of the old-timers to be loaded in new cases that are actually much better than the originals.

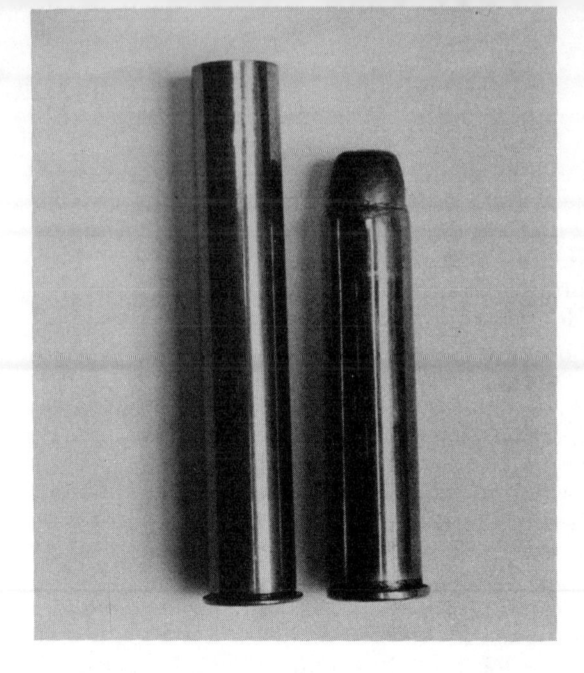

At left is a .50 basic BELL case, and at right is a fresh .50-110 Winchester handload with a lead bullet. The basic case shown has the thin "British rim," but BELL also makes this case with the standard "American rim" shown on the .50-110.

tage to using pistol primers. As mentioned elsewhere in this volume, rifle primers are better matched dimensionally to rifle cases, so I think it's best to go that route.

If you're shooting or loading for a good single-shot rifle which you feel should give better accuracy, some improvement can sometimes be obtained by seating a grease or wax wad over the powder beneath the bullet. Such wads can be made from a sheet of beeswax or bullet lubricant formed by either melting the material and letting it harden in a thin sheet, or by simply softening it and pressing or rolling it out to a thickness of about $^3/_{32}$ inch. Either way, the simplest way of forming and seating wads is to simply press the sheet of lubricant or wax over the case mouth, cutting out a disc, after the powder charge is in place. Seating the bullet will then force the wad down snugly against the powder. It's usually a good idea to reduce the powder charge to compensate for the space that will be occupied by the wad.

Left is an original U.M.C. .50-70 case, compared with the new D.G.W. case, shown complete and sectioned.

BULLETS FOR BLACK-POWDER LOADS

Black-powder calibers were originally loaded with very soft lead bullets. Plain unhardened scrap lead will generally do quite well for casting such bullets; it should be no harder than a $^1/_{20}$ alloy. Jacketed bullets suitable for some of the old calibers are available, but most of the original guns have soft-steel barrels which will be worn a great deal more by jacketed bullets than by lead. Considering that little is to be gained in bullet performance on game by jacketed bullets, lead ones are really the best choice. Most black-powder numbers won't drive bullets fast enough to produce significant expansion in game, and so there's little justification for the more costly bullets.

At one time or another, Lyman offered molds for all the black-powder bullets. Most of them are no longer catalogued and very few are stocked these days, but at least one or two bullets may still be special-ordered for most of those calibers at some delay in delivery and additional cost. There are also custom mold makers, who will supply excellent molds for almost any size, weight, and type of black-powder bullets.

Many of the black-powder bullets may be loaded without sizing; they can be lubricated right from the mold by dipping or setting them in molten lubricant and then removing them with a cake cutter, or by simply smearing bullet lubricant into the grooves by hand. Bullet molds were originally designed when reloading equipment was very basic, so bullet diameters were established as those which could be loaded without forcing the individual to buy or make sizing equipment. The more modern bullets will usually require sizing, and the makers of lubricator-sizers offer a wide variety of die and punch diameters to make this possible.

Generally speaking, it's best to stick with original black-powder bullet designs and weights for the caliber involved. However, lighter or heavier bullets may be used within the limitations imposed by the gun. Single-shot rifles will often accommodate ammunition with the bullet seated to a greater-than-original length. In fact, many of them will produce their best accuracy with the bullet seated out so that it actually touches the rifling when the round is fully chambered. Often this makes it possible to load a

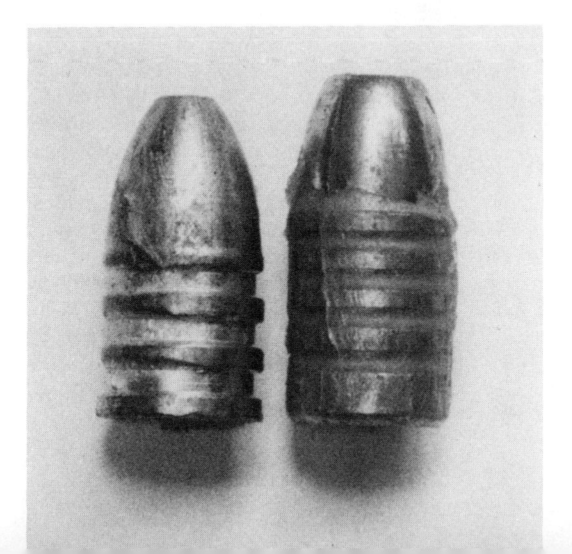

Typical black-powder bullet designs with several wide lubricant grooves and cast of soft lead. The bullet at left is as cast, while the one at right has been lubricated by simply smearing lubricant into the grooves with the fingers.

heavier charge of powder, and if the recoil isn't objectionable, this will produce a more efficient load. The heavier powder charge should be determined just as previously described. If you don't want to use the additional space for more powder when loading a lighter-than-standard bullet, best results will be obtained if the powder is held in place by a tight-fitting card wad seated firmly upon it. Many of the older repeating rifles have feed mechanisms which are not very tolerant of variations in overall cartridge length. For this reason, standard length should be adhered to rather closely, regardless of the weight and length bullet used.

CRIMPING

Though a tight bullet/case assembly is not necessary for efficient combustion of black powder, almost all of the old repeating rifles use tubular magazines. This makes a heavy roll crimp necessary if bullets are to be retained securely under the influence of recoil and long, stiff magazine springs. Actually, what really causes the problem is that the cartridges tend to stand still as the gun recoils rearward, compressing the magazine spring; then, when recoil movement stops, the spring slams the column of cartridges hard to the rear, and with as many as a dozen cartridges, one on top of the other, the one at the bottom receives a helluva thump. If the bullet isn't held very tightly, it will be shoved deeper into the case, as far as the powder charge will allow. Then, in many guns, that short cartridge won't feed correctly. If this magazine problem seems like a small thing, imagine for a moment a lightweight .45-70 Winchester '86 carbine with a half-dozen rounds in the magazine. Each bullet weighs over an ounce, and the case and the powder add the better part of another ounce. That's two-thirds to three-quarters of a pound of lead, brass, and powder slamming against the nose of the rearmost cartridge in the magazine. It takes a stiff crimp to withstand that amount of force.

Though full charges of black powder are most often used, small charges may be employed where less power and recoil are desired. If the charge occupies less than about half of the available case volume, performance may be improved by seating a tight-fitting card wad over it to hold it back against the head of the case.

FOULING—AND AN ALTERNATIVE

Though black powder is romantic, it does have its disadvantages in the vast amount of black, sooty fouling it generates. Approximately 56 percent of black powder's weight remains behind as ash. While a large amount of this makes that delightful cloud of pungent white smoke at the muzzle, some of it remains in the gun and accumulates into a thick, gummy coating. If you find this objectionable, there is a recently developed substitute for black powder that produces essentially the same performance with the same volume of propellant, makes a lovely cloud of white smoke, and, in fact, possesses all the traditional characteristics of black powder *except* the objectionable fouling. This propellant is called Pyrodex and was developed by the late Dan Pawlak, who died in early 1977 as a result of an explosion at the original Pyrodex plant near Seattle. Developed originally for muzzleloading guns, Pyrodex is also produced in "CTG Grade" specifically for metallic cartridges. It is loaded bulk-for-bulk with black powder. However, because of its somewhat different density, it cannot be loaded *weight-for-weight* with black powder. The proper charge of Pyrodex is achieved by simply using the same volume as of black powder.

The simplest way of doing this is to cut down a cartridge case to make a charge cup that will hold the proper black-powder charge, then use it for the Pyrodex. Alternatively, set an adjustable measure to throw the proper charge of black powder, and then it will throw the correct charge of Pyrodex, though the latter will weigh less.

Pyrodex requires substantial compression in order to ignite and burn efficiently. For this reason, the charge should be adjusted so that substantial pressure will be exerted upon it when the bullet is seated; and this in turn requires a tight bullet/case assembly and a heavy roll crimp applied simultaneously with or immediately following seating to prevent the bullet from being forced back out by the propellant.

SMOKELESS POWDER IN BLACK-POWDER CALIBERS

Some loading manuals contain a limited number of smokeless-powder loads for those black-powder calibers which have survived in manufacture until now. However, with the single exception of the *Lyman Cast Bullet Handbook,* most of them concentrate on jacketed-bullet loads. The Lyman book is the principal source of lead-bullet loads in these calibers, which are .25-20, .32-20, .38-40, .44-40, .45 Colt, .38-55, and .45-70. This smokeless-powder loading data is carefully developed with the limitations of original guns in mind. They are, of necessity, limited to pressures that the weakest of the old guns will withstand. Consequently, for example, .44-40 loads are limited to the capabilities of the M1873 Winchester. They can be increased, but only for use in guns known to be stronger, such as the Winchester single-shot, or the Winchester M1892 rifle. Likewise, unless otherwise identified, .45-70 loads are limited to what the trapdoor Springfield will withstand. Again, for the stronger Winchester single-shot and M1886 rifles, the loads may be increased considerably.

CLEANING FIRED BLACK-POWDER CASES

Loading with black powder differs from smokeless (or Pyrodex, for that matter) in that after firing, the cases need immediate additional attention before they are laid aside to await their next loading. After firing they will be thickly coated inside with sooty black-powder fouling, and perhaps to a lesser degree on the outside as well. If it is left there the fouling will not only corrode the brass, but will harden and be very difficult to remove later—and will spoil your resizing die if it isn't removed. As soon as is practical after firing, decap the cases manually, then dump them in a bucket of hot water to which a bit of detergent has been added. Let them soak for a while, then agitate them a bit to loosen the fouling. The exterior fouling will wipe off easily enough, but to get it all out of the inside you may have to use a small bottle brush or a bore-cleaning brush. In any event, get rid of all that fouling, then rinse in hottest water and dry before putting the cases away. Cases seem to last forever when treated this way, but if they are not thoroughly cleaned after firing, they may not even be suitable for a second loading six months later.

Except for the slight variations in technique described earlier in this chapter, the actual operations and processes for loading black-powder calibers are exactly the same as described in Chapter 4. Cases are resized, decapped, and reprimed, and the necks are expanded. Then they are charged with powder, and bullets are seated and crimped or not crimped as the circumstances dictate.

Careful handloading of the old black-powder calibers opens up a whole new world of shooting fun. Century-old designs fairly reek with history and tradition. There's something about shooting an old Colt Lightning or Winchester '73 rifle that simply can't be matched by a modern high-velocity magnum rifle in spite of the latter's vast technological superiority. Billy the Kid and Pat Garrett never used a bolt-action magnum, and there were no Winchester Model 70s at the Battle of San Juan Hill or fighting the Moros in the Philippines.

14

Case Forming: Making What You Need from What You've Got

IN THE CLOSING DAYS OF WWII, there were lots of souvenir 8 × 57mm Mauser rifles that had made their way back to the U.S. Unfortunately, there was virtually no commercial ammunition available to fit them, and as soon as the few rounds that accompanied the rifles were shot up, the owners were looking for more. The fired German military cases couldn't be reloaded because there were no Berdan primers available to fit. In fact, at that time there were damned few primers of any sort to be had. After all, there was a war on. But, there being a war on, and soldiers being what they are the world over, it wasn't difficult to pick up military .30-06 ammunition. A number of ingenious people discovered very quickly that one could pull the bullet and dump the powder from the .30 caliber cartridges, then resize the cases in an 8 × 57mm die, trim them to length, and have brand-new 8mm Mauser primed cases ready for loading. The really resourceful handloader could even use those .30 bullets in the 8mm case by simply bumping them up to a larger diameter; however, that's an *advanced* handloading project which we can't cover here. In any event, needing ammunition for some Mauser rifles, I ordered some of that stuff loaded in reformed .30-06 cases from George Spence down in Steele, Missouri. That was my introduction to case forming, for I immediately deduced how he'd done the job. From that day onward, I made thousands of cases in other calibers from recovered military brass, and even got so involved in converting one case to another that fifteen years later I wrote a book on the subject, titled *Cartridge Conversions*. If this sort of thing turns you on, that book is still available, and may be obtained without too much difficulty.

As it turns out, the many different calibers you see in ammunition catalogs are loaded in cases that are not as different as you might first think.

This fine old Winchester M1886 rifle is chambered for the .40-82 Winchester cartridge, which was discontinued about 40 years ago. Handloading combined with case forming is the only way in which this gun, and tens of thousands like it, can ever hope to be placed in action again. With modern reformed cases and proper loads, this old gun is just as effective a hunting rifle now as it was 85 years go. It can drive a 260-grain bullet at nearly 2000 feet per second, making it a superb gun for almost any North American game at ranges up to 100-150 yards. It gives one a deep feeling of satisfaction and accomplishment to make up with his own hands *good* ammunition for one of these rifles and put it back into service.

For example, ther are three basic types of case heads—rimless, rimmed, and belted—and they come in relatively few sizes. The .30-06 case head was originally copied from the 8mm Mauser head, and is common to over a score of domestic and European cartridges. The Holland & Holland belted case head, dating from 1912 or thereabouts, has been copied by all our domestic belted magnums with the single exception of the smaller and larger Weatherby calibers. Even the 105-year-old .45-70 case has the same head as nearly twenty, long-discontinued black-powder cases. Other head sizes are nearly as widely used.

This high degree of commonality among case-head types and sizes makes it possible to reshape one case to serve the purpose of another, as long as the two share the same type and size head. As an example, .30-06 brass may be reshaped (and sometimes shortened) to form perfectly good cases in calibers .22-250, .250-3000, .257 Roberts, 6mm Remington, .243 Winchester, .25-06, .270 Winchester, 7mm Mauser, .280 Remington, .300 Savage, .308 Winchester, 7.65mm Mauser, 8mm Mauser, 8 × 60mm, 9mm Mauser, .358 Winchester, 9.3mm Mauser, 9.5mm Mannlicher, 9.3 × 62mm, and quite a few others I can't call to mind at the moment. The .30-06 is probably the most useful for forming other calibers, but the .30-40, .45-70, .375 H&H, and a few others can also be quite useful. In addition to that, in recent years we have been offered special "basic" cases which are new cases with a cylindrical body made upon one of the standard head types and sizes. These cases are made primarily for reforming into various other calibers that are no longer available. Norma-Precision was the first to do this, offering cylindrical cases with .30-06 and belted magnum heads nearly twenty years ago. Almost that far back I had a substantial quantity of cases 3 1/4 inches long made on the .45-70 head for the same purpose. Since then, other makers have gotten into the act, the most recent being BELL (Brass Extrusion Laboratories Limited).

There are two reasons for making one caliber of case into another. The first and most compelling reason is to make cases that are no longer manufactured and therefore are not available. The second is to save money by

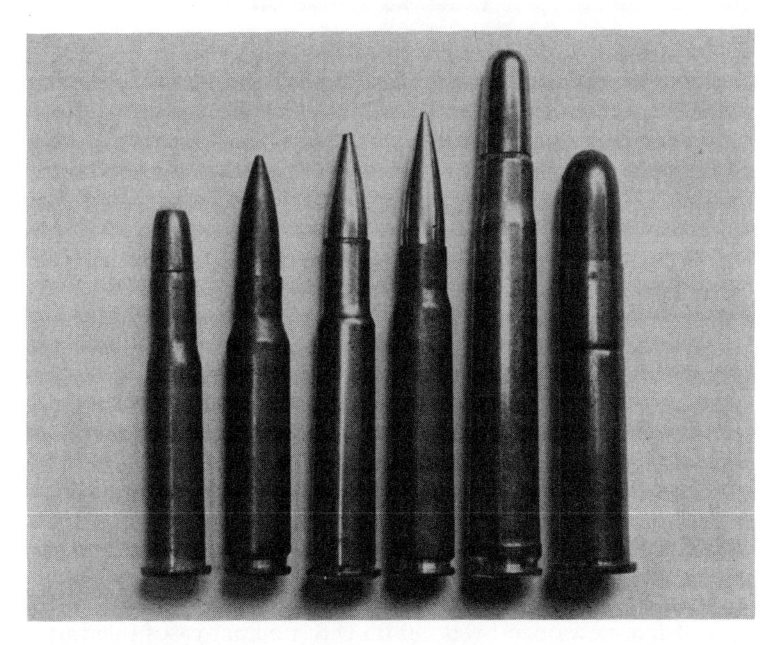

Six cartridges, five standard head shapes and sizes which are common to the bulk of modern rifle calibers and thus make case forming practical. Left to right, .30-30 Winchester, .308 Winchester (.30-06 head), .30-40, 7mm Mauser (.30-06 head), .375 H&H Magnum, .45-70

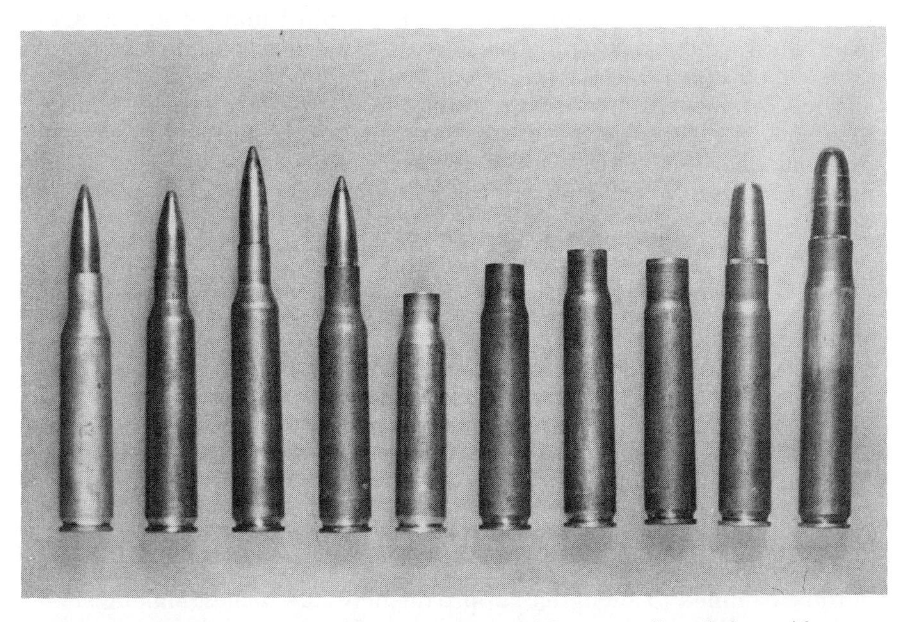

These ten different calibers, ranging from 6mm to 9.3mm, are all easily formed from the .30-06 case and constitute only about half of the practical possibilities.

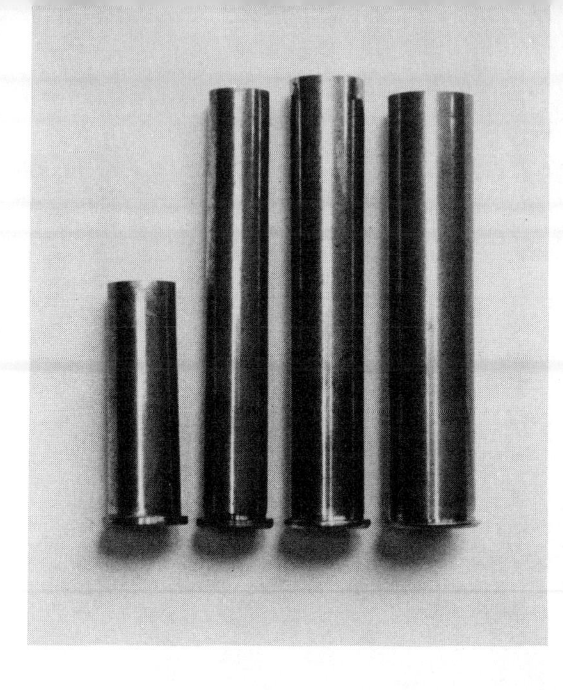

New "basic" cases are currently being manufactured specifically for reforming to other calibers. From left, D.G.W. .50-70, RCBS .45 basic, BELL .50 basic, and BELL .577.

making what you have into what you need. At one time, I had many thousands of like-new once-fired .30-06 U.S. military cases piled up in my garage. They had cost only a few cents per pound, so each case cost only a fraction of a cent. When I wanted to load, say, .270 Winchester or .308 ammunition, it would have been ridiculously wasteful to pay 10 cents each for new factory cases when I could make them so simply from that pile of .30-06 brass. And when I obtained a fine 7 × 64mm Brenneke rifle, not a single round of factory-loaded ammunition could I find for it, not at any price, but I could make quite satisfactory cases in that caliber from that same .30-06 brass.

The .30-06 won't do for everything, but everything can be achieved somehow. When I acquired a .40-60 caliber Winchester M1876 rifle, the cartridge had long been discontinued and none were available. I bought new .45-70 cases (not cheap, even then) and shortened and resized them to work perfectly in that old rifle.

Those examples should give you an idea of the usefulness of case forming. In its most elementary form, it consists of nothing more than simply resizing an existing case to form one of another caliber. Examples of this are resizing the .45-70 to the long-discontinued .40-65 or .38-56 blackpowder calibers, and running .30-06 cases into .270 Winchester or .25-06 Remington dies. The "basic" case (the one used to make what you need) in those examples not only has the correct head type and size, but the correct length. The entire job is done just as easily and quickly as resizing a fired case.

One step up the ladder in complexity are those reforming jobs which also require trimming the basic case. Making 7mm and 8mm Mauser cases from the .30-06 is an excellent example, for after the resizing operation they must be trimmed to a length of approximately 2.24 inches. Making .45-60 and .40-60 Winchester cases from the .45-70 requires the same operations—resize, then trim to length.

To the best of my knowledge, the first batch of this basic case was made up by Kynoch for me over twenty years ago; "Nonte Taylor" headstamp identifies these .45 × 3¼-inch cases, which have now become collector's items.

Trimming to another caliber usually involves removing far more brass than can be done conveniently on the typical hand-operated case trimmer. A power trimmer will knock off ½ inch of excess brass quickly and easily, but it is by no means necessary. Most die manufacturers make what is called a "form and trim die," and when the basic case is run into it, one simply hacksaws off the surplus protruding from the top of the die, then files the cut edge smooth and flush with the die surface, and the job is finished. Some form and trim dies resize the case fully, others simply do part of the job, so that after shortening it must be run into a proper full-length die. But you don't even need that to turn out enough cases to get a rifle talking again. Simply resize the case first, mark it at a point slightly greater than the finished length, and remove the bulk of the excess with either a tubing cutter or a hacksaw; then bring it to final length in an ordinary case trimmer.

When the basic case is a good deal longer than the one being formed, some makes and designs of dies will require that the decapping rod be re-

RCBS form and trim die in use: case run all the way in, excess being cut off with hacksaw.

A complete forming-die set offered by RCBS for making .250-3000 Savage cases from the .30-06. From left, die #1, which partially forms the new shoulder without affecting the neck; die #2, which reduces the neck partially; die #3, a form and trim die which brings the neck to the final outside diameter and permits trimming to correct length; and die #4, which is a neck-reaming die. The reamer protruding from the top of the die may be turned by hand or power to cut away excess brass inside the case neck. After die #4, the neck and shoulder of the case should be annealed, and the final operation in producing a ready-to-load case is running it into a full-length sizing die.

moved to prevent interference; others may require that part of the surplus length be chopped off before resizing because there simply isn't room in the die for it. These are minor points, and you'll discover them readily enough as they crop up.

When the neck diameter of a basic case is reduced a good deal, or when it is shortened substantially, the neck walls may become too thick. As the neck is reduced in diameter, the excess brass has to go somewhere, and so the walls are thickened; and as the case is shortened substantially, the new neck falls in a thicker part of the case walls. When a bullet of the proper diameter is seated in this thicker neck, its diameter may be too great to even enter the chamber, or it may enter well enough, but without adequate clearance, producing excessive pressures. This little problem is solved by either reaming the inside of the necks or turning the outside to reduce wall thickness. Because of variations in chambers and cases, it's difficult to predict at just what point reaming or turning may become necessary. Making either 7mm or 8mm cases from .30 cases never seems to require any such action but, reducing a .30 case to 6mm may require reaming, and reducing it further to .22 caliber will certainly require reaming.

All the situations we've discussed so far require the use of a basic case as long or longer than the one to be made. What happens if the case you need is substantially longer than an otherwise suitable basic case that is available? Well, it depends on how great the length difference might be. In some instances, as much as 1/8 inch difference will not have any serious effect, and

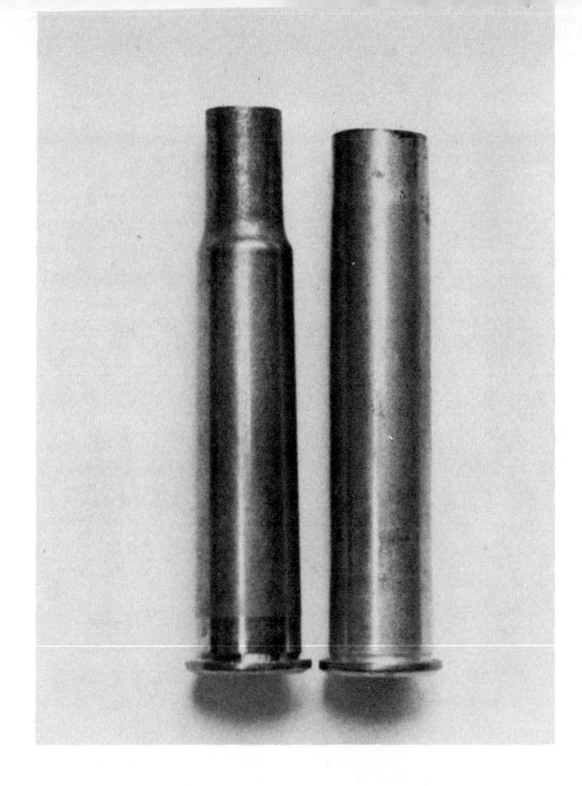

At left a fired .30-40 case, and at right the same case with its mouth expanded and fire-formed for use as a "short case" in the .405 Winchester. This case is about $^3/_{10}$ inch too short, but the long .405 bullet allows it to be used.

may simply be ignored. A classic example of this would be using the .30-40 case for the .35 Winchester. The Winchester case is approximately $^1/_8$ inch longer than the .30-40, but it has quite a long neck to begin with, so even coming up $^1/_8$ inch short, it will still have plenty of neck to support a bullet properly. The use of the shorter case means that $^1/_8$ inch of the chamber neck will not be covered by brass, so that portion of the chamber neck will eventually be roughened and eroded by powder gases, but this won't cause any serious problems unless a really great amount of ammunition is fired. It would take thousands of rounds to make that portion of the neck rough enough to cause extraction problems if full-length cases were used later. Using the .45-70 case for .45-90 loads is another example; the former is approximately $^3/_{10}$ inch shorter than the latter, but all other dimensions are the same. Bullets are simply seated to a greater (than .45-70) overall cartridge length, as long as a sufficient amount of the bullet is held within the case to resist the stresses of feeding through the magazine. This is an unusual example, and seldom will as much as $^3/_{10}$ inch shortage in the basic case be tolerated.

There isn't anything more that the individual in his home shop can do about this condition, but a very few specialists in this field have learned to re-draw basic cases to greater length. In this area, Robert Pomeroy draws .45-70 cases to .45-90 length, and he also stretches .30-40 out to .35 and .405 Winchester length. Occasionally it's worthwhile to purchase redrawn cases from one of these specialists to suit your needs. This is custom work and expensive, but it may be the only way out.

The new basic cases available from RCBS and BELL are all $3^1/_4$ inches long. They are made to this length because it is the longest that one might ever need. Yet they may be shortened by as much as half that amount in

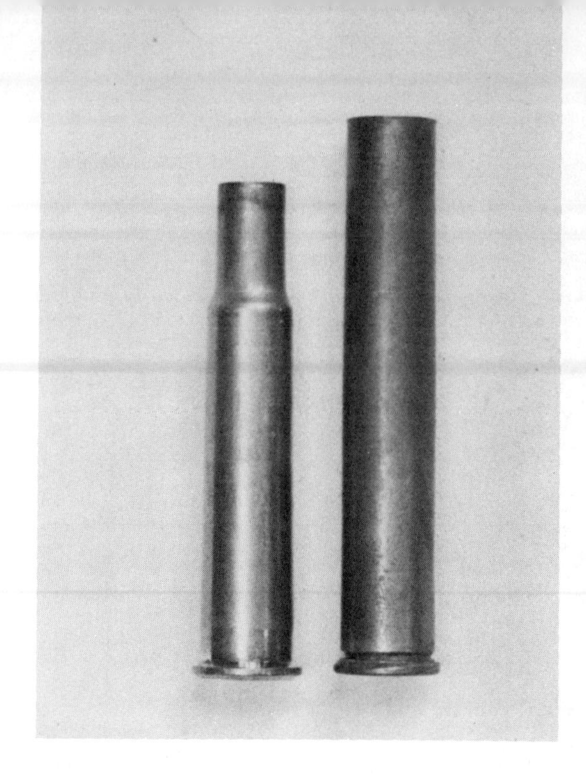

At left a fired .30-40 case, and at right the same thing redrawn by Pomeroy to the correct length for the .405 Winchester. It may then be resized to produce full-length cases in .35, .40-72, and .38-70 Winchester calibers.

some forming operations. For example, the .45 Basic has a .45-70 head, and may be cut all the way back to as little as 1.75 inches to produce the shortest of the old .45 caliber black-powder cases. Of course, it would be foolish to do so as long as .45-70 cases are available at a much lower cost. Generally, the .45 basic case is used only to make those calibers with cases longer than the .45-70.

When a basic case is shortened substantially and its neck diameter is reduced a good deal, problems are almost certain to be encountered unless it is annealed. The .30-06 may be shortened $^1/_2$ inch and necked down to make .243 brass, and the result will *look* very nice. However, the job places the new neck in a harder portion of the original case, and the considerable reshaping of the brass work-hardens it extensively. Unless the neck and shoulder are annealed, they're almost certain to split in short order. If loaded and fired right away, the splits may not show up for some time, but they may occur during bullet seating, or in storage after the cases are loaded. While relatively inexperienced in this area, I once made up a bunch of 6.5mm cases from '06 brass, loaded them without annealing, and set them up on the shelf awaiting future use. A few months later they were taken down, and it was discovered that over one-third of the necks had split. The combination of extensively work-hardened brass and very tight bullet/case assembly simply placed too much stress on the necks and after a while they simply gave up and split.

Traditionally, cases have been annealed by heating the neck/mouth/shoulder area to a dull red with a small torch flame, then immediately quenching the entire case in cold water. This softens the brass in the heated area, increasing its ductibility. However, this is an imprecise method at best, usually resulting in wide variations between cases simply

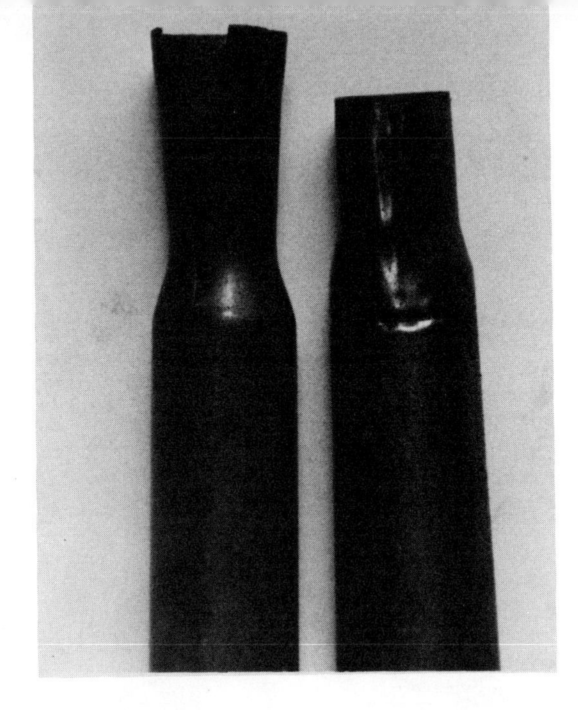

Common problems in necking down basic cases a large amount: At left is a neck, which split upon being run over an expander plug after having been reduced in one pass from 9.3mm to 7mm. At right is a fold in a .45-70 case produced when it was necked down to .33 caliber in one pass.

because heat cannot be applied and judged uniformly.

A far better method consists of immersing the affected portion of the case in molten bullet alloy for a specific period of time, thus insuring uniform heating of the brass. The cases should be prepared by decapping and cleaning and dipping the part to be annealed in light oil or finely-powdered graphite. If cases are not decapped, air will be compressed inside and will prevent molten lead from rising to the proper level; if oil or graphite is not applied, molten lead may "solder" itself to the case (less likely in plated cases), creating a very difficult removal problem. With cases prepared, bullet metal should be melted, then allowed to stabilize at a temperature just high enough to insure that the mix remains entirely fluid. Case mouths are then immersed vertically in the lead to the depth of the bullet seat, or, in the instance of bottle-neck calibers, to the rear of the shoulder. Five seconds is a good starting immersion time, but may be adjusted (less for harder, more for softer) to suit the caliber and your preference. The case is then withdrawn, given a flip of the wrist to throw off lead that might be clinging to the surface, then dropped into a container of cool water. As soon as cases have cooled, dried and been degreased, they are ready for further reloading operations. Unplated cases will show a dull, blue-gray or brownish color over the annealed area; this is not harmful, but may be polished off if you desire.

Cases reformed from another caliber will normally possess thicker walls and therefore less internal capacity than if originally manufactured in the same caliber. The greater the amount of reduction, the greater the degree of this condition. Resizing a .30-06 case to .270 Winchester has virtually no effect on volume; however, squeezing the same case down to 7mm Mauser or to .22-250 results in substantially reduced volume. This means simply that loading data intended for cases originally manufactured in a particular caliber will produce higher pressures in a reformed case. For this reason,

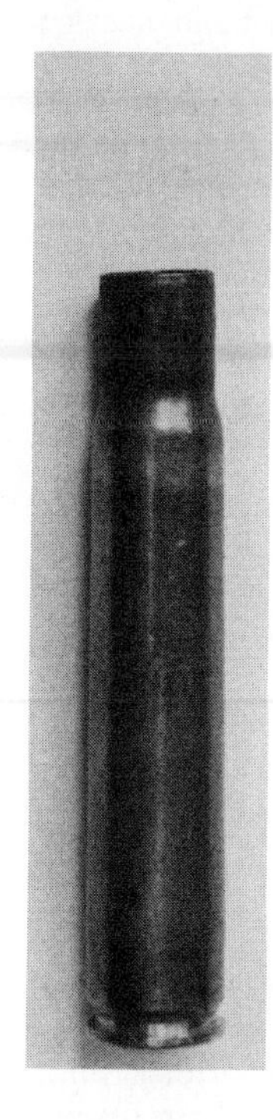

Expanding this .30-06 neck to .35 caliber (for the .35 Whelen) in the conventional manner produced this off-center and out-of-square condition. Not visible is the wide variation in the neck-wall thickness also produced by the expanding operation; the neck is hardly half as thick on the left as it is on the right.

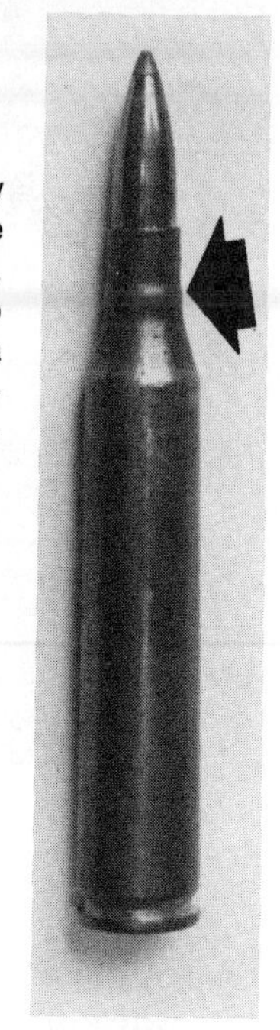

The arrow shows the secondary shoulder formed when this .30-06 case was necked down to .280 Remington. This slight shoulder allows the case to be supported in the chamber by a "crush fit" so that the shoulder fire-forms to match the chamber without excessive stretching of the case.

one should always reduce the powder charge by 5 to 10 percent when switching from original-manufacture to reformed cases in any caliber. If a maximum load proved safe in original-manufacture 7mm Mauser cases is used in reformed .30-06 cases, chamber pressures are almost certain to be excessive and perhaps even dangerous. Keep this in mind when loading reformed cases.

Occasionally, reforming will involve *increasing* neck diameter rather than reducing it. You might very well have a supply of 7mm cases and want to use them in 8mm caliber; and while opening up the neck seems simple enough, often it isn't. Simply running an ordinary expander plug into the neck to open it up will usually move the neck off center and may also drag one side down a bit, producing an out-of-square case mouth. The off-square condition won't introduce any functional problems, and the off-center neck can be cleared up by resizing. However, the off-center condition will have made one side of the neck much thinner than the other, and resizing won't cure that. This problem can be reduced in severity by performing the expansion in successive small stages with highly-polished tapered expanding plugs combined with plenty of resizing lubricant. The necks and mouths will come out better this way, but they still won't be perfect. Really, your best bet is to use a case longer than needed, and depend upon reduction of the neck and trimming to produce a better job.

Fire-forming constitutes an important part of case forming. This means simply that a reformed case comes out a bit undersize at the shoulder and thus its volume is less than it should be, and it is expanded to the proper shape and volume by firing it in the gun. A typical example is reforming the .30-06 to .280 Remington. The Remington shoulder is a few thousandths of an inch farther from the case head than that of the '06. This would normally set up a condition of excess headspace, but when the .30 neck is reduced to .280 caliber, the die leaves a small secondary shoulder at the junction of neck and shoulder, and for that first shot, this provides sufficient contact to eliminate the excess-headspace condition. Then, when the loaded cartridge is fired, the short shoulder is "blown out" into contact with the chamber shoulder and thus assumes the correct shape and dimensions. A more extreme example would be the making of .225 Winchester cases from .30-30 brass. After resizing, the new case would have a shoulder that is incomplete and of the incorrect angle, and it would be substantially undersize as well. Firing will blow this area out to fit the chamber, giving the case its final and correct shape. The amount of fire-forming in this instance is quite substantial, and it is not uncommon for a case to split under those conditions. Another example is found in forming .308 cases from '06 brass. The resizing die shoves the shoulder back to the proper location, and trimming establishes the correct length. However, the '06 case tapers more sharply than the .308 and is about .015 inch smaller in diameter at the shoulder. Fire-forming corrects this condition.

While fire-forming is an essential part of case forming, it should be held to the minimum by selecting the basic case carefully. Very light loads with fast-burning powders have often been recommended in the past for fire-forming; however, I've always obtained better results with fairly stiff loads.

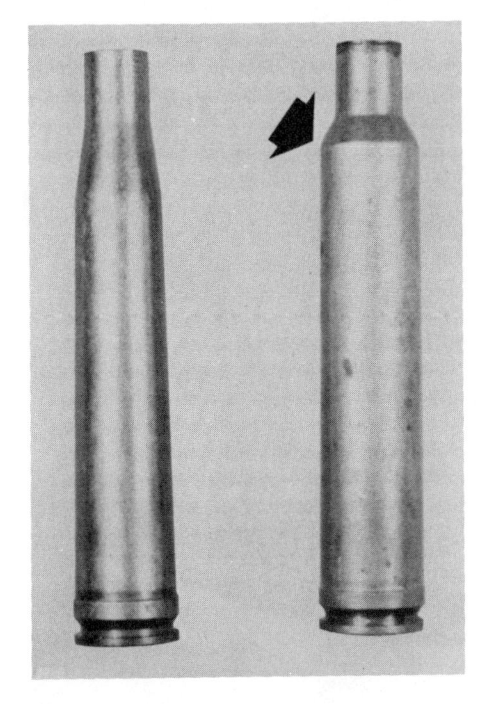

A typical fire-forming operation. At left is the .300 H&H Magnum and at right is the same case fired in an "improved" version of the chamber, producing the much sharper shoulder angle and larger shoulder diameter at arrow.

Multiple forming steps for the fairly difficult job of making 6.5mm Remington Magnum cases from 7mm Magnum brass. At left is the fired 7mm case, followed by the same case with the shoulder partially formed as a first operation, then the neck and shoulder brought to final dimensions and form by a second die, and finally, the case after it has been trimmed to length in a form and trim die. At this point, the case will require annealing of the neck and shoulder or it is likely to split in only one or two firings.

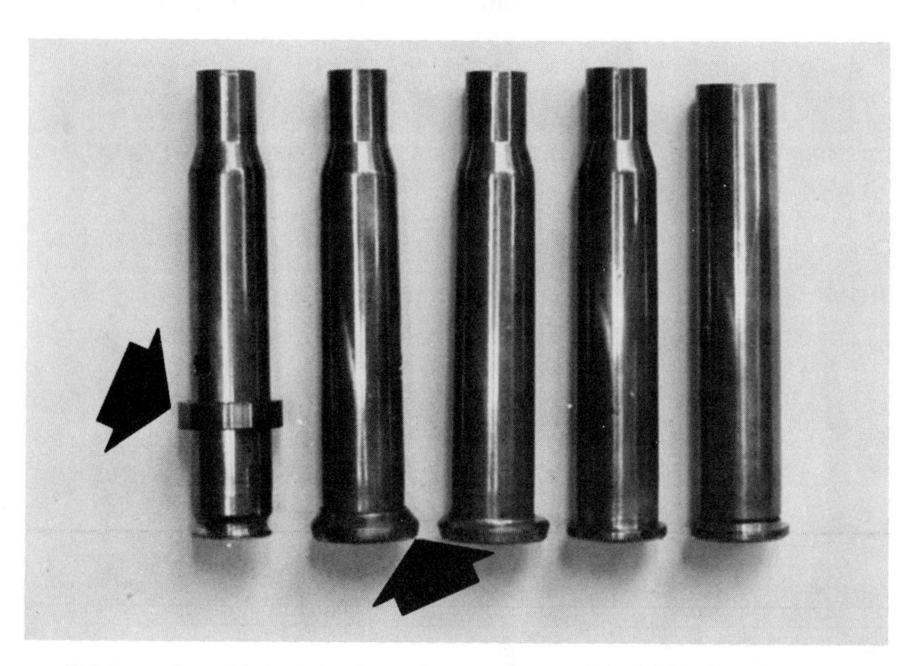

This is a truly sophisticated and complex case-forming job which indicates just how far you may go if you get deeply into the game. At left is a .30-06 case over which has been slipped a turned brass ring. Next, the ring has been forced to the case head and swaged into the extraction groove. The ring has then been swaged in a second operation which locked it permanently to the case head. A new rim was then turned from the swaged ring to .405 Winchester configuration. Last, the case was fire-formed and trimmed to fit the .405 Winchester chamber. This type of job is definitely not for the neophyte or the amateur.

Medium loads—for the reformed caliber taken from loading manuals—usually do the job best. In the interest of economy, cast bullets can be used in a load that falls somewhere between the midrange and full-charge classes.

There are a rather goodly number of other, more complex, case-forming operations that can be used by the advanced handloader. However, I think those not so advanced should stick with the basic jobs which involve only resizing, trimming, reaming or turning, and fire-forming. Toward that end, I've prepared a table listing the forming jobs you're most likely to encounter, along with the basic case (the most commonly available one), comparative dimensions of the two, and the operations necessary to complete the job. Referring to the table when a job comes up may save a lot of research in other references.

CASE-FORMING TABLE

With some batches of cases, neck reduction of more than about .020 inch may have to be done in more than one stage. An example is reducing the .308 to .243. A proper intermediate step would be to first reduce the neck in a 7mm die, then to .243. That much reduction will also usually require annealing of the neck and shoulder.

Caliber	Make from	Operations
.219 Zipper	.30–30	Resize .25–35; resize full-length; ream neck
.222 Remington	.223/.222 Mag.	Resize full length; trim to 1.70″
.22–250	.250–3000 Sav.	Resize full-length
.243 Winchester	.308/7.62 mm	Resize full-length; ream neck
6mm Remington	.30–06	Resize 7mm Mauser; trim to 2.24″; resize full-length; ream neck
.25–35 Winchester	.30–30	Resize full-length
.257 Roberts	.30–06	Resize 7mm Mauser; trim to 2.23″; resize full-length
.25–06	.30–06	Resize full-length
.270 Winchester	.30–06	Resize full-length
7mm Mauser	.30–06	Resize full-length; trim to 2.24″
7 × 64mm	.30–06	Resize full-length; fire-form
.280 Remington	.30–06	Resize full length; fire-form
.300 Sav.	.30–06 (.308)	Resize full-length; trim to 1.87″; ream neck
.300 H&H	.375 H&H	Resize full-length
.300 Winchester Mag.	.300 H&H	Resize full-length; trim to 2.60″; fire-form
.308 Winchester	.30–06	Resize full-length; trim to 2.00″; fire-form

Continued on next page

Case-Forming Table *(continued)*

Caliber	Make from	Operations
7.65mm Mauser	.30–06	Resize full-length; trim to 2.09″
7.7mm Japanese	.30–06	Resize full-length; trim to 2.28″; fire-form
.32 Special	.30–30	Resize full-length
8mm Mauser	.30–06	Resize full-length; trim to 2.24″
.33 Winchester	.45–70	Resize full-length; trim to 2.10″
.358 Winchester	.30–06	Resize full-length; trim to 2.00″
.35 Winchester	.30–40 Pomeroy redraw	Resize full-length
.38–55 Winchester	.30–30	Expand neck; fire-form
.38–56 Winchester	.45–70	Resize full-length
.38–70 Winchester	45 RCBS Basic	Resize full-length; trim to 2.34″
.38–72	.30–40 Pomeroy redraw	Trim to 2.58″; resize full-length
.40–60 Winchester	.45–70	Resize full-length; trim to 2.58″
.40–70 BN Sharps	.45 RCBS Basic	Trim to 2.25″; resize full-length
.40–82	.45 RCBS Basic	Trim to 2.40; resize full-length
.40–90 BN Sharp	.45 RCBS Basic	Trim to 2.63″; resize full-length
.405 Winchester	.30–40 Pomeroy redraw	Resize full-length
.45–60 Winchester	.45–70	Trim to 1.89″
.45–75 Winchester	.50 Bell Basic	Trim to 1.86″; resize full-length
.45–90 Winchester	.45 RCBS Basic	Trim to 2.40″
.45–2 ⅞″ Sharps	.45 RCBS Basic	Trim to 2.875″
.577–450 Martini	.577 Bell	Trim to 2.34″; resize full-length
.50–70 U.S.	.50 Bell Basic	Trim to 1.75″
.50–110 Winchester	.50 Bell Basic	Trim to 2.40″

15

Problems and Solutions

THE ODDS ARE EVEN that if you start out with good equipment, excellent-condition fired or new cases, carefully chosen components, and wisely selected loads, and stick with the more or less standard calibers and don't go in for the real hotshot magnums and maximum-velocity .22s, it may be a long time before you encounter any problems.

Of course, inattention and carelessness will cause problems right away. But ambition also causes problems. Ambition in attempting to use hotter and hotter loads or to branch out into the more potent magnum cartridges. Ambition in attempting for one reason or another to use unsuitable powders and bullets or to stretch case life beyond what it would normally be. Whatever the reason, though, sooner or later the problems will crop up.

CASE SEPARATIONS

The time may come when you notice a brightly polished ring not too far in front of the case head. That is, if you're lucky, it will be just a bright ring, though it might show up as a crack extending partway around the case. At its worst, the crack will go all the way around the case, and when you open the action, the head will separate and come out alone, leaving the rest of the case in the chamber. This is called a "case separation"; if there's only a slight crack, it's called an "incipient separation." The bright ring is a sign it's coming, and indicates that each loading and firing has been stretching the case just a little bit more, producing a thinned ring just above where the walls join the head. When you first notice the bright ring, make a short right-angle bend in the end of a thin piece of spring wire and probe inside the case down near the head; you'll feel a shallow groove there which is a clear indication that the case is approaching separation.

This can be caused by either excess headspace in the gun or an excess headspace condition in the case produced by improper adjustment of the resizing die.

Separations develop whenever there is more clearance than there should be between the shoulder of the case and the shoulder of the chamber, and it develops regardless of whether rimmed-case or belted-case headspace might be perfect. It's often said that if headspace is correct, cases won't separate; but that applies *only* to rimless cases, which normally headspace upon the shoulder. Belted, rimmed, and semi-rimmed cases will stretch and eventually separate if there is excess shoulder clearance, no matter how perfect headspace may be.

Here is what happens: When firing occurs, the propellant gas expands in all directions and forces the brass into contact with chamber walls and bolt face. If the case headspaces on some sort of rim, this pressure thrusts the shoulder forward to fill the chamber; if the case headspaces on its shoulder, it is driven forward by firing-pin blow and primer thrust, placing the shoulder in firm contact with the chamber shoulder, after which the expanding gas drives the head back against the bolt face. The result is the same either way—the case walls are stretched—and that stretching manifests itself in a thinning just ahead of the solid web. Unless the condition is very severe, a single firing won't cause separation, but if the case is resized in such a manner that the shoulder is pushed back to its original position, then as little as two to four firings will stretch the case to the point that it cracks at the thinned area.

There's really nothing you can do about this condition in the first firing of a new case, or a case that has already been resized. However, once you've identified the condition in a particular gun, you can give the fired cases a treatment which will virtually eliminate the problem in future loadings. After the first firing, set up the resizing die in your press, but back it out about 1/2 turn from its original adjustment. Then, with a candle, apply a thin coat of soot to the neck and shoulder area of a fired case. Make sure there's a thin film of lubricant on the die first, because this is not the time for a stuck case. Run the case into the die, then extract it and look at it without disturbing the soot coating; you'll see the soot scraped from most of the neck and part of the body behind the shoulder, but it should be undisturbed on the shoulder proper. Turn the die into the press just a wee bit, and repeat the process. Keep repeating this until you can see disturbance in the soot coating on the shoulder that indicates the die shoulder has just barely made contact with the case shoulder. Verify that the case will chamber freely, then lock the die in this position. Now you can resize the rest of that batch of cases without pushing the shoulder back and thus creating the excess shoulder clearance that results in case separations. Incidentally, it's a good idea to remove the decapping stem while this is being done, mainly to prevent overworking the neck and perhaps spoiling that particular case. Also, clean the soot from the die afterward.

Take note of the fact that case separations are far more common in rimmed and belted cases than in the rimless type. This stems from the fact that manufacturers of both guns and ammunition hold the head-to-shoulder dimension much more closely in rimless cases simply because they headspace on the shoulder; in the other types, they get a little bit sloppy with this dimension while concentrating on rim or belt dimensions where the case headspaces technically. I've seen belted magnum chambers and ammunition so poorly matched in the shoulder area that even the very first firing produced a distinct thinning of the case and as few as three firings produced a separation.

PRIMER LEAKS

There's another form of case failure you may eventually encounter and that is a primer leak. In its mildest form, this is indicated just by a smoky black smudge on the case head at the edge of the primer pocket. It may completely encircle the primer, or it may involve only a small segment. Initially it's difficult to determine whether this resulted from the primer or the case condition. Punch out the fired primer and examine the primer pocket closely. If there are no irregularities and if a new primer seats tightly, then the case is probably okay. However, if there are deep scratches or gouges in the pocket and if a new primer seats easily or loosely, the case is at fault and should be discarded. Primer leaks may or may not be accompanied by excessive flattening of the primer, but when the latter is present, it indicates excessive pressures—usually, but not always. If the primer pocket is so oversize that a new primer slips in easily or won't stay in at all, then it has expanded either because of excessive pressure or because the head itself is too soft. Either way, discard the case.

Another problem in this area is a pierced primer. It may be produced by excessive pressure, by a combination of excess pressure and weak firing-pin spring or poor firing-pin shape, or entirely by defects in the gun. A pierced primer normally doesn't harm the case, so if a new primer seats tightly, consider the case satisfactory for further use.

PRIMER EXTRUSION

Primer extrusion is another problem that is usually the fault of the gun, but it may be enhanced by high pressures. It is usually caused by excessive clearance between the firing-pin nose and its hole in the bolt face; the primer cup flows back into this gap, raising a distinct rim around the perimeter of the firing-pin dent. The condition can be severe enough that this entire section of the primer cup blows out, leaving an apparently pierced or perforated primer. If you see this rim around the firing-pin dent, check the bolt face closely—and you'll probably find a substantial gap between the pin and its hole. The only cure is to have the gun repaired, though you can continue using it by going to lighter loads where the pressure is not sufficient to cause primer extrusion.

CASE BULGES

There will normally be very slight expansion of the case just ahead of the rim or extraction groove. This is the normal transition from the case walls being supported by the chamber walls to the solid head. However, if this expanded area becomes more than about .005 inch greater than head diameter, either pressures are excessive or the chamber is oversize, and this may be interpreted to mean that the pressure is too high for that gun.

Fired cases may occasionally show an eccentric bulge forward of the head and of considerable size. This usually occurs in autoloading pistols, but may also occur in some repeating or autoloading rifles where either inadvertently or by design the feed ramp cuts away a small portion of the chamber wall and thus eliminates case support at that point. Under severe conditions, a hole may be blown in the case at that point. When acquiring fired cases in military-pistol calibers, it's a good idea to watch closely for this condition—submachine guns produce it to a greater degree than pistols, and cases fired in them often find their way on the market.

DISHED SHOTSHELL HEADS

In shotshell cases, particularly with the paper type and to a lesser degree in the built-up plastic type, there is a phenomenon known as the "dished head." When this occurs, the head of the fired cases is pushed in at the center, creating a readily visible concave condition. It may appear to be difficult to find an explanation for this condition, but actually it results from a small amount of gas escaping around the primer and expanding between the standing breech and the case head, pushing the head metal forward to form that concavity. Generally, such a case should be discarded, because the primer pocket is not tight enough, or gas wouldn't have escaped to cause the problem in the first place.

DISTORTED SHOTSHELL RIMS

Another problem encountered in shotshell cases is a very substantial thickening of the rim and a radiusing of the rear perimeter of the head. This is usually an indication of substantial excess headspace in the gun, and poor base-wad condition which has allowed gas to flow back under it and into the folded metal rim of the case. Such cases really should be discarded, though they can sometimes be restored to limited serviceability in a shell reconditioner. In any event, the gun should certainly be repaired, because eventually a case rim will rupture, and gas will escape and may damage the gun or injure the shooter.

DAMAGED CASE MONTHS

Occasionally after resizing a straight case, you'll note a small segment of the mouth turned over or folded. This is usually the result of the mouth being out of round, and thus catching on the mouth of the resizing die; it can also occur with good cases if you're careless about seating them properly in the shell holder.

ACCORDIONED CASES

After seating a bullet, you may discover that a narrow strip of the neck is neatly accordion-folded beneath the base of the bullet. Naturally, both case and bullet are ruined. This is caused by too little chamfering or mouth flaring, and also by poor bullet alignment before seating. It is more likely to occur with bullets having very sharp-edged bases. You may also notice a small segment of the mouth buried in the side of the bullet, and this can also happen with jacketed bullets. It can be caused by a burr on the inside of the case mouth, an irregularity on the surface of the bullet jacket, or even by a bit of foreign material in the loading die. Most of the time the case can be salvaged, and the load may be fired safely enough, though I'd not expect it to hit much.

After seating and crimping a bullet, you may notice a slight rippling in the surface of the case; it may be severe enough to actually cause accordion-like folds. This can occur with any type of case, and in sharply bottlenecked calibers, it may take the form of the shoulder being pushed neatly in upon itself in a perfect ring fold. In any event, it is caused by too much seating pressure or too much crimping pressure. Unless the shoulder is folded, the cartridge may be fired if it will enter the chamber, and will be okay afterward.

BENT CASE RIMS

A case which entered the shell holder freely enough for resizing may show a reluctance to do so when you're preparing to seat bullets. If the shell holder is clean and unobstructed, look closely at the rim and you'll probably find it is bent rearward a bit at one point or another. This can be produced by excessive force necessary to extract the case from the sizing die. This is invariably the result of forgetting to lubricate during resizing, or grit or other foreign material on the case or in the die. If the rim is only slightly bent and not cracked, simply tapping it back into approximate alignment will salvage the case.

BRITTLE BLACK-POWDER CASES

If you're working with some old obsolete black-powder cases that appear to be in good condition and yet are excessively hard and brittle, doubtless they were fired originally with mercuric primers. The mercury released by the primer has amalgamated with the brass and weakened it badly. The case may crack or crumble during reloading operations, or it may fail during firing. Regardless, it should not be used if the neck is so hard that it cannot be deformed by thumb pressure.

OLD AMMUNITION

Occasionally you may have an opportunity to purchase some old ammunition cheaply from which you can salvage the cases for reloading. It won't be unusual if such ammunition exhibits a few split necks, and if it does, a good many more are likely to split on firing. Rather than that, pull the bullets and dump the powder, then anneal those necks which aren't split. Then the cases can be reloaded and will probably stand up well. The original splits resulted from the brass being too hard and gripping the bullet too tightly.

You'll have heard reference to "corrosive primers," and their propensity for causing bore rust and pitting. Naturally, this will be uppermost in your mind when you have an opportunity to purchase military-surplus ammunition. Almost all U.S. military ammunition in .45 and .30-06 calibers utilized corrosive primers until early 1950. Consequently, a headstamp of 1951 or later ensures noncorrosive primers. On the other hand, all U.S. 9mm Parabellum, .38 Special, and .30 carbine ammunition was loaded with commercial noncorrosive primers from the beginning, so you need not fear it. With very few exceptions, virtually all foreign military ammunition from WWII up into the late 1950s was assembled with corrosive primers. In fact, some used corrosive primers until the late 1960s. There is simply no way to be genuinely certain that foreign military ammunition you might encounter is *not* loaded with corrosive primers.

You can conduct a test that is reasonably accurate in ordinary or damp climates, but it isn't reliable in very dry climates. Pull the bullets and dump the powder from two or three of the suspect cartridges, then polish a piece of steel plate clean and bright, and fire the primed cases in a gun with the muzzle very close to the plate. This will deposit primer residue on the plate. If a spot of rust appears there within forty-eight hours, you can be certain the primer is corrosive. On the other hand, absence of rust is no guarantee that the primers are not corrosive.

At some point you may encounter a batch of fired steel cartridge cases—most likely in .45 ACP caliber, but some .30-06 and quite a bit of 8mm Mauser ammunition was loaded in steel cases. There were other steel cases, including Russian and Italian rifle ammunition and U.S. .30 Carbine. Generally speaking, there's no point whatever in attempting to reload the foreign steel cases because they are relatively hard, and require hard-to-get Berdan primers and complex decapping methods. However, steel U.S. cases with headstamps dating after the middle 1950s will reload fairly well if in good clean uncorroded condition. Unfortunately, they'll seldom be found that way, because firing breaks the corrosion-resistant coating and they rust very quickly thereafter.

OIL DENTS

In Chapter 4, we mentioned oil dents. These are dents that appear generally in the shoulder area of the case when too much resizing lubricant has been used. It becomes trapped between the case and die, and the case yields to make space for the incompressible fluid, producing the dent. If the dent hasn't produced a fold or split, the case can usually be salvaged by firing it with an ordinary load. Most of the time the dent will be removed by case expansion, but just occasionally the case will split in the process. A split of this sort does not harm the gun. The split case must be discarded, but most oil-dented cases can be salvaged in this manner.

PULLING BULLETS FROM MILITARY CASES

Military rifle ammunition is usually assembled more tightly than comparable commercial cartridges. The bullet is not only crimped strongly in place, but is bedded in mouth sealer. This is done to enable it to resist the heavy impacts of feeding through automatic gun mechanisms. You may decide to break down a batch of this ammunition in order to use the cases, and find that pulling the bullets is very difficult. There is a simple way to break the bond between case and bullet, after which the bullets may be pulled easily. Simply set up a bullet-seating die to push the bullet about 1/16 inch deeper into the case. Then run all the cartridges through the seating die, and your problem is solved. The deeper seating of the bullet breaks the bond formed by the neck sealer, after which relatively little effort is required to extract the bullet.

SCRATCHED RESIZING DIES

Sooner or later, you'll probably mess up the inside of a resizing die. It takes only one case with grit on it to produce longitudinal scratches in the die, and also to imbed some of that grit in the cavity walls so that every case resized thereafter is badly scratched. Generally this won't interfere with the function of the case, and doesn't present any safety hazard, but it looks terrible. Once you've gotten the die in this condition, it can usually be polished back into serviceability if you're careful.

Remove all lubricant and grease with acetone or similar solvent on a swab, then make a hacksaw cut longitudinally in a piece of dowel or rod which will enter the die with about 1/16-inch clearance. Fit fine-grit "Gritcloth" in the slot and wrap it loosely around the dowel so that it's a moderately snug fit in the die cavity. Chuck this in your portable electric drill, set it for low speed, and spin the Gritcloth inside the die cavity, constantly moving it in and out and rotating it slightly at the rear so that it never bears on any one spot for any length of time. Don't overdo this, but after a few seconds of polishing, flush out the grit and steel particles thoroughly then run a lubricated case into the die and check for scratches. Repeat this until the scratches on the case either disappear or are substantially reduced. If the die is badly scored, you won't be able to polish it out without making it much oversize, but you really don't need to remove scratches. As long as you polish out the burrs and imbedded grit particles, resized cases will look good. If somehow one of your dies picks up a bit of rust inside, this same treatment will often restore its serviceability.

NO PROPER DIES

There's bound to be a time when you're in a hurry to load a few rounds of a caliber for which you do not have proper dies. Well, if you have new or fired cases which will chamber in the gun all right, very often it will be possible to partially size the case and seat bullets with dies you already have at hand. For example, .284 Winchester dies will neck-size, expand necks, and seat bullets in almost any 7mm caliber whose case is longer than 2 inches. A set of .308 Winchester dies can be used to do the same with .30-30, .30-40, .300 Savage, and .30-06, and produce entirely acceptable handloads. Substitution of dies in this fashion requires only that the dies be adjusted in the press to accommodate the different length of the new case. Adjust the resizing die so that it sizes as much of the neck as possible, but does not set the shoulder back. Adjust the bullet-seating die so the proper overall cartridge length is produced. If the neck of the new cartridge is at least as long as the caliber for which the dies were made, it can be adjusted to crimp the case as well. Many handloaders substitute dies as a routine measure of economy in handgun calibers. For example, .38 Special dies serve for .357 Magnum when readjusted, .45 ACP dies may also be used for .45 Colt, and .44 Special dies will do nicely for the .44 Magnum. Anytime a situation of this sort arises, just compare the cartridge to be loaded with those for which you have dies, and quite often a satisfactory substitution will be apparent.

BERDAN PRIMERS

It's even money that sooner or later you'll start wondering if you can reload some of those Berdan-primed foreign cases. Well, it is possible, provided you can locate a supply of the proper size of Berdan primers. They are available in this country, but only sporadically, and from just a few sources. Shopping around by mail among the importers and specialty shops will usually uncover a source of the primers you need.

Decapping the fired cases then remains the only real obstacle. The main problem is that the two very tiny flash holes in Berdan cases don't provide for pin-decapping. A Berdan-type decapping tool is available from RCBS. It consists of a steel rod over which the case is placed, and a chisel-pointed tool which punches through the Berdan primer cup and then pries it out.

A reasonably practical alternative which may be used is hydraulic decapping. It consists of making up a rod or dowel which fits closely in the case mouth, then filling the case with water, setting it over a block of wood containing a hole large enough to admit the primer, placing the rod in the case mouth, and rapping it smartly with a hammer. The force of the hammer blow is transmitted to the water, which flows through the small flash holes and forces the fired primer out. It's messy and it's slow, but it works.

After Berdan cases have been decapped by one means or another, proper-size new primers can be placed mouth-up on a steel plate, and the case started over the primer and then tapped down with a dowel and stick or light hammer to seat the primer flush with the case head. Again, it's slow, but it works quite well. RCBS—and perhaps other makers—also offers special Berdan-size primer seating punches of its regular design. If you have a fair number of cases to prime, this is the best route.

CASE STUCK IN DIE

Sooner or later you'll find a case stuck in a resizing die. You may try hard to get it out in the usual way, and likely the rim will pull off. The case is stuck tight, and the decapping stem closes off the upper end, so a punch can't be gotten in to drive it out. Some dies, notably RCBS dies, are made so that the decapping stem may be used as a jackscrew to push the case out if it isn't stuck too tightly. Just loosen the lock nut, then use a screwdriver in the slotted tip to turn the stem in against the case head. Further turning will loosen the case if it isn't stuck too tight. If this fails, unscrew and remove the bushing through which the stem passes, along with the lock nut. Slip a fired case over the top of the stem and drive the case out with a hammer. Take care, though, because the stem is slender and will bend easily if you strike it wrong.

If you're really hung up and none of those methods works, you'll have to obtain one of the commercial stuck-case removers and follow the maker's instructions. Usually this consists of taking the die from the press, drilling out the primer pocket, then turning in a threaded stud which will fit into the ram head or shell holder. Then enough beef on the press handle will pull the case out. It's best, though, to keep dies and cases clean, and to lubricate cases unless you're using a tungsten-carbide die.

If you stay with the handloading game, doubtless other problems will arise as you move along. I don't have room to cover them all here, and by the time you've whipped those I've outlined, you'll probably be able to devise solutions to any others that come up without any real trouble. Just remember that careful study of any problem is necessary before you jump in with both feet. Hurried and unresearched solutions turn out to be more often wrong than right.

This book has been intended only as a basic guide. There are several other quite good references that go into the subject in great detail. Once you've exhausted this source, you'll be well advised to expand your library with other books, such as Phil Sharpe's classic *Complete Guide to Handloading,* the *NRA Reloading Guide,* and, perhaps, even my own *Modern Handloading.* Building up a four- or five-volume handloading library isn't expensive, and it's the best way to prepare yourself in advance for solving problems and enjoying and benefiting from the game to the fullest.

Index